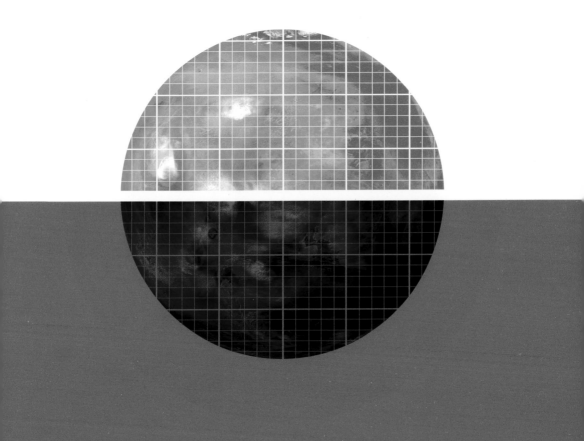

MARS

The fourth planet from the Sun and the second-smallest planet in the solar system, Mars is named after the Roman god of war. It is also often described as the "Red Planet" due to its reddish appearance. Mars is a terrestrial planet with a thin atmosphere composed primarily of carbon dioxide.

MARS PLANET PROFILE

»	EQUATORIAL DIAMETER	6,792 km
»	POLAR DIAMETER	6,752 km
»	MASS	6.42 x 10^23 kg (10.7% EARTH)
»	MOONS	2 (PHOBOS & DEIMOS)
»	ORBIT DISTANCE	227,943,824 km (1.52 AU)
»	ORBIT PERIOD	687 days (1.9 YEARS)
»	SURFACE TEMPERATURE	-153 to 20 °C

REDLINE

WRITTEN BY **NEAL HOLMAN**

ILLUSTRATED BY **CLAYTON McCORMACK**

COLORED BY **KELLY FITZPATRICK**

LETTERED BY **CRANK!**

EDITED BY
JAMES LUCAS JONES
AND **ROBIN HERRERA**

DESIGNED BY
DYLAN TODD

AN ONI PRESS PUBLICATION

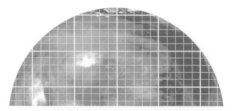

THIS VOLUME COLLECTS ISSUES 1–5 OF THE ONI PRESS SERIES REDLINE

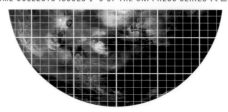

PUBLISHED BY ONI PRESS, INC.

JOE NOZEMACK, FOUNDER & CHIEF FINANCIAL OFFICER
JAMES LUCAS JONES, PUBLISHER
CHARLIE CHU, V.P. OF CREATIVE & BUSINESS DEVELOPMENT
BRAD ROOKS, DIRECTOR OF OPERATIONS
RACHEL REED, MARKETING MANAGER
MELISSA MESZAROS MACFADYEN, PUBLICITY MANAGER
TROY LOOK, DIRECTOR OF DESIGN & PRODUCTION
HILARY THOMPSON, GRAPHIC DESIGNER
KATE Z. STONE, JUNIOR GRAPHIC DESIGNER
ANGIE KNOWLES, DIGITAL PREPRESS LEAD
ARI YARWOOD, EXECUTIVE EDITOR
ROBIN HERRERA, SENIOR EDITOR
DESIREE WILSON, ASSOCIATE EDITOR
ALISSA SALLAH, ADMINISTRATIVE ASSISTANT
JUNG LEE, LOGISTICS ASSOCIATE

onipress.com
facebook.com/onipress
twitter.com/onipress
onipress.tumblr.com
instagram.com/onipress

@NealHolman
@DeadMeatComic
@wastedwings
@ccrank
@bigredrobot

FIRST EDITION: JANUARY 2018
ISBN 978-1-62010-459-0
EISBN 978-1-62010-460-6

LIBRARY OF CONGRESS CONTROL NUMBER: 2017943796
1 2 3 4 5 6 7 8 9 10

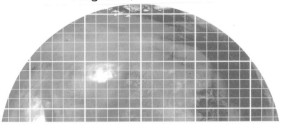

C H A P T E R   01

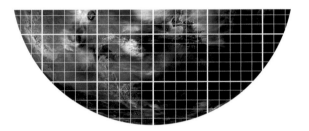

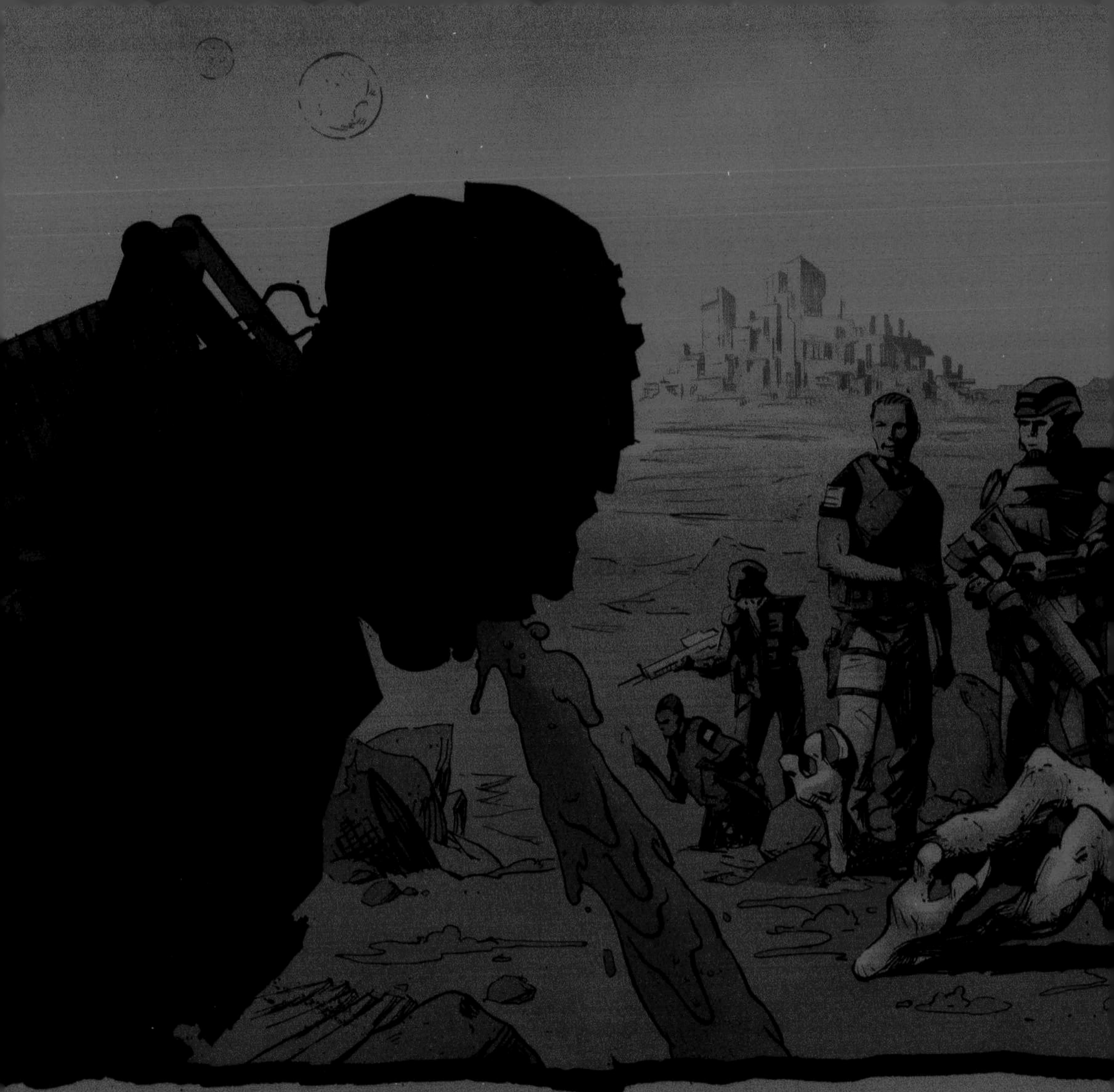

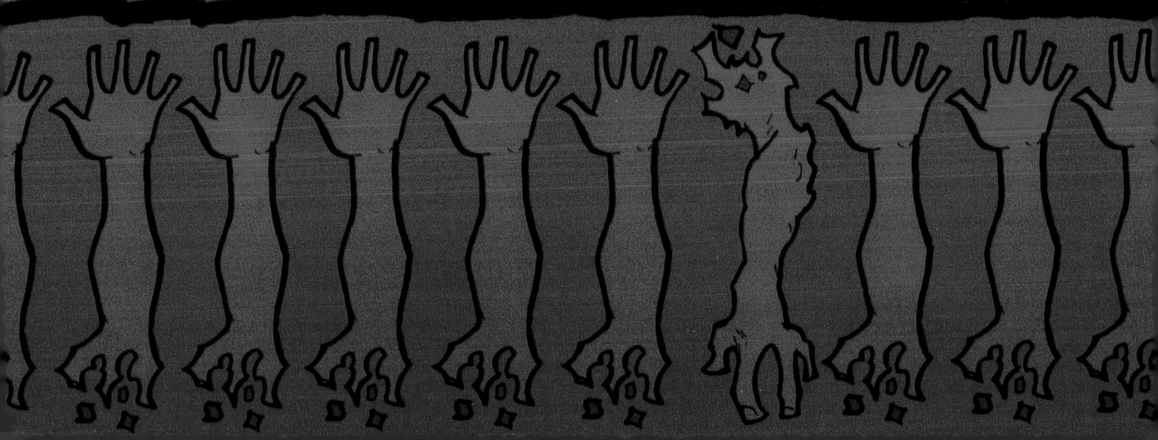

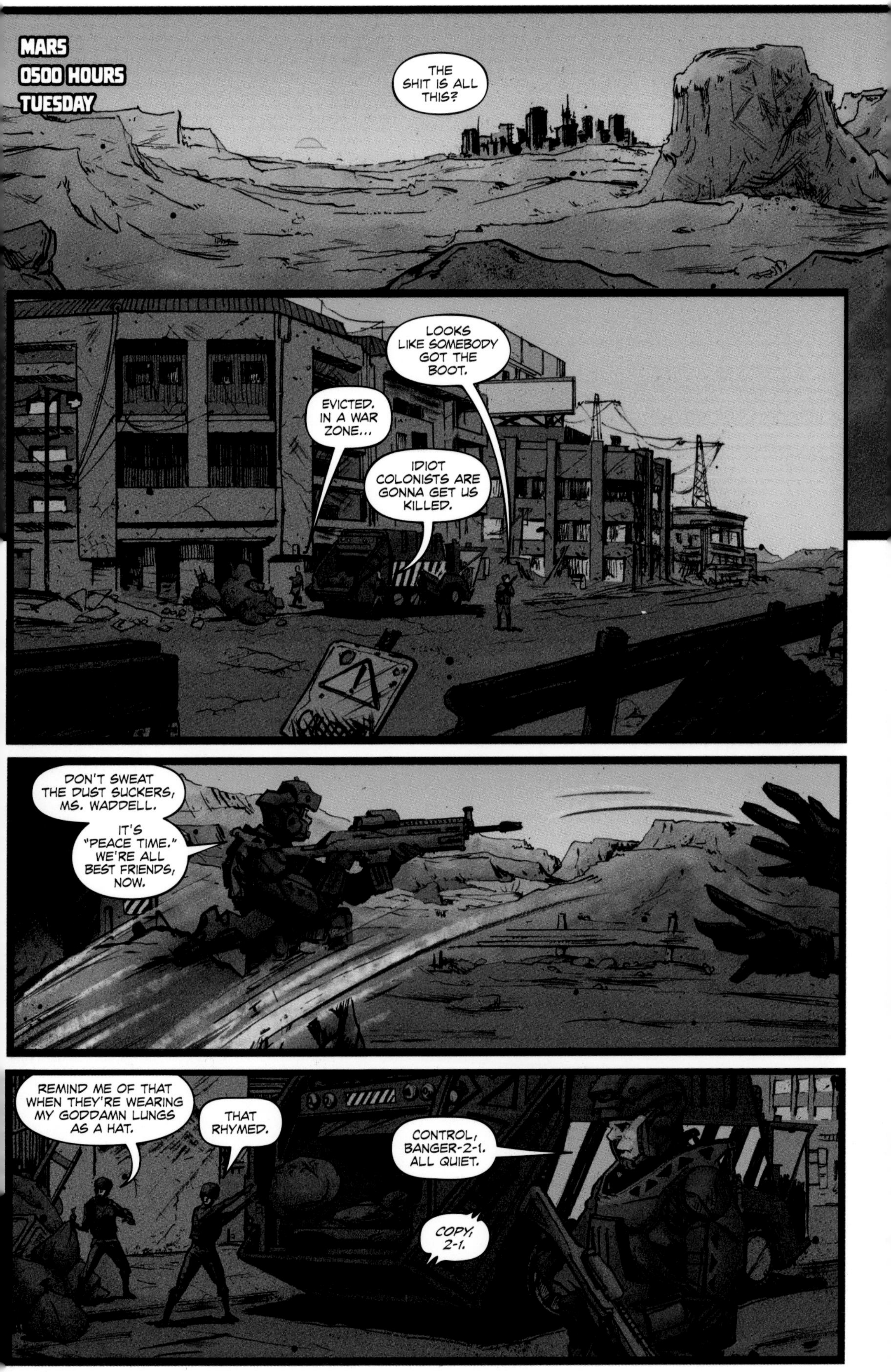
MARS
0500 HOURS
TUESDAY
THE SHIT IS ALL THIS?
LOOKS LIKE SOMEBODY GOT THE BOOT.
EVICTED. IN A WAR ZONE...
IDIOT COLONISTS ARE GONNA GET US KILLED.
DON'T SWEAT THE DUST SUCKERS, MS. WADDELL.
IT'S "PEACE TIME." WE'RE ALL BEST FRIENDS, NOW.
REMIND ME OF THAT WHEN THEY'RE WEARING MY GODDAMN LUNGS AS A HAT.
THAT RHYMED.
CONTROL, BANGER-2-1. ALL QUIET.
COPY, 2-1.

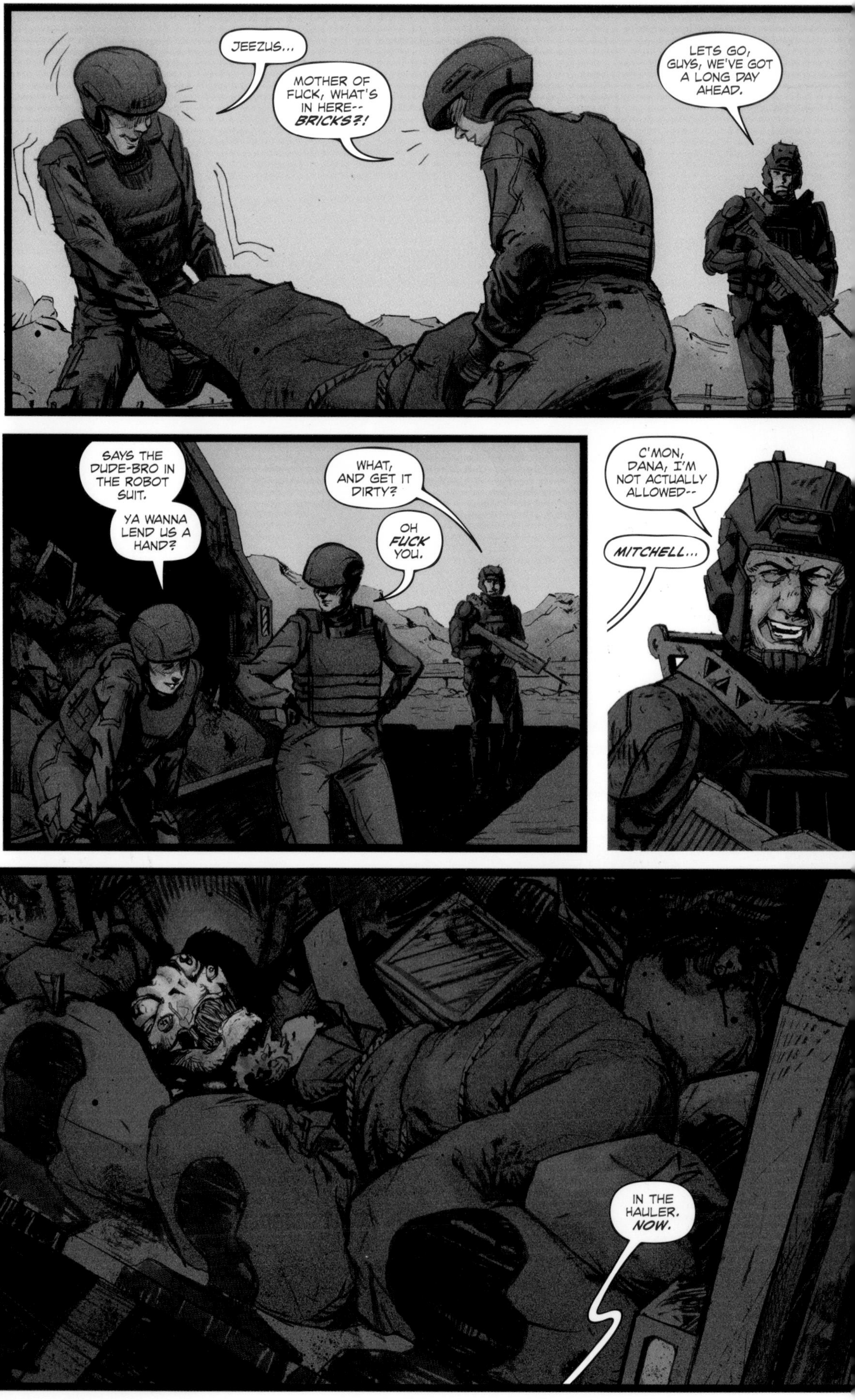
JEEZUS...
MOTHER OF FUCK, WHAT'S IN HERE-- *BRICKS?!*
LETS GO, GUYS, WE'VE GOT A LONG DAY AHEAD.
SAYS THE DUDE-BRO IN THE ROBOT SUIT.
YA WANNA LEND US A HAND?
WHAT, AND GET IT DIRTY?
OH *FUCK* YOU.
C'MON, DANA, I'M NOT ACTUALLY ALLOWED--
MITCHELL...
IN THE HAULER. *NOW.*

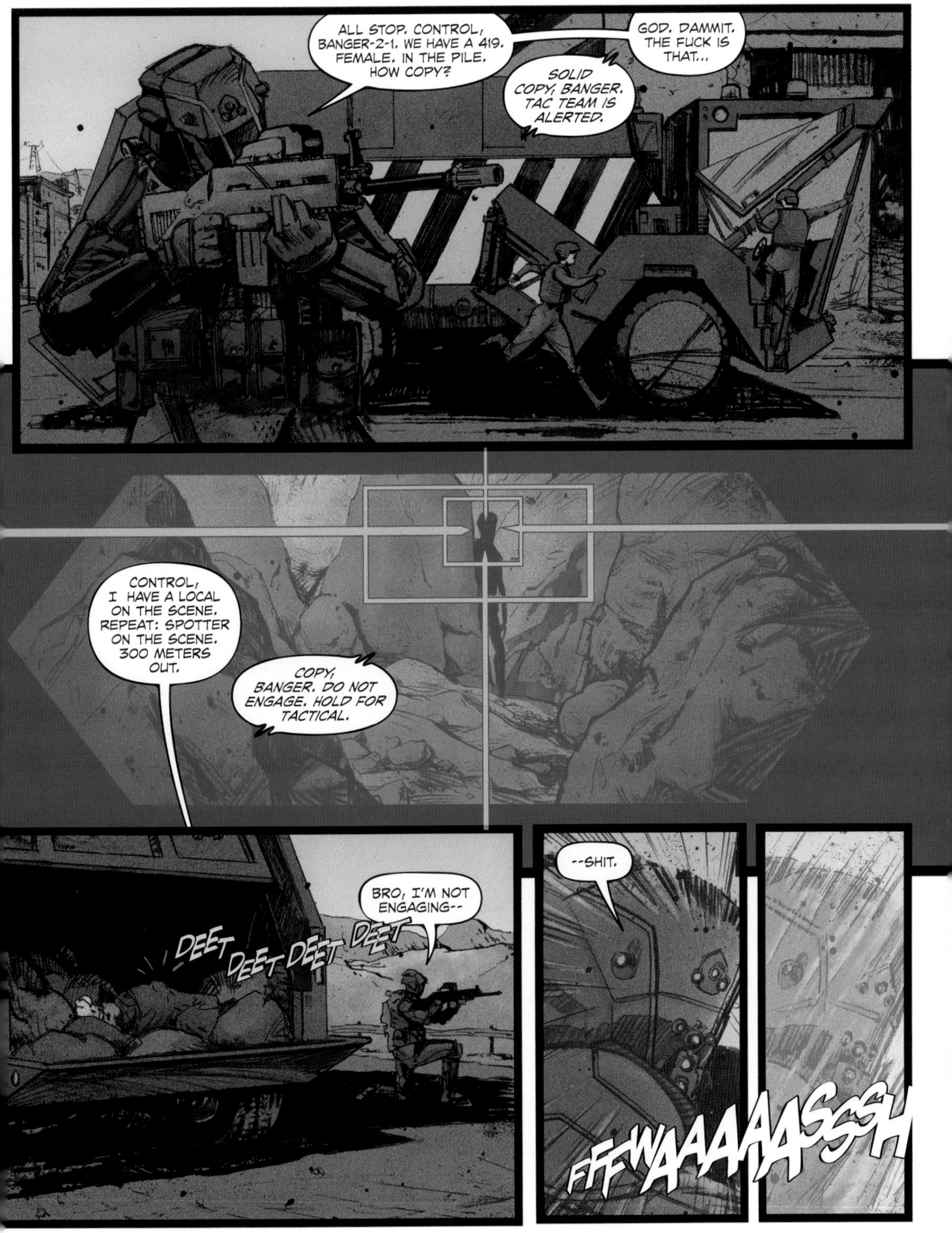
ALL STOP. CONTROL, BANGER-2-1. WE HAVE A 419. FEMALE. IN THE PILE. HOW COPY?
GOD. DAMMIT. THE FUCK IS THAT...
SOLID COPY, BANGER. TAC TEAM IS ALERTED.
CONTROL, I HAVE A LOCAL ON THE SCENE. REPEAT: SPOTTER ON THE SCENE. 300 METERS OUT.
COPY, BANGER. DO NOT ENGAGE. HOLD FOR TACTICAL.
DEET DEET DEET DEET
BRO, I'M NOT ENGAGING--
--SHIT.
FFFWAAAAASSSH

CHAPTER 01

For a heart stained in anger, grows weak and grows bitter...

John Prine, "Bruised Orange"

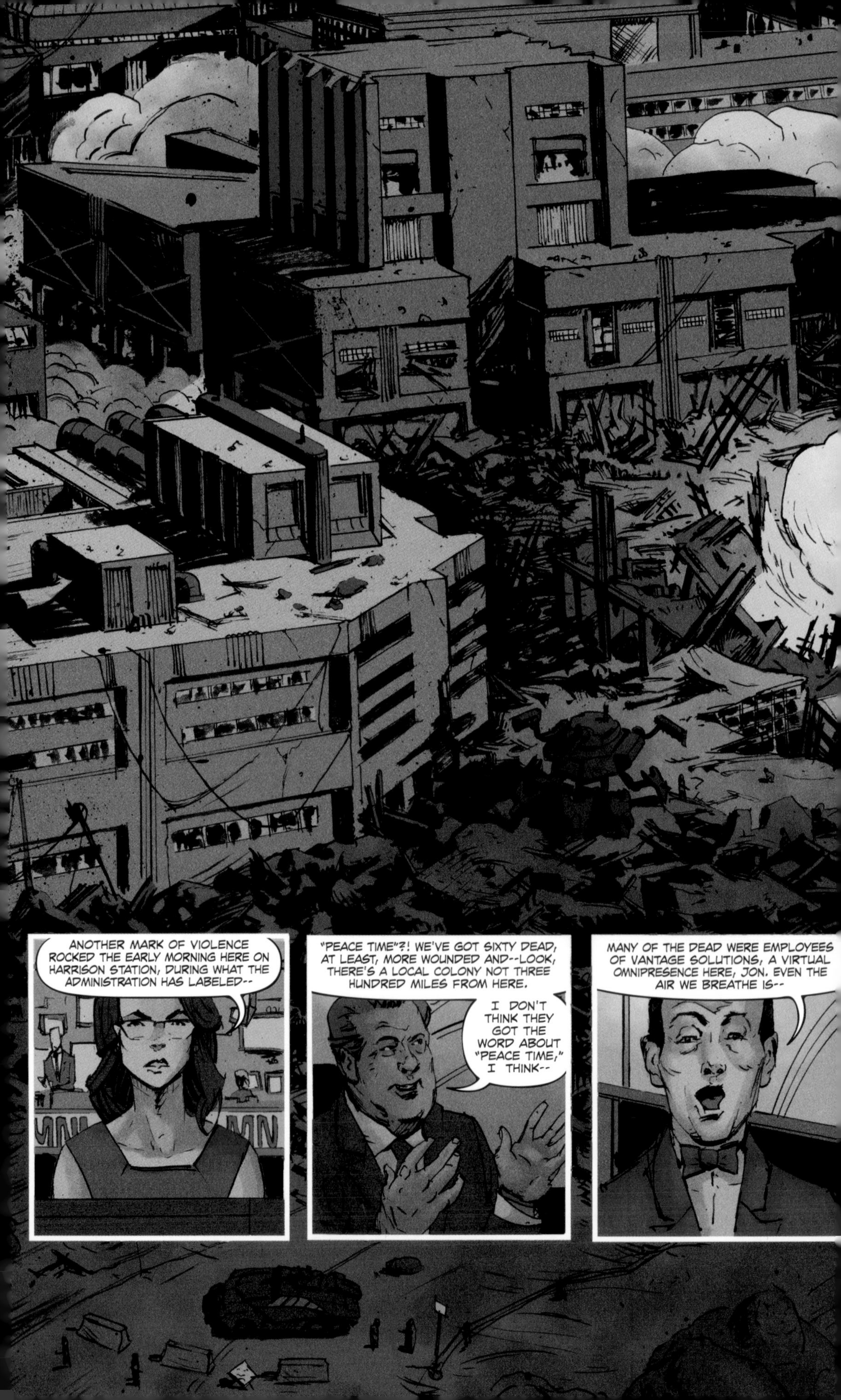

ANOTHER MARK OF VIOLENCE ROCKED THE EARLY MORNING HERE ON HARRISON STATION, DURING WHAT THE ADMINISTRATION HAS LABELED--
"PEACE TIME"?! WE'VE GOT SIXTY DEAD, AT LEAST, MORE WOUNDED AND--LOOK, THERE'S A LOCAL COLONY NOT THREE HUNDRED MILES FROM HERE.
I DON'T THINK THEY GOT THE WORD ABOUT "PEACE TIME," I THINK--
MANY OF THE DEAD WERE EMPLOYEES OF VANTAGE SOLUTIONS, A VIRTUAL OMNIPRESENCE HERE, JON. EVEN THE AIR WE BREATHE IS--

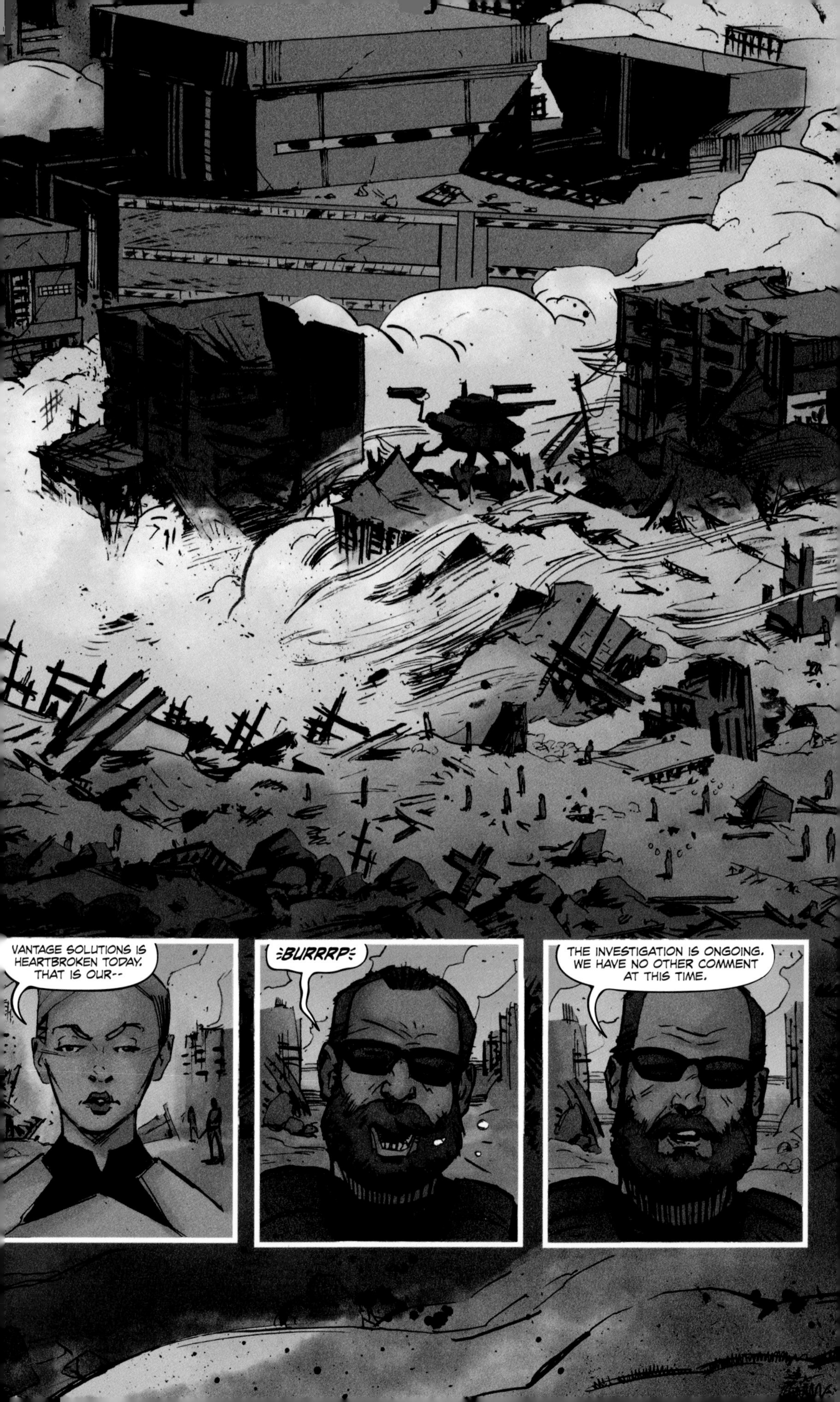
VANTAGE SOLUTIONS IS HEARTBROKEN TODAY. THAT IS OUR--
BURRRP
THE INVESTIGATION IS ONGOING. WE HAVE NO OTHER COMMENT AT THIS TIME.

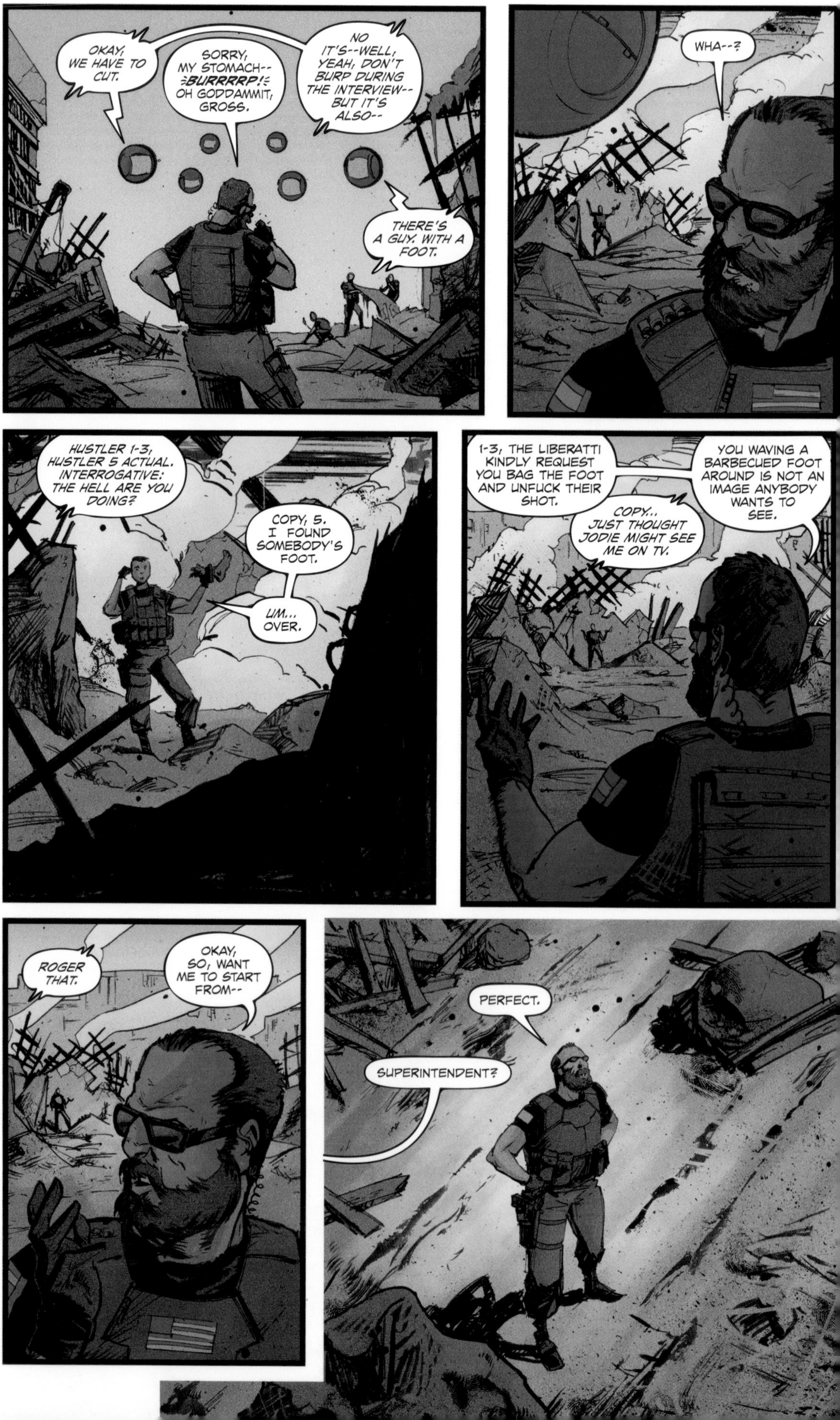
OKAY, WE HAVE TO CUT.
SORRY, MY STOMACH-- BURRRRP! OH GODDAMMIT, GROSS.
NO IT'S--WELL, YEAH, DON'T BURP DURING THE INTERVIEW-- BUT IT'S ALSO--
THERE'S A GUY. WITH A FOOT.
WHA--?
HUSTLER 1-3, HUSTLER 5 ACTUAL. INTERROGATIVE: THE HELL ARE YOU DOING?
COPY, 5. I FOUND SOMEBODY'S FOOT.
UM... OVER.
1-3, THE LIBERATTI KINDLY REQUEST YOU BAG THE FOOT AND UNFUCK THEIR SHOT.
YOU WAVING A BARBECUED FOOT AROUND IS NOT AN IMAGE ANYBODY WANTS TO SEE.
COPY... JUST THOUGHT JODIE MIGHT SEE ME ON TV.
ROGER THAT.
OKAY, SO, WANT ME TO START FROM--
PERFECT.
SUPERINTENDENT?

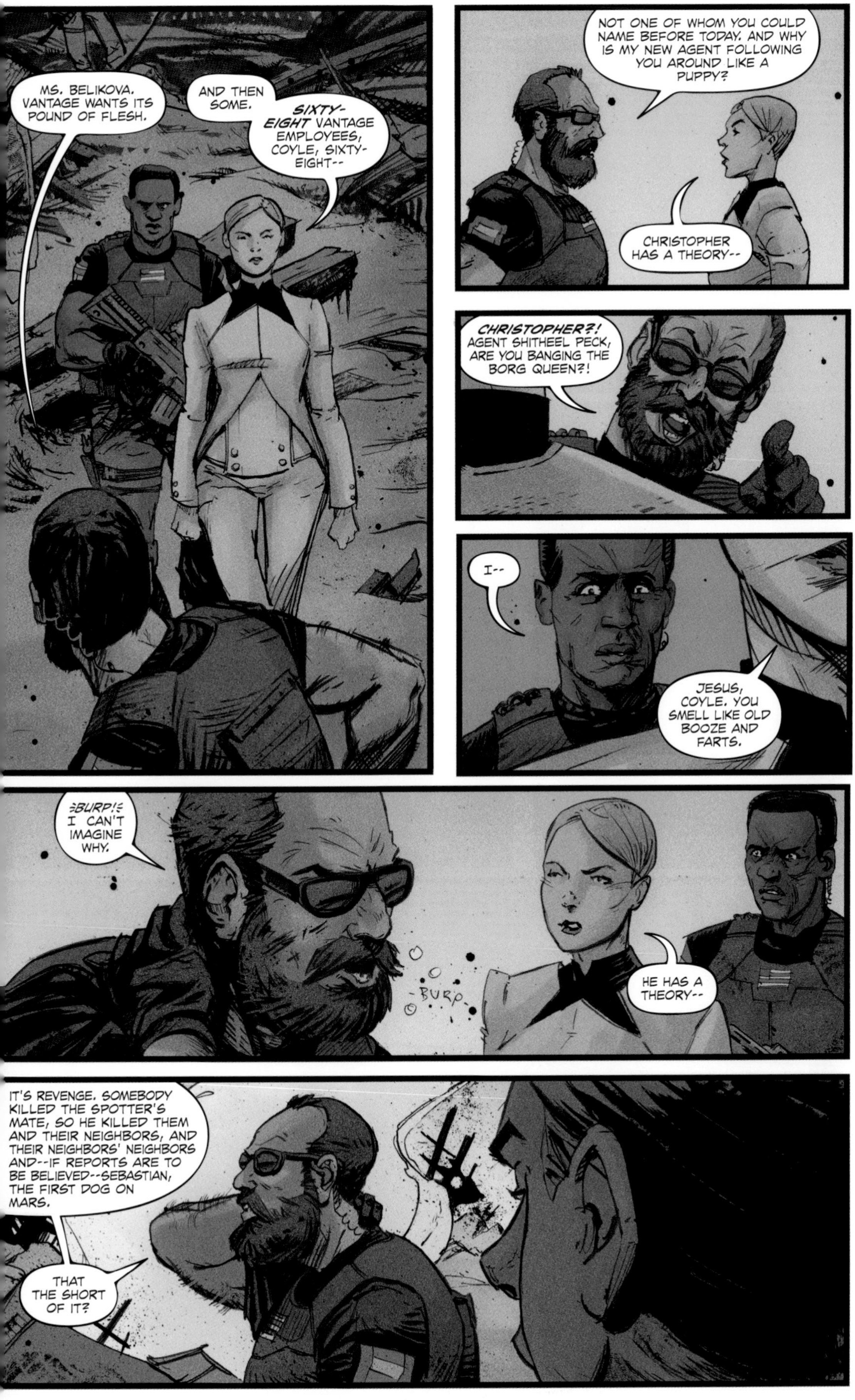

MS. BELIKOVA. VANTAGE WANTS ITS POUND OF FLESH.
AND THEN SOME.
SIXTY-EIGHT VANTAGE EMPLOYEES, COYLE, SIXTY-EIGHT--
NOT ONE OF WHOM YOU COULD NAME BEFORE TODAY. AND WHY IS MY NEW AGENT FOLLOWING YOU AROUND LIKE A PUPPY?
CHRISTOPHER HAS A THEORY--
CHRISTOPHER?! AGENT SHITHEEL PECK, ARE YOU BANGING THE BORG QUEEN?!
I--
JESUS, COYLE. YOU SMELL LIKE OLD BOOZE AND FARTS.
BURP! I CAN'T IMAGINE WHY.
-BURP-
HE HAS A THEORY--
IT'S REVENGE. SOMEBODY KILLED THE SPOTTER'S MATE, SO HE KILLED THEM AND THEIR NEIGHBORS, AND THEIR NEIGHBORS' NEIGHBORS AND--IF REPORTS ARE TO BE BELIEVED--SEBASTIAN, THE FIRST DOG ON MARS.
THAT THE SHORT OF IT?

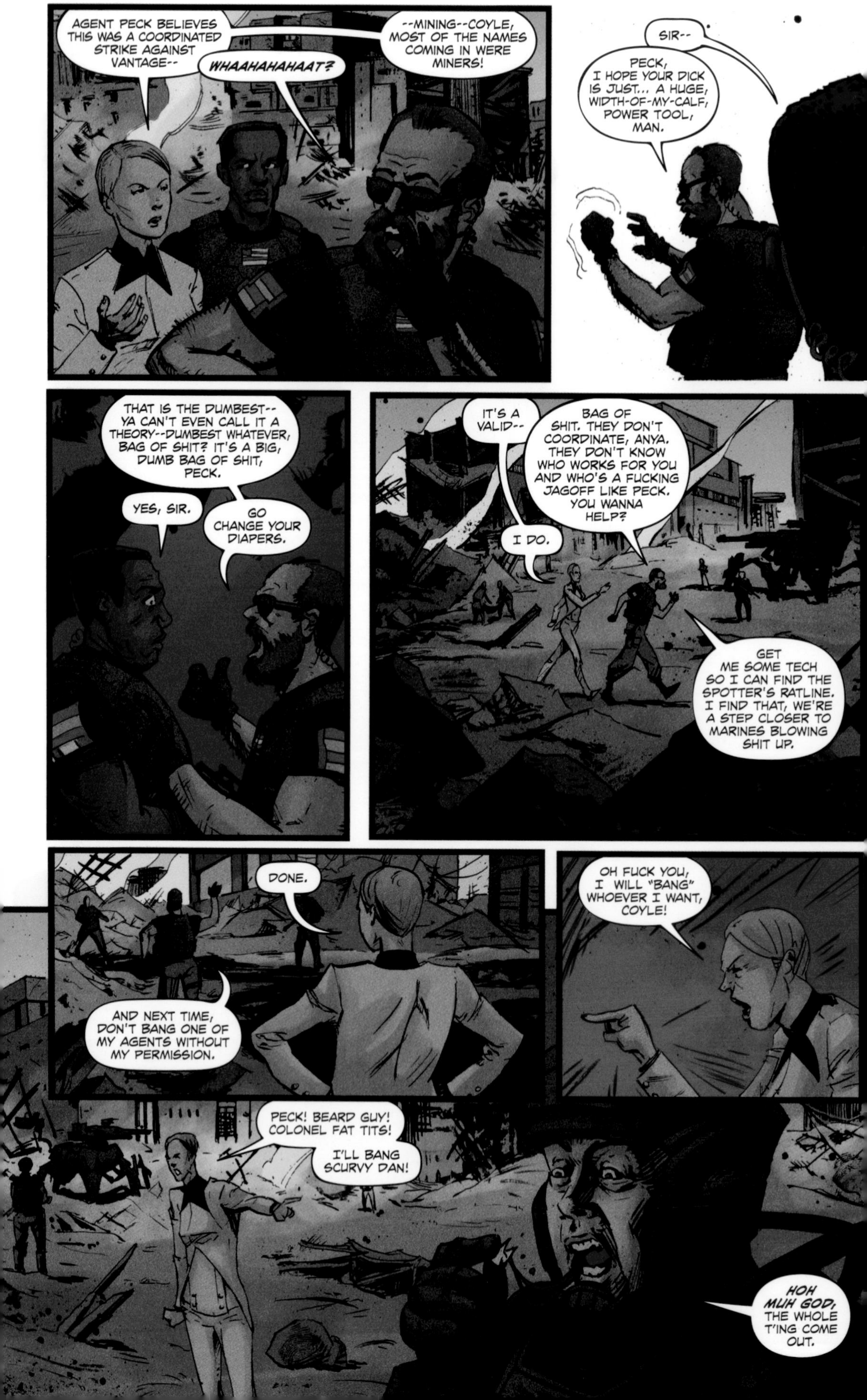
AGENT PECK BELIEVES THIS WAS A COORDINATED STRIKE AGAINST VANTAGE--
WHAAAHAHAHAAT?
--MINING--COYLE, MOST OF THE NAMES COMING IN WERE MINERS!
SIR--
PECK, I HOPE YOUR DICK IS JUST... A HUGE, WIDTH-OF-MY-CALF, POWER TOOL, MAN.
THAT IS THE DUMBEST--YA CAN'T EVEN CALL IT A THEORY--DUMBEST WHATEVER, BAG OF SHIT? IT'S A BIG, DUMB BAG OF SHIT, PECK.
YES, SIR.
GO CHANGE YOUR DIAPERS.
IT'S A VALID--
BAG OF SHIT. THEY DON'T COORDINATE, ANYA. THEY DON'T KNOW WHO WORKS FOR YOU AND WHO'S A FUCKING JAGOFF LIKE PECK. YOU WANNA HELP?
I DO.
GET ME SOME TECH SO I CAN FIND THE SPOTTER'S RATLINE. I FIND THAT, WE'RE A STEP CLOSER TO MARINES BLOWING SHIT UP.
DONE.
AND NEXT TIME, DON'T BANG ONE OF MY AGENTS WITHOUT MY PERMISSION.
OH FUCK YOU, I WILL "BANG" WHOEVER I WANT, COYLE!
PECK! BEARD GUY! COLONEL FAT TITS!
I'LL BANG SCURVY DAN!
HOH MUH GOD, THE WHOLE T'ING COME OUT.

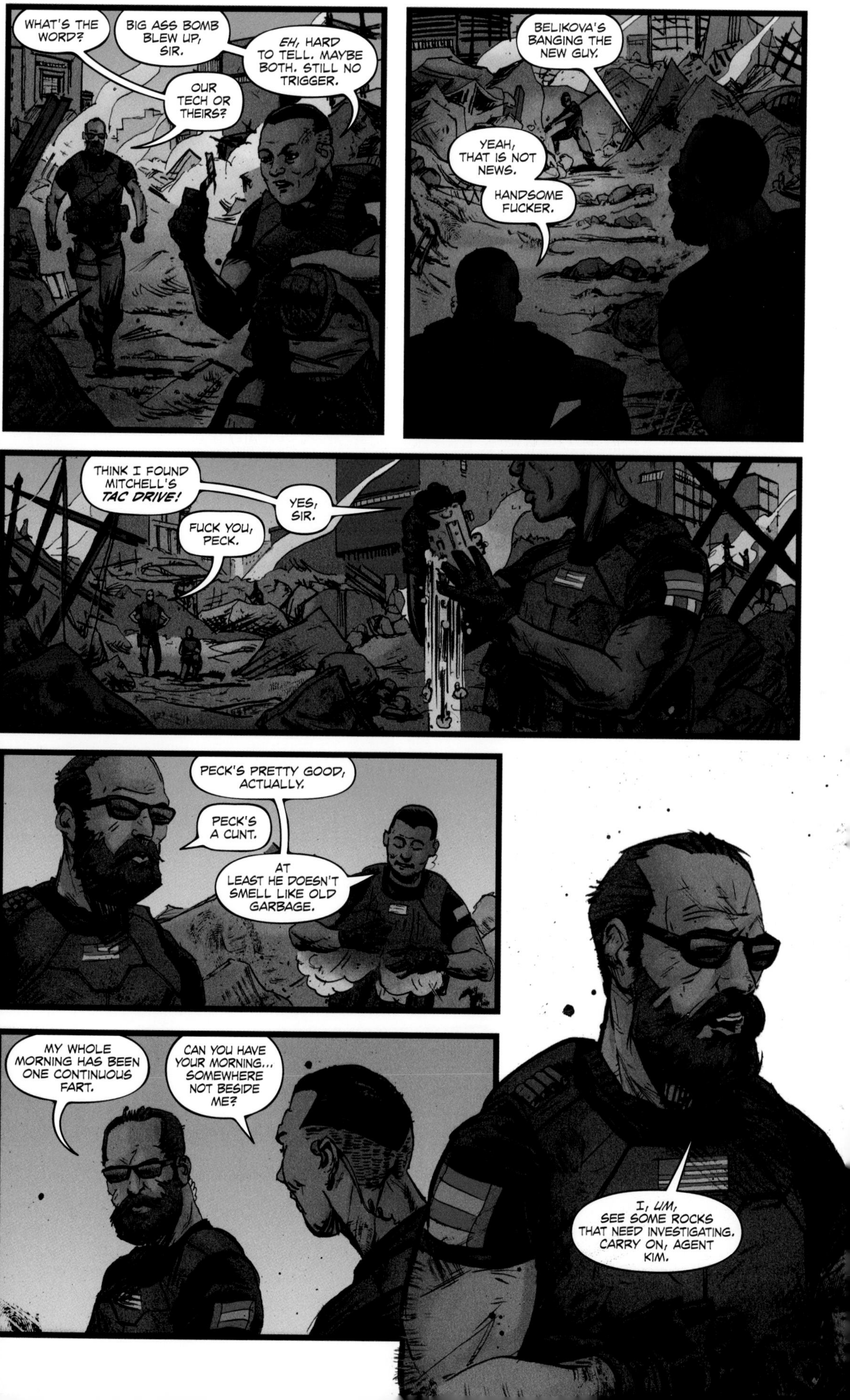

WHAT'S THE WORD?
BIG ASS BOMB BLEW UP, SIR.
OUR TECH OR THEIRS?
EH, HARD TO TELL. MAYBE BOTH. STILL NO TRIGGER.
BELIKOVA'S BANGING THE NEW GUY.
YEAH, THAT IS NOT NEWS.
HANDSOME FUCKER.
THINK I FOUND MITCHELL'S TAC DRIVE!
YES, SIR.
FUCK YOU, PECK.
PECK'S PRETTY GOOD, ACTUALLY.
PECK'S A CUNT.
AT LEAST HE DOESN'T SMELL LIKE OLD GARBAGE.
MY WHOLE MORNING HAS BEEN ONE CONTINUOUS FART.
CAN YOU HAVE YOUR MORNING... SOMEWHERE NOT BESIDE ME?
I, UM, SEE SOME ROCKS THAT NEED INVESTIGATING. CARRY ON, AGENT KIM.

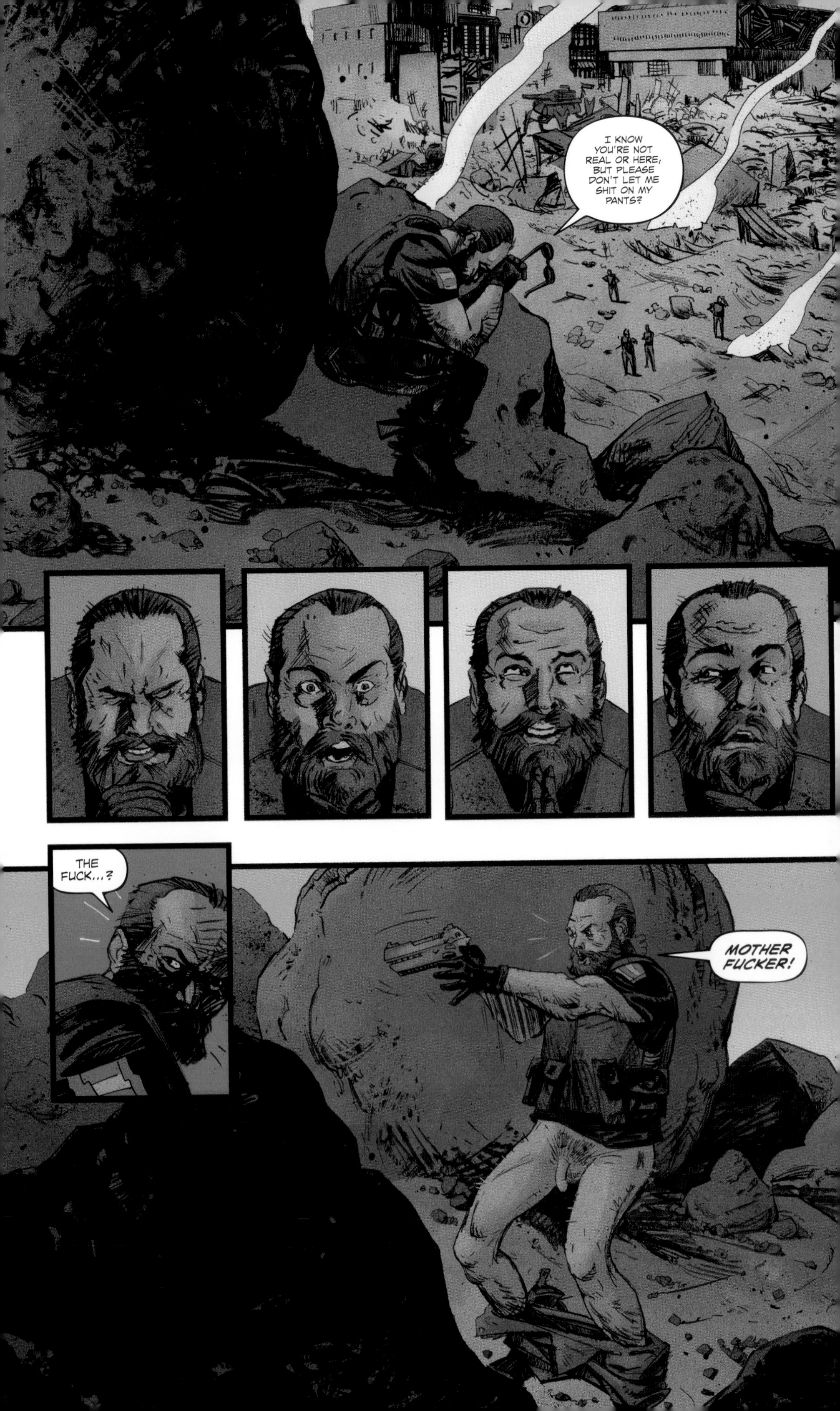

I KNOW YOU'RE NOT REAL OR HERE, BUT PLEASE DON'T LET ME SHIT ON MY PANTS?
THE FUCK...?
MOTHER FUCKER!

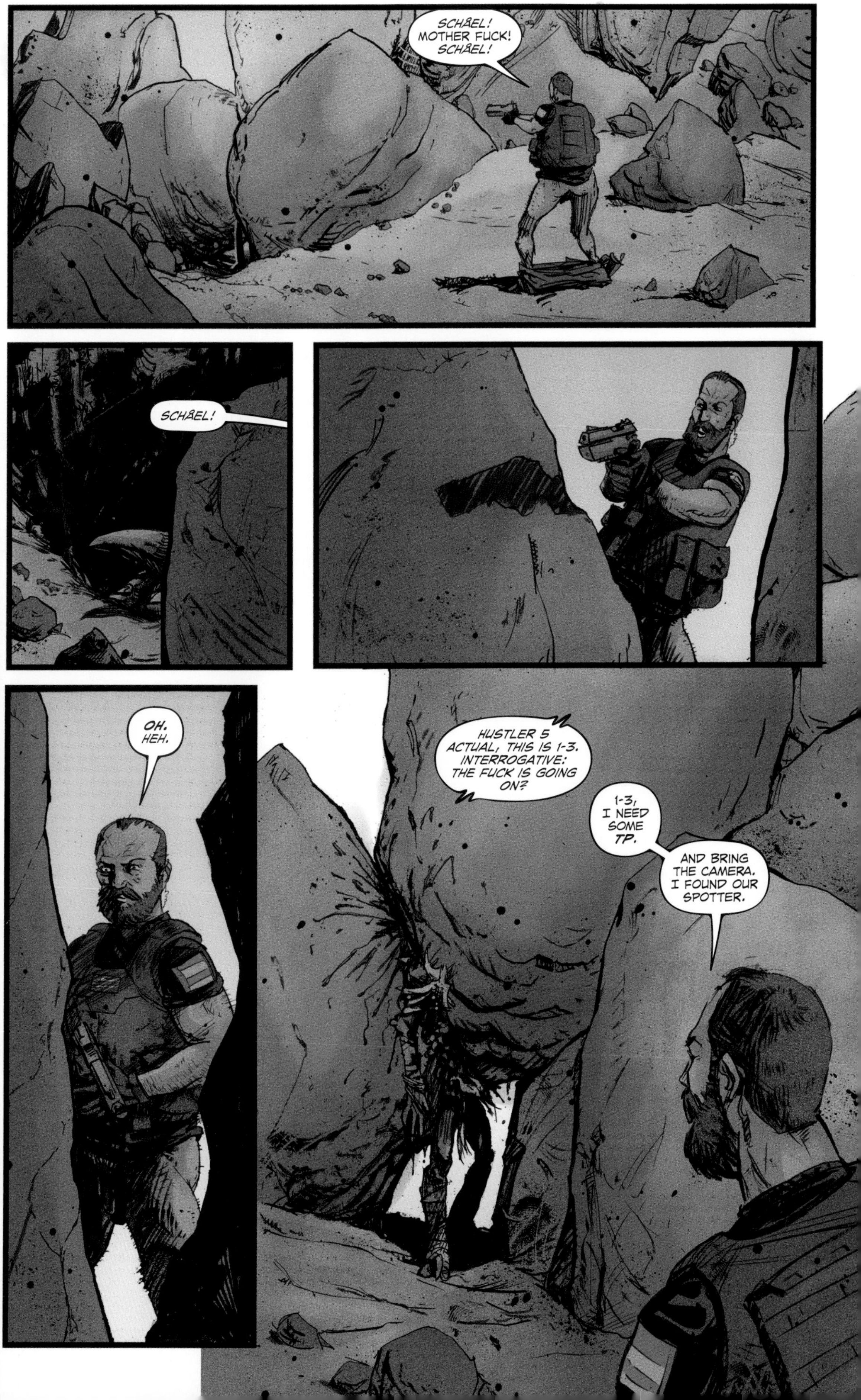
SCHÄEL! MOTHER FUCK! SCHÄEL!
SCHÄEL!
OH. HEH.
HUSTLER 5 ACTUAL, THIS IS 1-3. INTERROGATIVE: THE FUCK IS GOING ON?
1-3, I NEED SOME TP.
AND BRING THE CAMERA. I FOUND OUR SPOTTER.

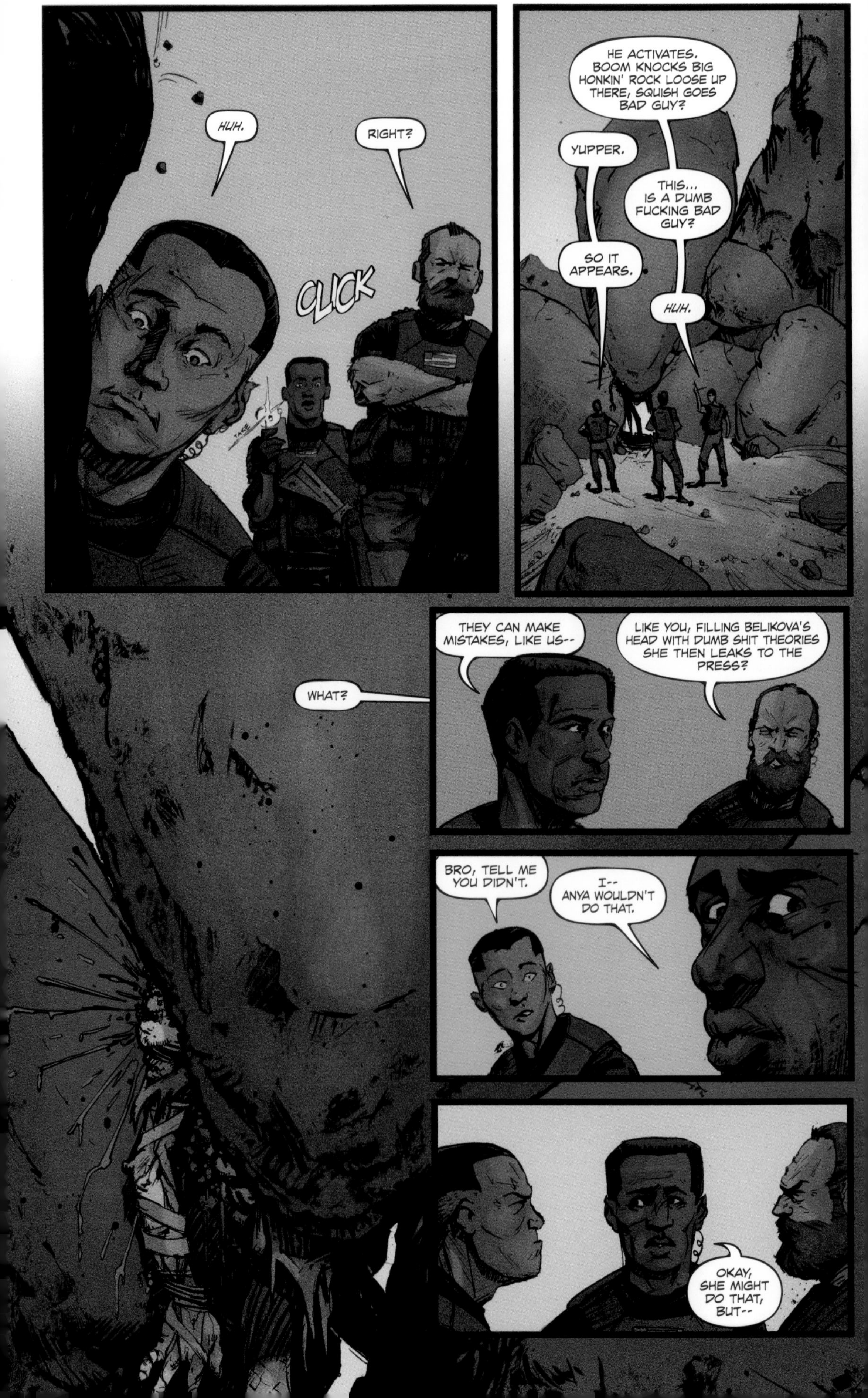
HUH.
RIGHT?
CLICK
TAKE
HE ACTIVATES. BOOM KNOCKS BIG HONKIN' ROCK LOOSE UP THERE, SQUISH GOES BAD GUY?
YUPPER.
THIS... IS A DUMB FUCKING BAD GUY?
SO IT APPEARS.
HUH.
WHAT?
THEY CAN MAKE MISTAKES, LIKE US--
LIKE YOU, FILLING BELIKOVA'S HEAD WITH DUMB SHIT THEORIES SHE THEN LEAKS TO THE PRESS?
BRO, TELL ME YOU DIDN'T.
I-- ANYA WOULDN'T DO THAT.
OKAY, SHE MIGHT DO THAT, BUT--

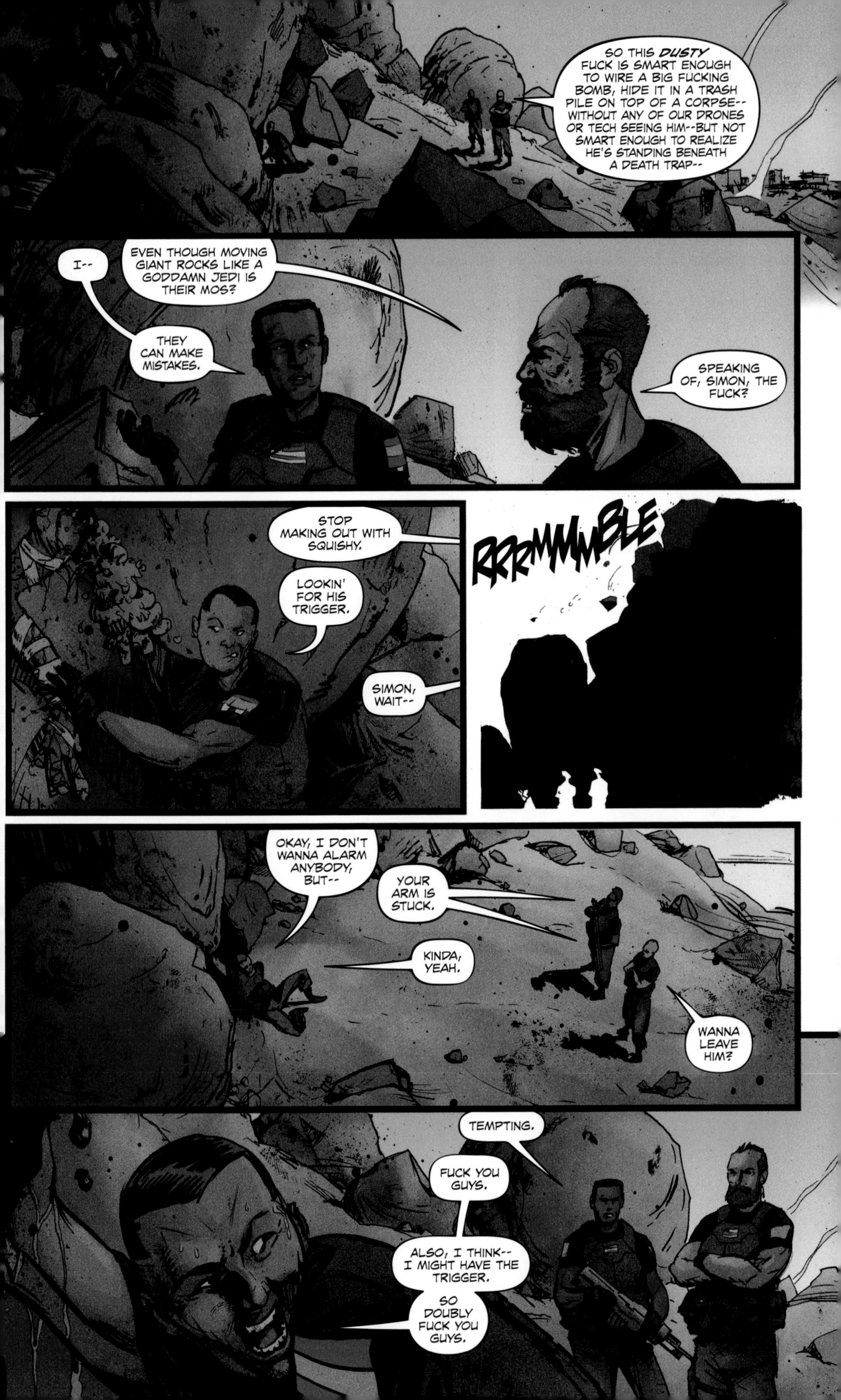
SO THIS DUSTY FUCK IS SMART ENOUGH TO WIRE A BIG FUCKING BOMB, HIDE IT IN A TRASH PILE ON TOP OF A CORPSE--WITHOUT ANY OF OUR DRONES OR TECH SEEING HIM--BUT NOT SMART ENOUGH TO REALIZE HE'S STANDING BENEATH A DEATH TRAP--
EVEN THOUGH MOVING GIANT ROCKS LIKE A GODDAMN JEDI IS THEIR MOS?
I--
THEY CAN MAKE MISTAKES.
SPEAKING OF, SIMON, THE FUCK?
STOP MAKING OUT WITH SQUISHY.
LOOKIN' FOR HIS TRIGGER.
SIMON, WAIT--
RRRMMMMBLE
OKAY, I DON'T WANNA ALARM ANYBODY, BUT--
YOUR ARM IS STUCK.
KINDA, YEAH.
WANNA LEAVE HIM?
TEMPTING.
FUCK YOU GUYS.
ALSO, I THINK--I MIGHT HAVE THE TRIGGER.
SO DOUBLY FUCK YOU GUYS.

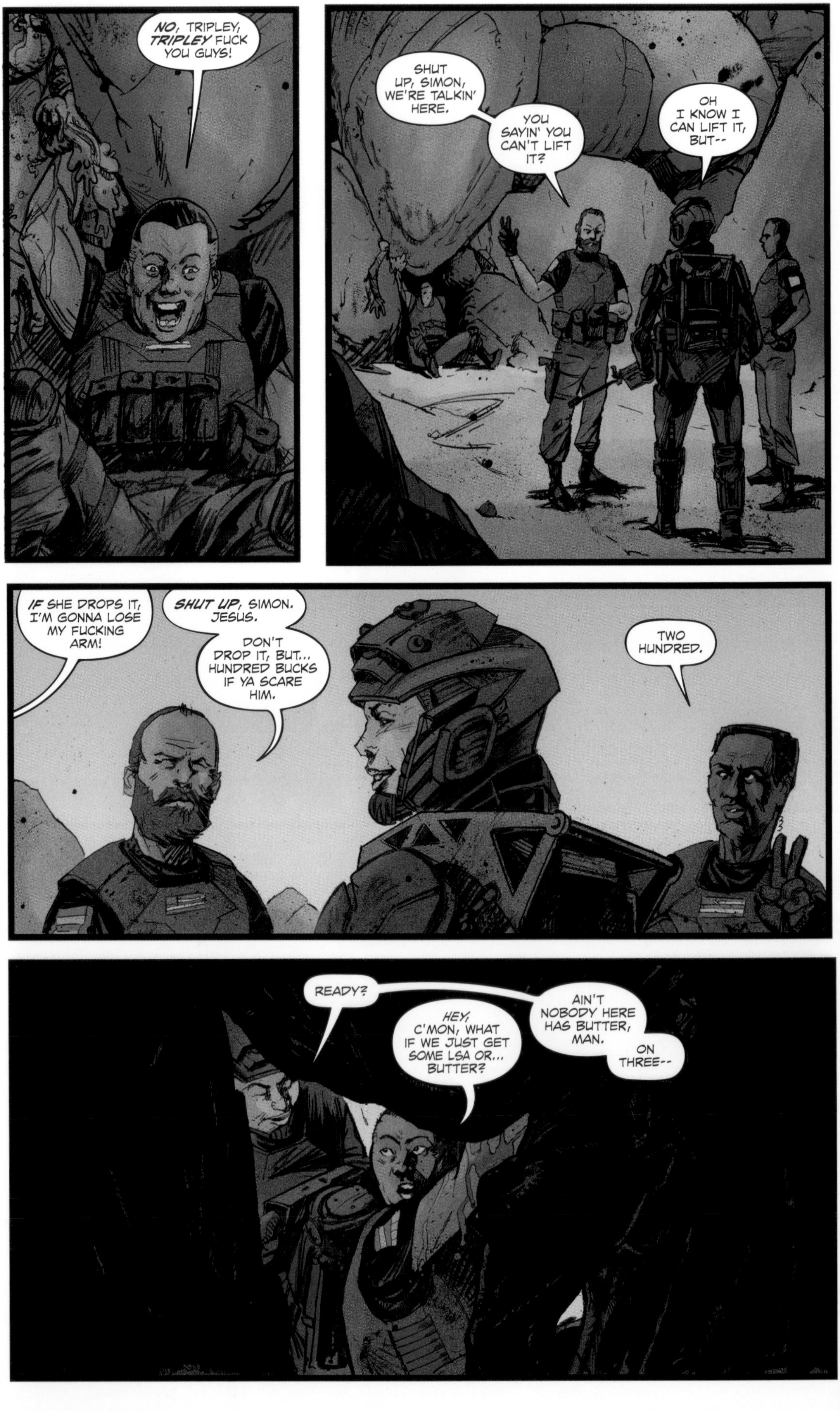
NO, TRIPLEY, TRIPLEY FUCK YOU GUYS!
SHUT UP, SIMON, WE'RE TALKIN' HERE.
YOU SAYIN' YOU CAN'T LIFT IT?
OH I KNOW I CAN LIFT IT, BUT--
IF SHE DROPS IT, I'M GONNA LOSE MY FUCKING ARM!
SHUT UP, SIMON. JESUS.
DON'T DROP IT, BUT... HUNDRED BUCKS IF YA SCARE HIM.
TWO HUNDRED.
READY?
HEY, C'MON, WHAT IF WE JUST GET SOME LSA OR... BUTTER?
AIN'T NOBODY HERE HAS BUTTER, MAN.
ON THREE--

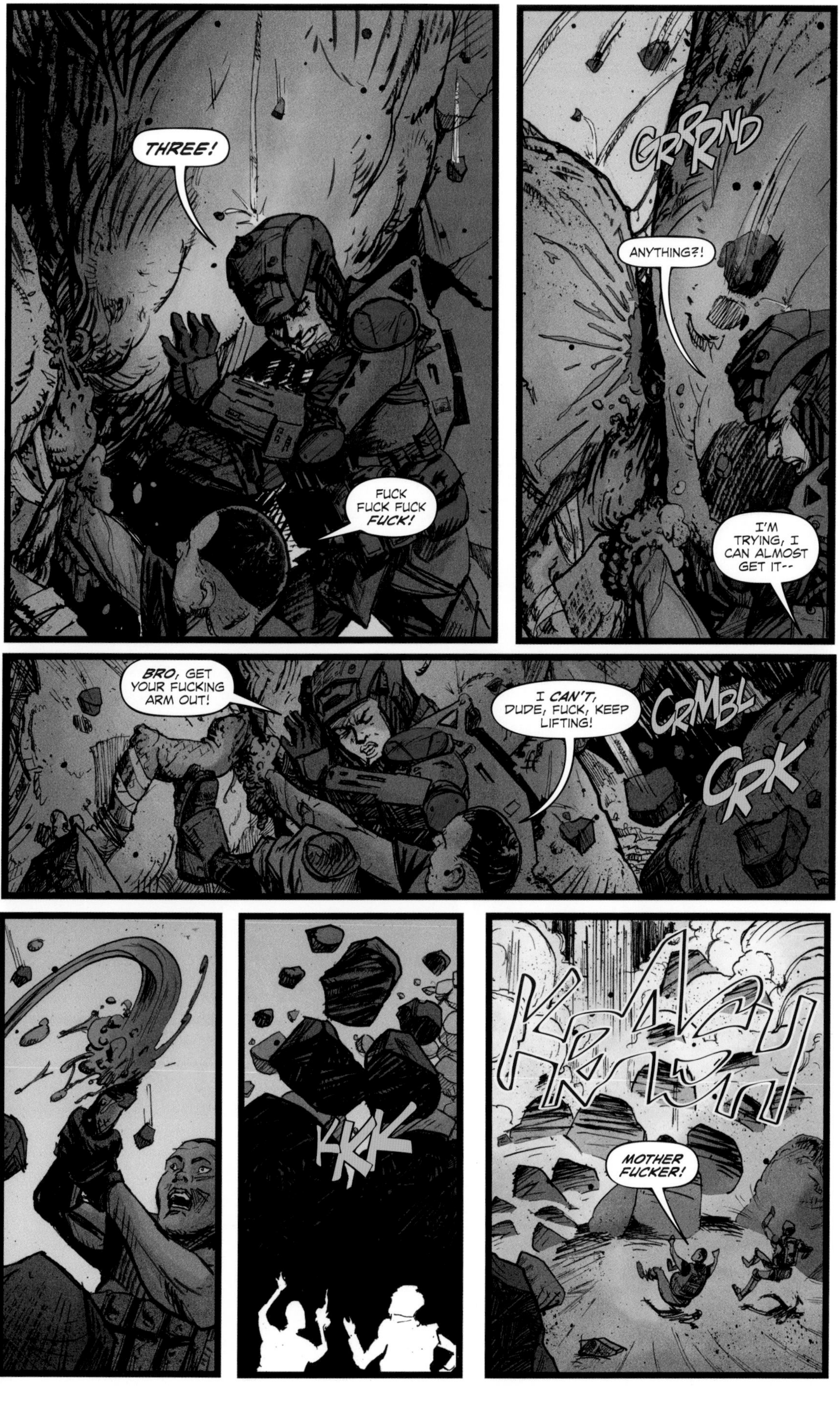
THREE!
FUCK
FUCK FUCK
FUCK!
GRRRND
ANYTHING?!
I'M
TRYING, I
CAN ALMOST
GET IT--
BRO, GET
YOUR FUCKING
ARM OUT!
I CAN'T,
DUDE, FUCK, KEEP
LIFTING!
CRMBL
CRK
KRK
KRACH
KRASH
MOTHER
FUCKER!

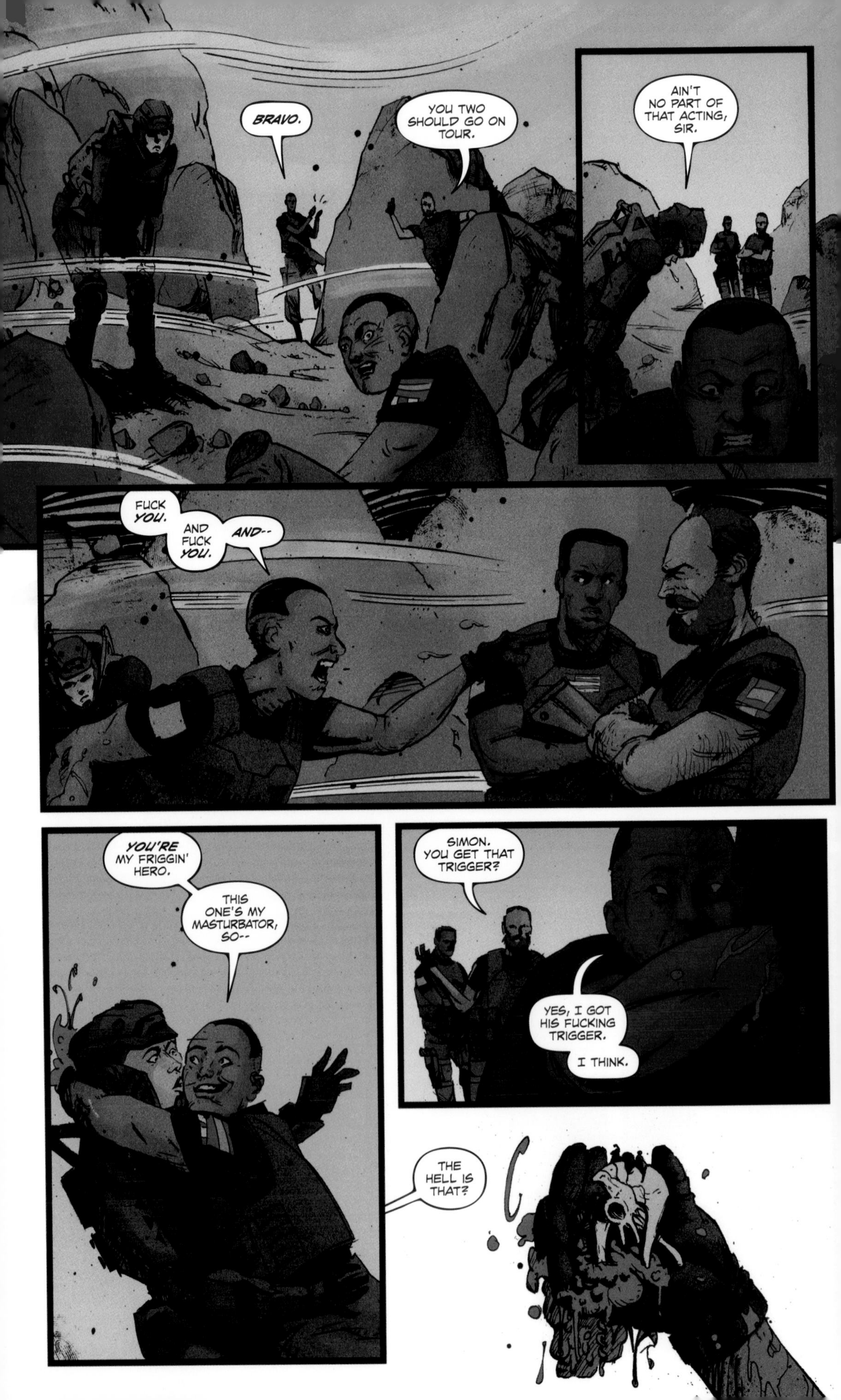
BRAVO.
YOU TWO SHOULD GO ON TOUR.
AIN'T NO PART OF THAT ACTING, SIR.
FUCK YOU.
AND FUCK YOU.
AND--
YOU'RE MY FRIGGIN' HERO.
THIS ONE'S MY MASTURBATOR, SO--
SIMON. YOU GET THAT TRIGGER?
YES, I GOT HIS FUCKING TRIGGER.
I THINK.
THE HELL IS THAT?

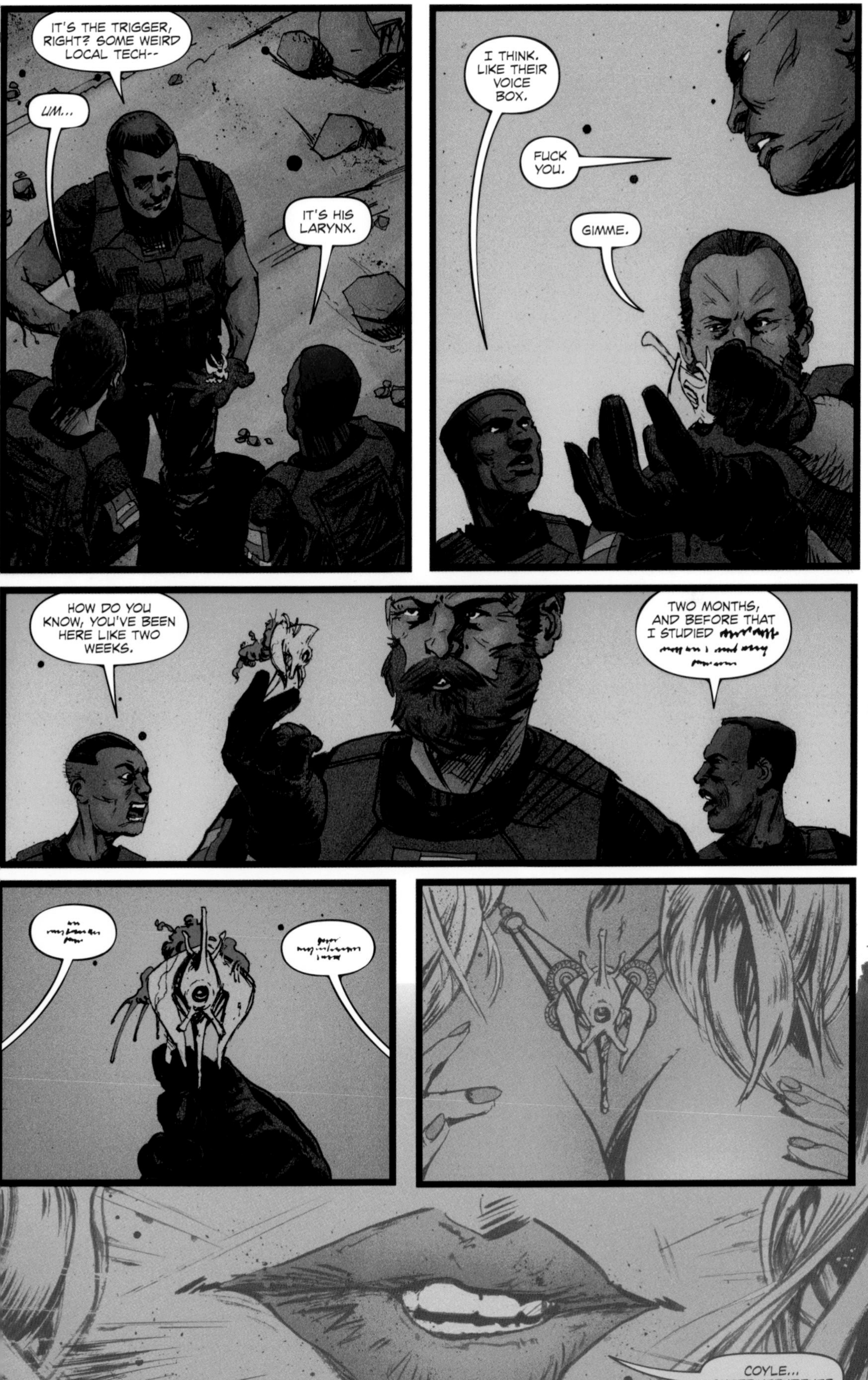
IT'S THE TRIGGER, RIGHT? SOME WEIRD LOCAL TECH--
UM...
IT'S HIS LARYNX.
I THINK. LIKE THEIR VOICE BOX.
FUCK YOU.
GIMME.
HOW DO YOU KNOW, YOU'VE BEEN HERE LIKE TWO WEEKS.
TWO MONTHS, AND BEFORE THAT I STUDIED
COYLE... SUPERINTENDENT?

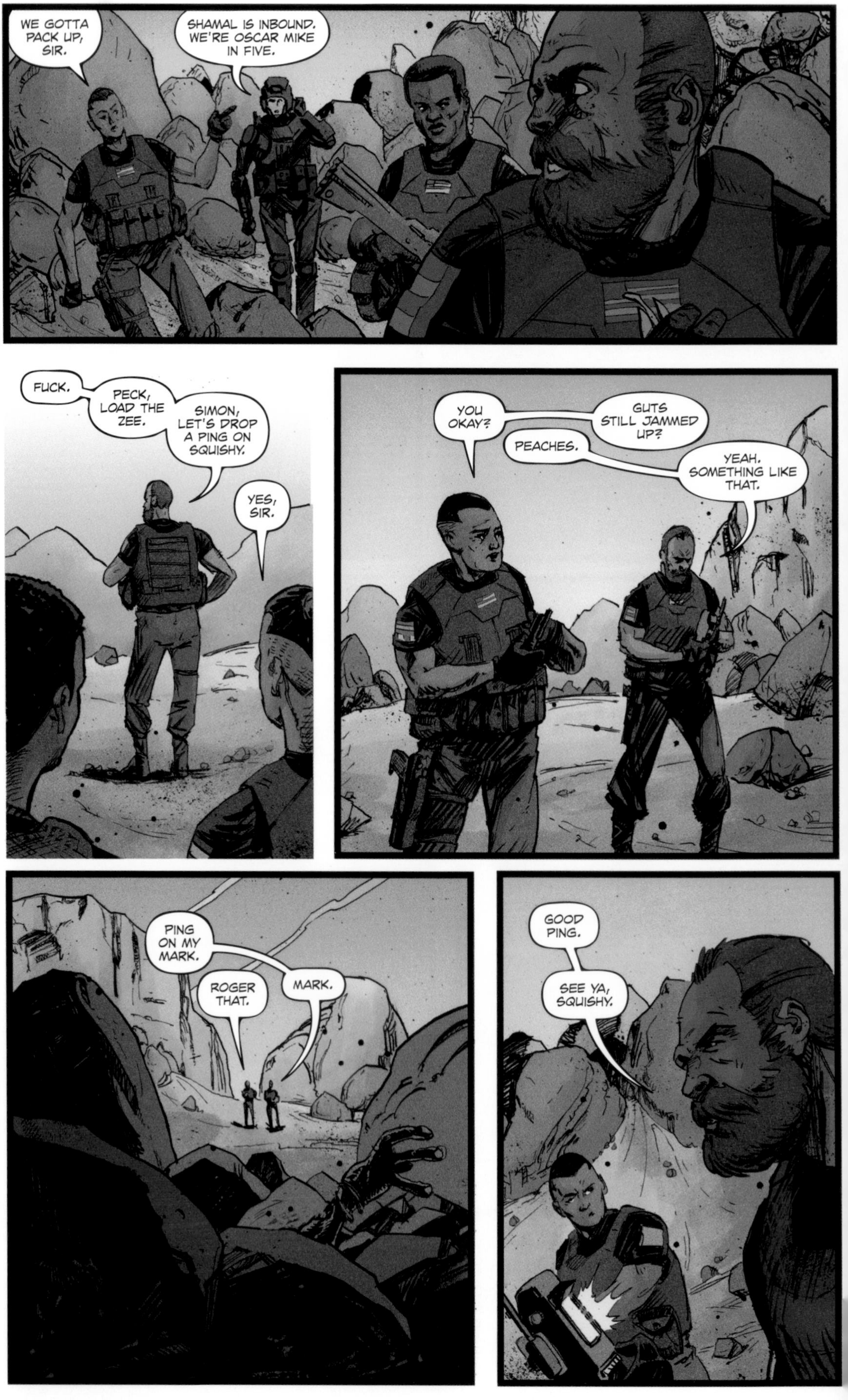
WE GOTTA PACK UP, SIR.
SHAMAL IS INBOUND. WE'RE OSCAR MIKE IN FIVE.
FUCK.
PECK, LOAD THE ZEE.
SIMON, LET'S DROP A PING ON SQUISHY.
YES, SIR.
YOU OKAY?
GUTS STILL JAMMED UP?
PEACHES.
YEAH. SOMETHING LIKE THAT.
PING ON MY MARK.
ROGER THAT.
MARK.
GOOD PING.
SEE YA, SQUISHY.

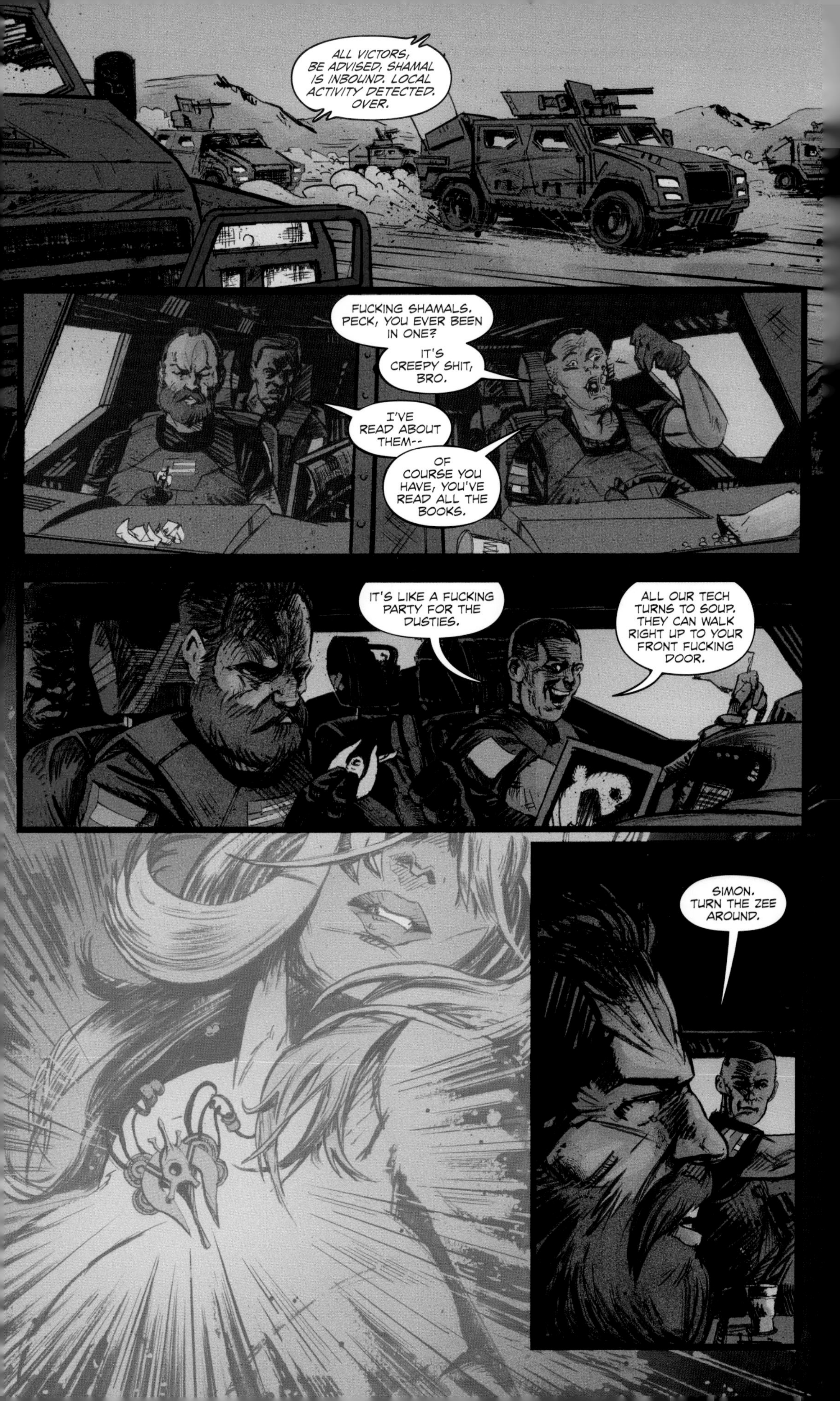
ALL VICTORS, BE ADVISED, SHAMAL IS INBOUND. LOCAL ACTIVITY DETECTED. OVER.
FUCKING SHAMALS. PECK, YOU EVER BEEN IN ONE?
IT'S CREEPY SHIT, BRO.
I'VE READ ABOUT THEM--
OF COURSE YOU HAVE, YOU'VE READ ALL THE BOOKS.
IT'S LIKE A FUCKING PARTY FOR THE DUSTIES.
ALL OUR TECH TURNS TO SOUP. THEY CAN WALK RIGHT UP TO YOUR FRONT FUCKING DOOR.
SIMON. TURN THE ZEE AROUND.

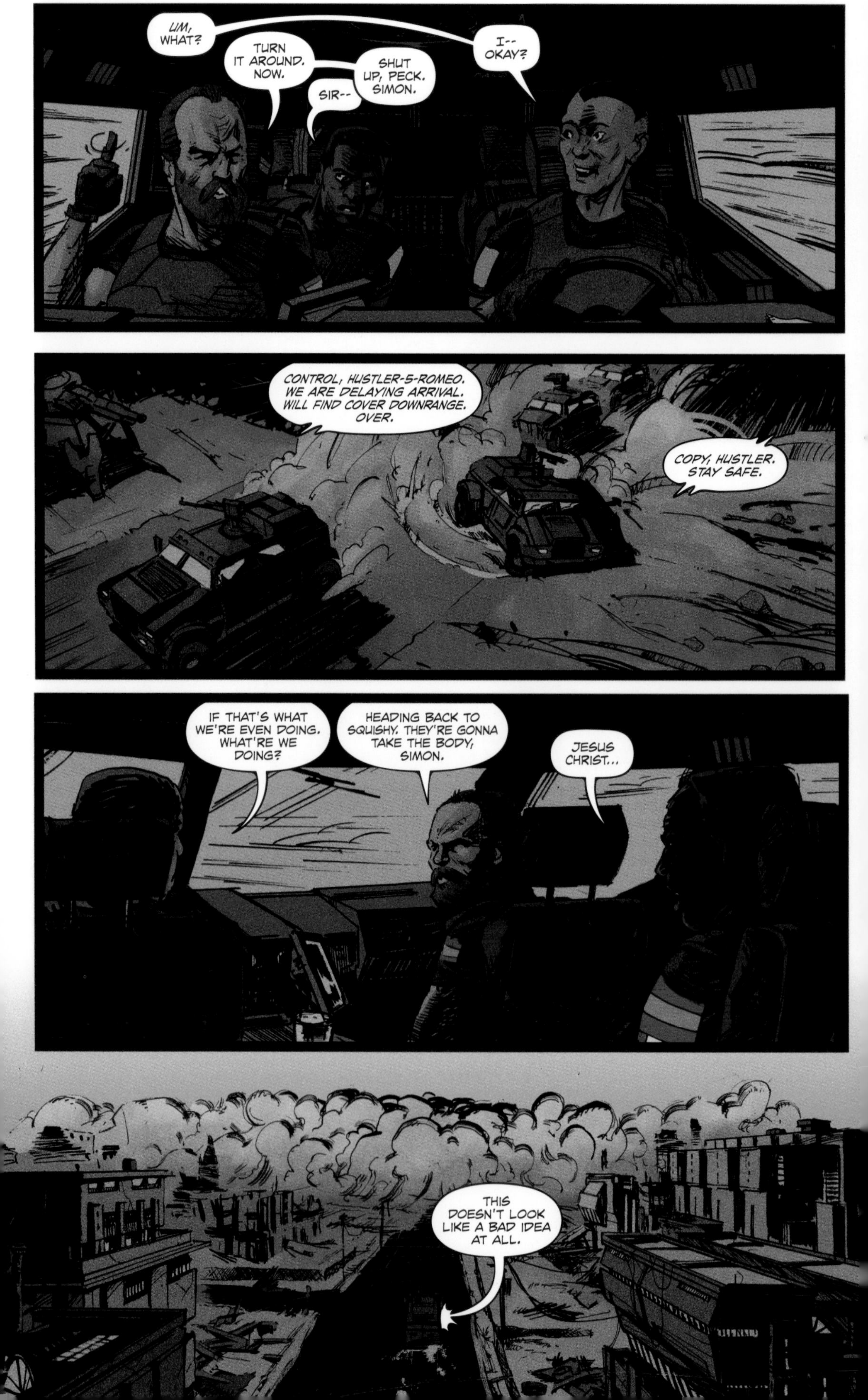
UM, WHAT?
TURN IT AROUND. NOW.
SIR--
SHUT UP, PECK. SIMON.
I-- OKAY?
CONTROL, HUSTLER-5-ROMEO. WE ARE DELAYING ARRIVAL. WILL FIND COVER DOWNRANGE. OVER.
COPY, HUSTLER. STAY SAFE.
IF THAT'S WHAT WE'RE EVEN DOING. WHAT'RE WE DOING?
HEADING BACK TO SQUISHY. THEY'RE GONNA TAKE THE BODY, SIMON.
JESUS CHRIST...
THIS DOESN'T LOOK LIKE A BAD IDEA AT ALL.

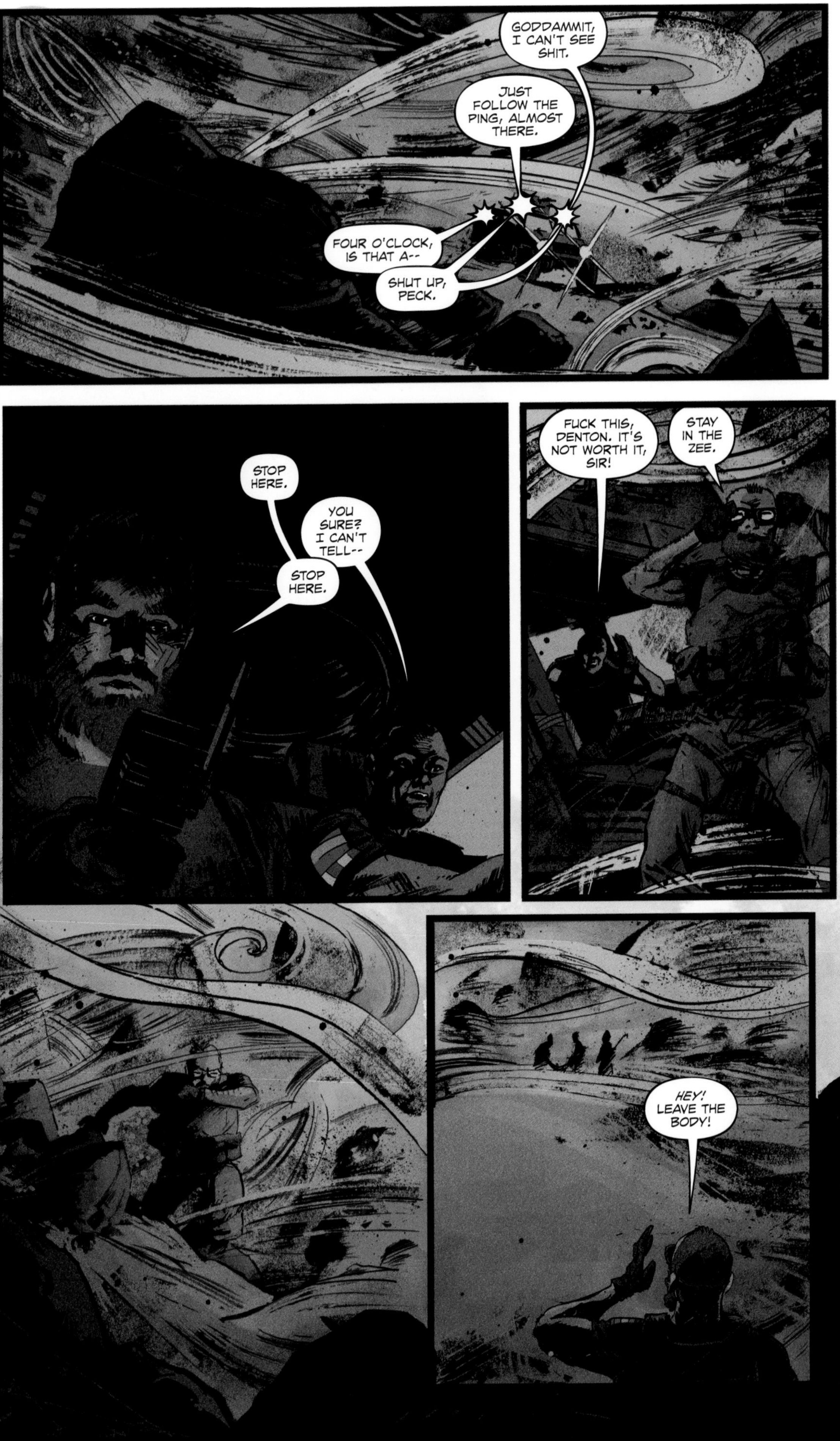
GODDAMMIT, I CAN'T SEE SHIT.
JUST FOLLOW THE PING, ALMOST THERE.
FOUR O'CLOCK, IS THAT A--
SHUT UP, PECK.
STOP HERE.
YOU SURE? I CAN'T TELL--
STOP HERE.
FUCK THIS, DENTON. IT'S NOT WORTH IT, SIR!
STAY IN THE ZEE.
HEY! LEAVE THE BODY!

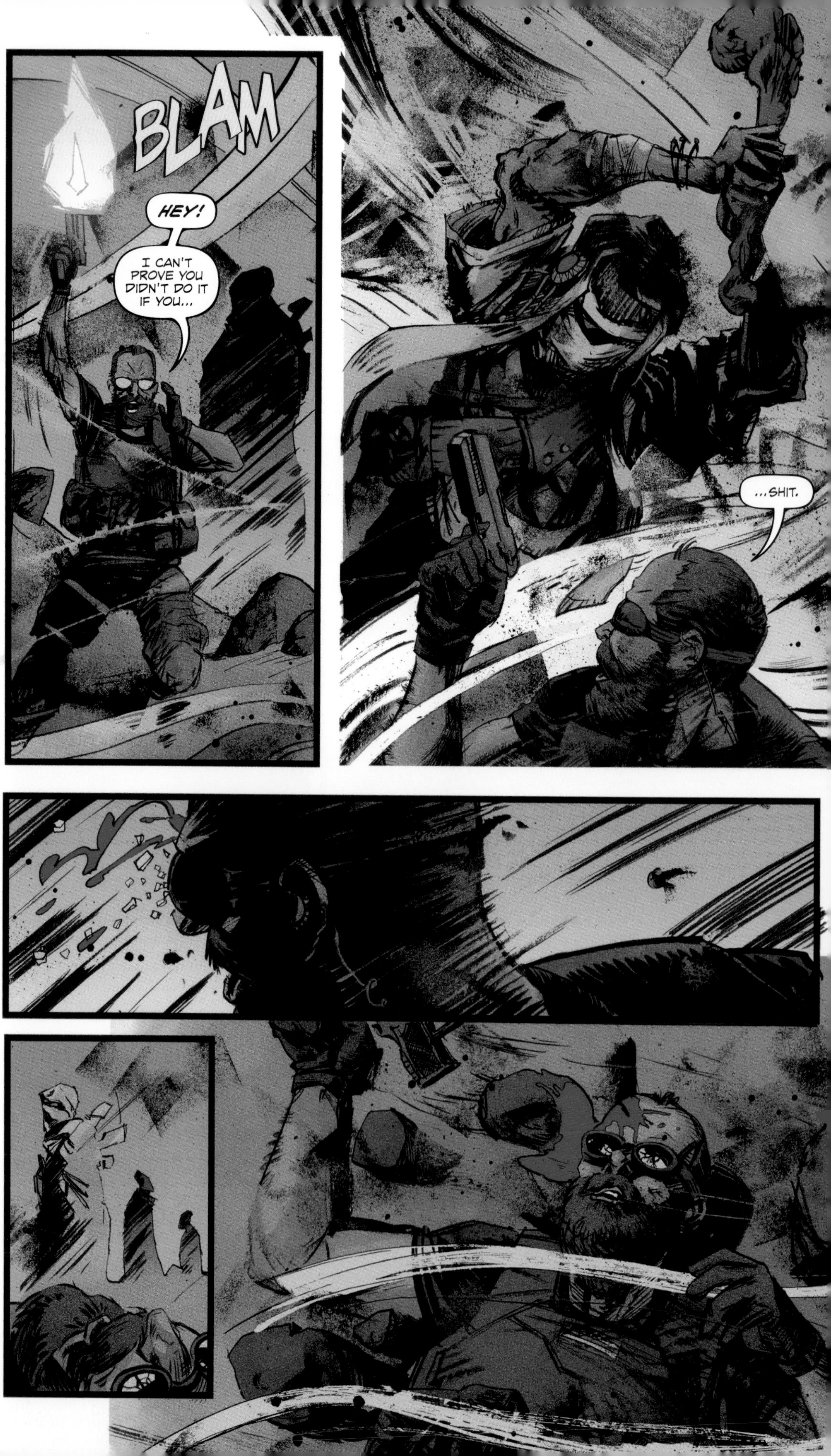
BLAM
HEY!
I CAN'T PROVE YOU DIDN'T DO IT IF YOU...
...SHIT.

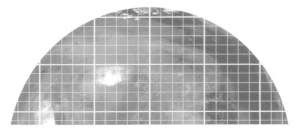

CHAPTER 02

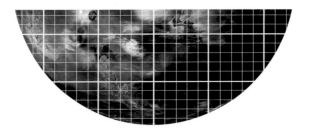

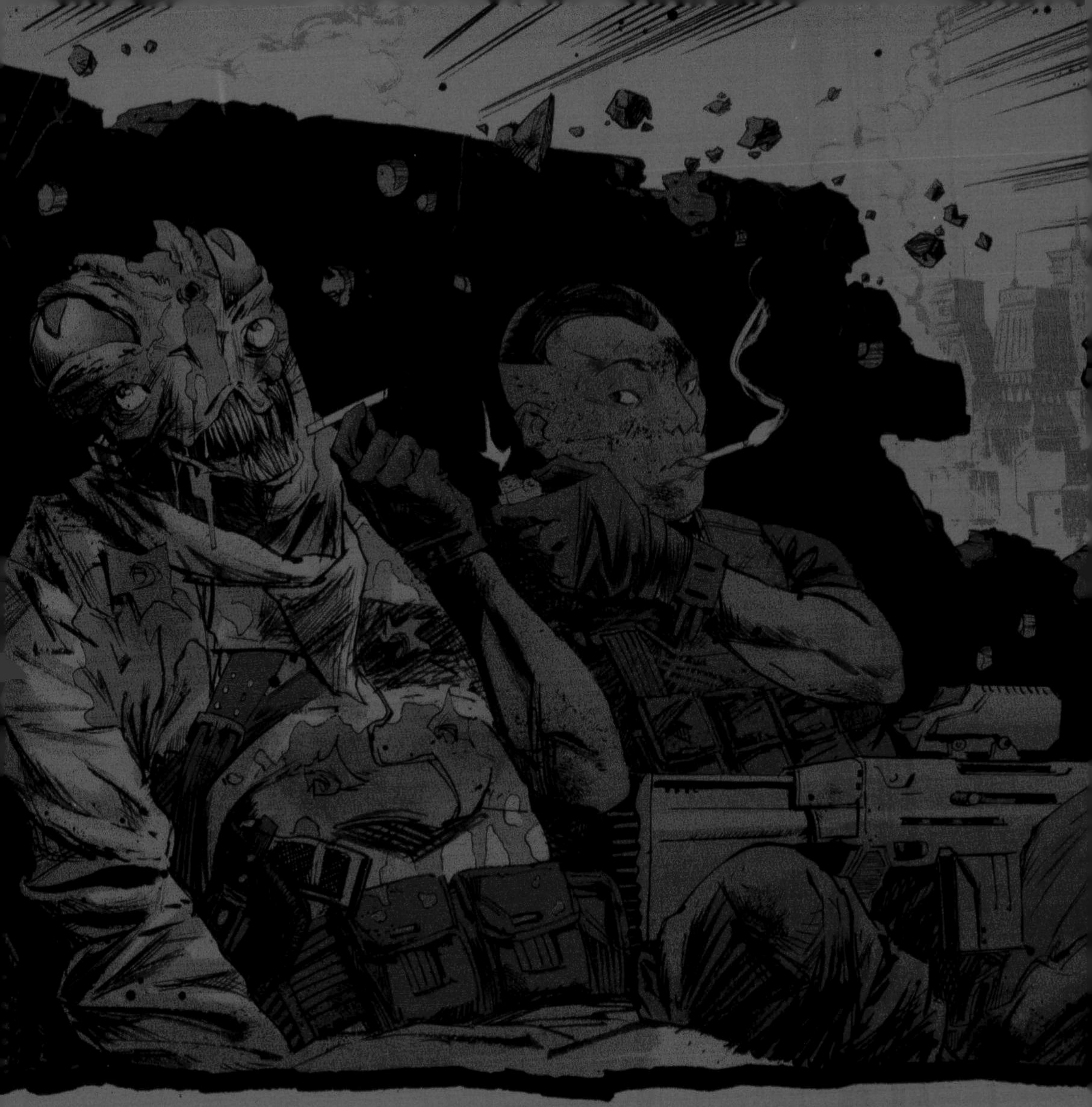

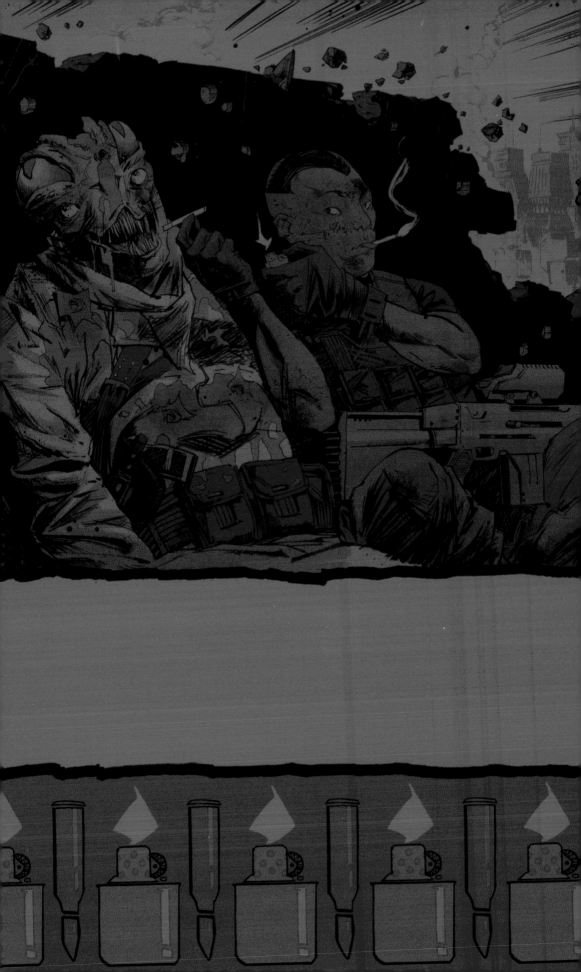

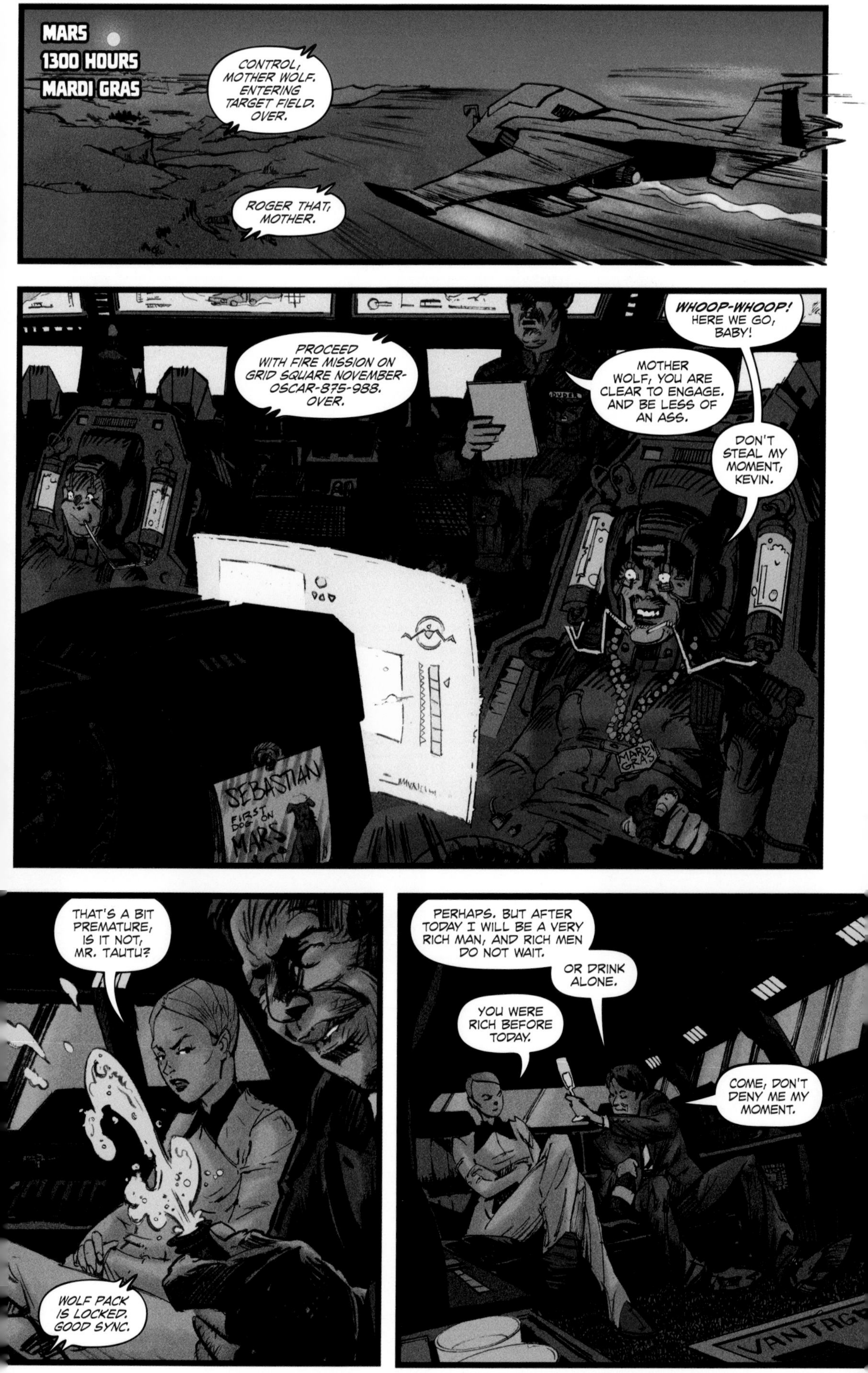
MARS
1300 HOURS
MARDI GRAS
CONTROL, MOTHER WOLF. ENTERING TARGET FIELD. OVER.
ROGER THAT, MOTHER.
PROCEED WITH FIRE MISSION ON GRID SQUARE NOVEMBER-OSCAR-875-988. OVER.
WHOOP-WHOOP! HERE WE GO, BABY!
MOTHER WOLF, YOU ARE CLEAR TO ENGAGE. AND BE LESS OF AN ASS.
DON'T STEAL MY MOMENT, KEVIN.
MARDI GRAS
SEBASTIAN FIRST DOG ON MARS
THAT'S A BIT PREMATURE, IS IT NOT, MR. TAUTU?
WOLF PACK IS LOCKED. GOOD SYNC.
PERHAPS. BUT AFTER TODAY I WILL BE A VERY RICH MAN, AND RICH MEN DO NOT WAIT.
OR DRINK ALONE.
YOU WERE RICH BEFORE TODAY.
COME, DON'T DENY ME MY MOMENT.

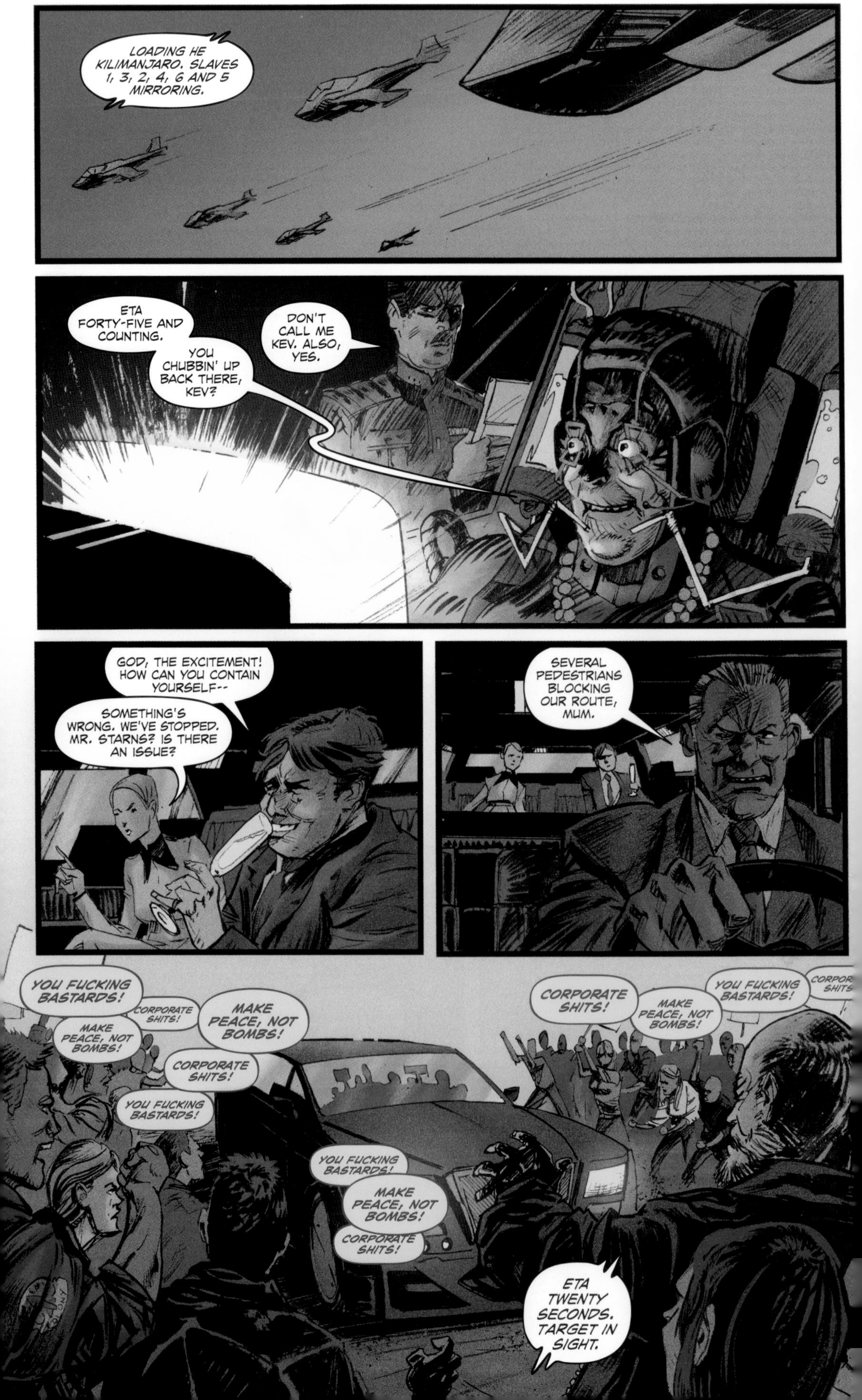
LOADING HE KILIMANJARO. SLAVES 1, 3, 2, 4, 6 AND 5 MIRRORING.
ETA FORTY-FIVE AND COUNTING.
YOU CHUBBIN' UP BACK THERE, KEV?
DON'T CALL ME KEV. ALSO, YES.
GOD, THE EXCITEMENT! HOW CAN YOU CONTAIN YOURSELF--
SOMETHING'S WRONG. WE'VE STOPPED. MR. STARNS? IS THERE AN ISSUE?
SEVERAL PEDESTRIANS BLOCKING OUR ROUTE, MUM.
YOU FUCKING BASTARDS!
CORPORATE SHITS!
MAKE PEACE, NOT BOMBS!
MAKE PEACE, NOT BOMBS!
CORPORATE SHITS!
YOU FUCKING BASTARDS!
YOU FUCKING BASTARDS!
MAKE PEACE, NOT BOMBS!
CORPORATE SHITS!
CORPORATE SHITS!
MAKE PEACE, NOT BOMBS!
YOU FUCKING BASTARDS!
ETA TWENTY SECONDS. TARGET IN SIGHT.

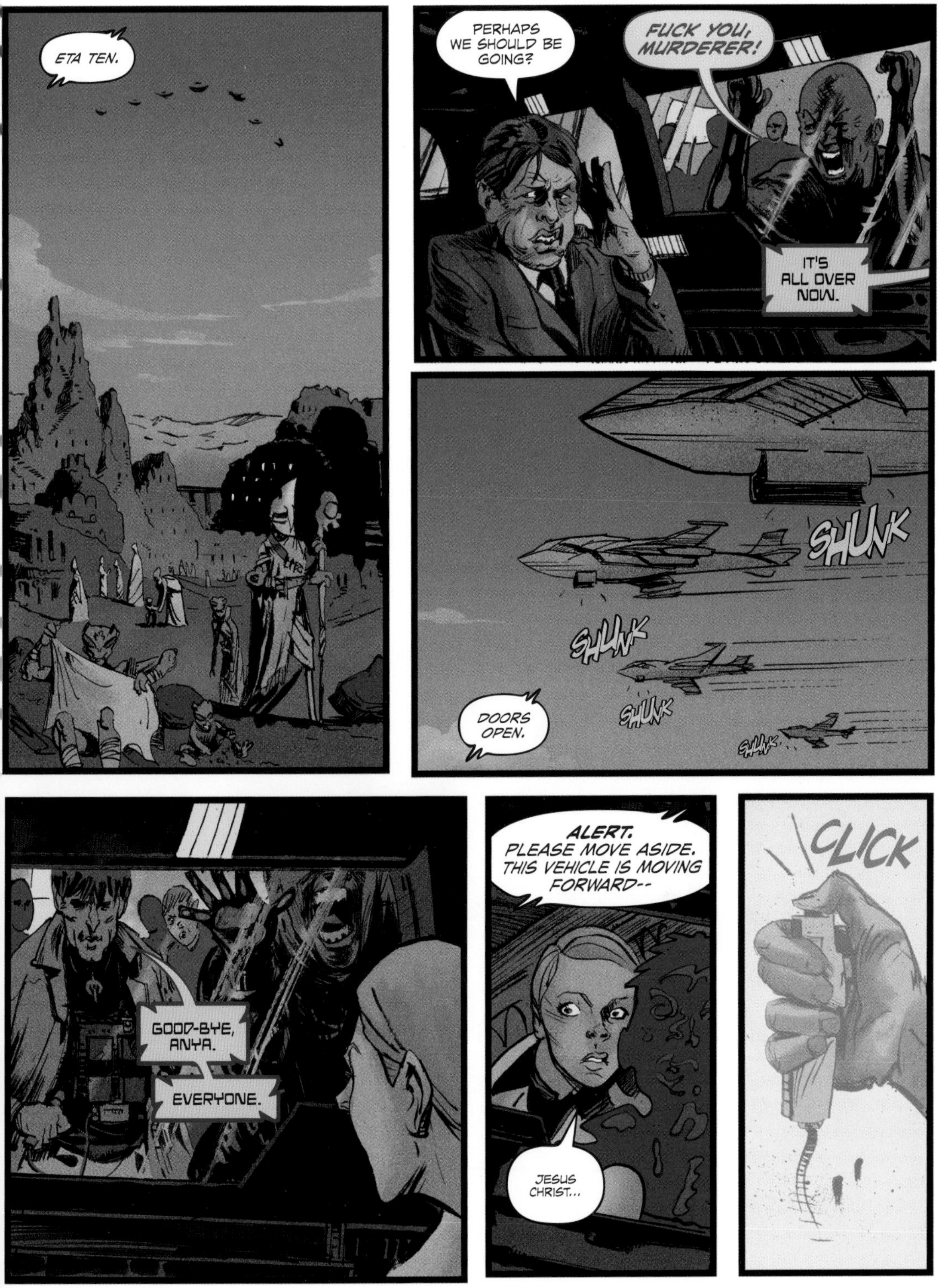
ETA TEN.
PERHAPS WE SHOULD BE GOING?
FUCK YOU, MURDERER!
IT'S ALL OVER NOW.
SHUNK
SHUNK
SHUNK
SHUNK
DOORS OPEN.
GOOD-BYE, ANYA.
EVERYONE.
ALERT. PLEASE MOVE ASIDE. THIS VEHICLE IS MOVING FORWARD--
JESUS CHRIST...
CLICK

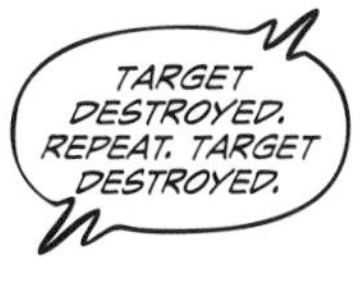
TARGET DESTROYED. REPEAT. TARGET DESTROYED.

CHAPTER 02

And out of darkness came the hands
That reach thro' nature, moulding men.

Alfred, Lord Tennyson

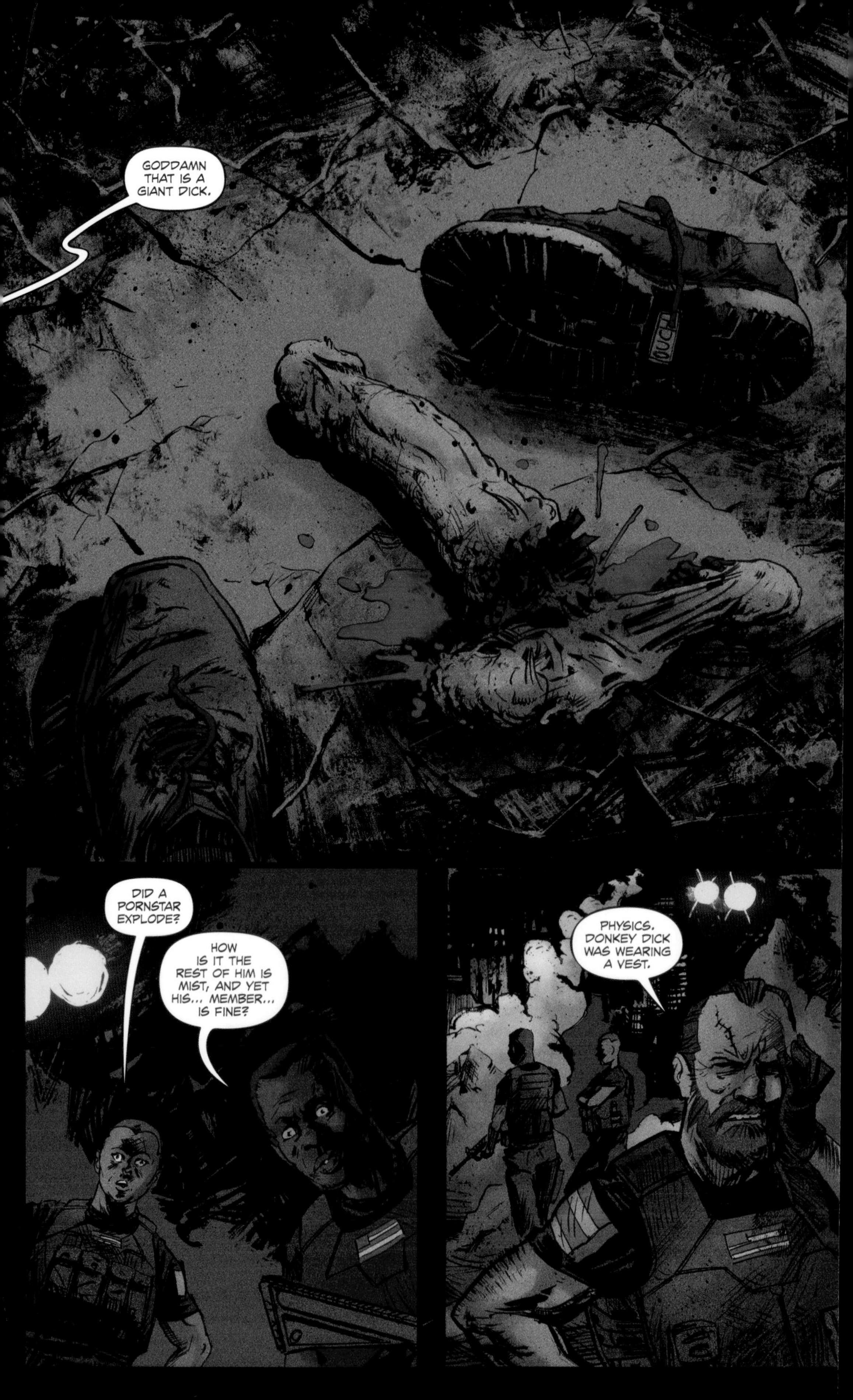
GODDAMN THAT IS A GIANT DICK.
DID A PORNSTAR EXPLODE?
HOW IS IT THE REST OF HIM IS MIST, AND YET HIS... MEMBER... IS FINE?
PHYSICS. DONKEY DICK WAS WEARING A VEST.

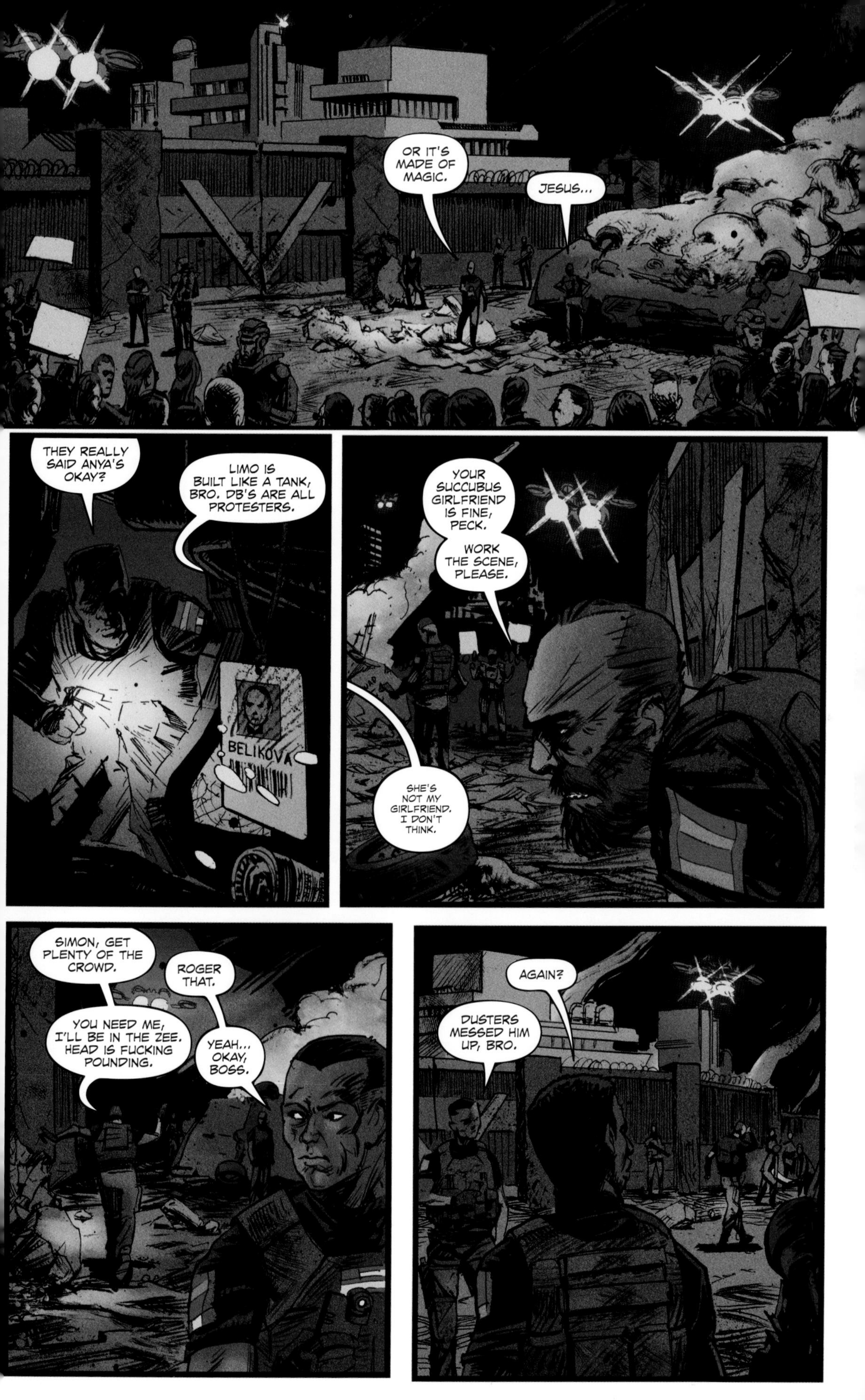
OR IT'S MADE OF MAGIC.
JESUS...
THEY REALLY SAID ANYA'S OKAY?
LIMO IS BUILT LIKE A TANK, BRO. DB'S ARE ALL PROTESTERS.
BELIKOVA
YOUR SUCCUBUS GIRLFRIEND IS FINE, PECK.
WORK THE SCENE, PLEASE.
SHE'S NOT MY GIRLFRIEND. I DON'T THINK.
SIMON, GET PLENTY OF THE CROWD.
ROGER THAT.
YOU NEED ME, I'LL BE IN THE ZEE. HEAD IS FUCKING POUNDING.
YEAH... OKAY, BOSS.
AGAIN?
DUSTERS MESSED HIM UP, BRO.

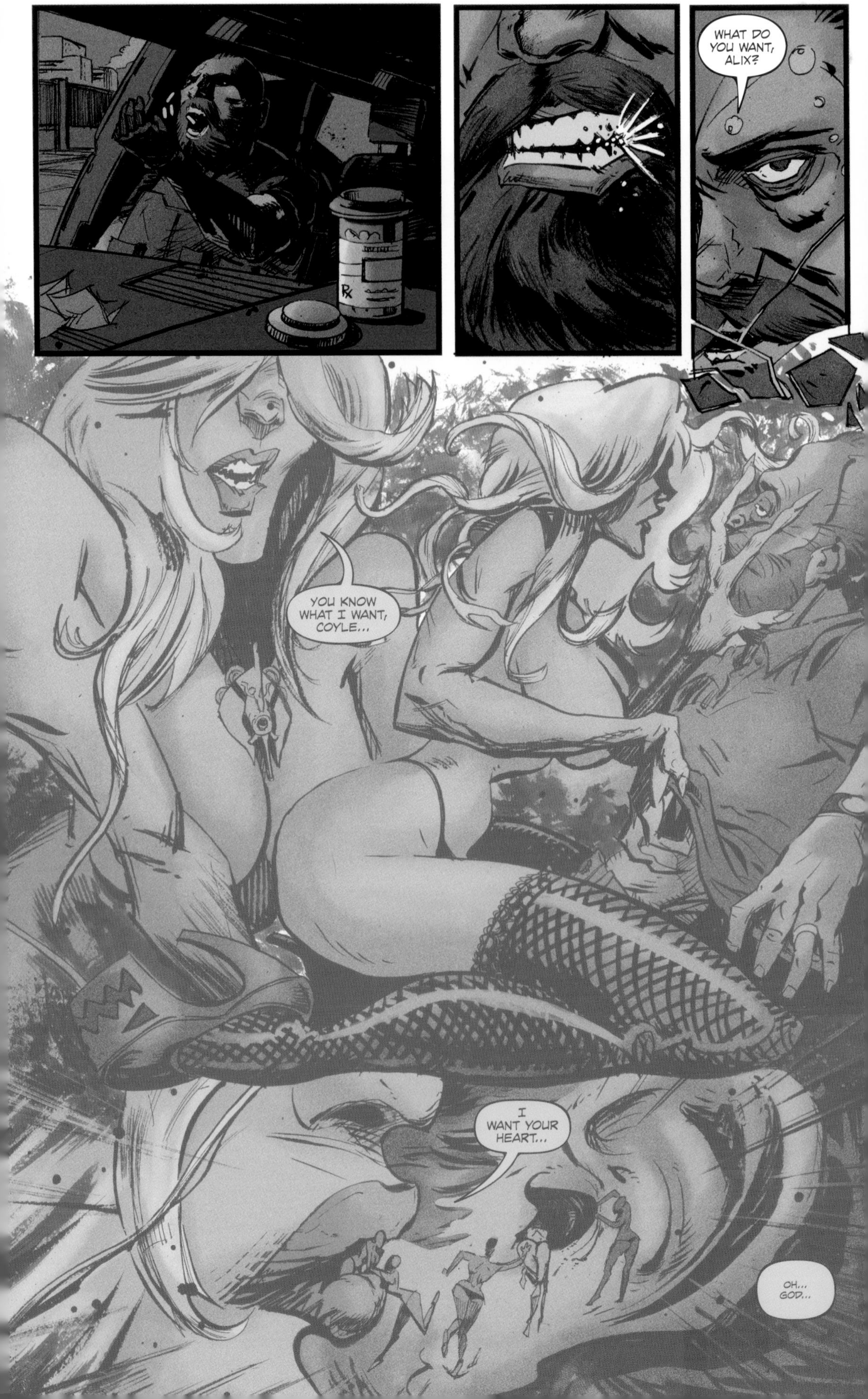
WHAT DO YOU WANT, ALIX?
YOU KNOW WHAT I WANT, COYLE...
I WANT YOUR HEART...
OH... GOD...

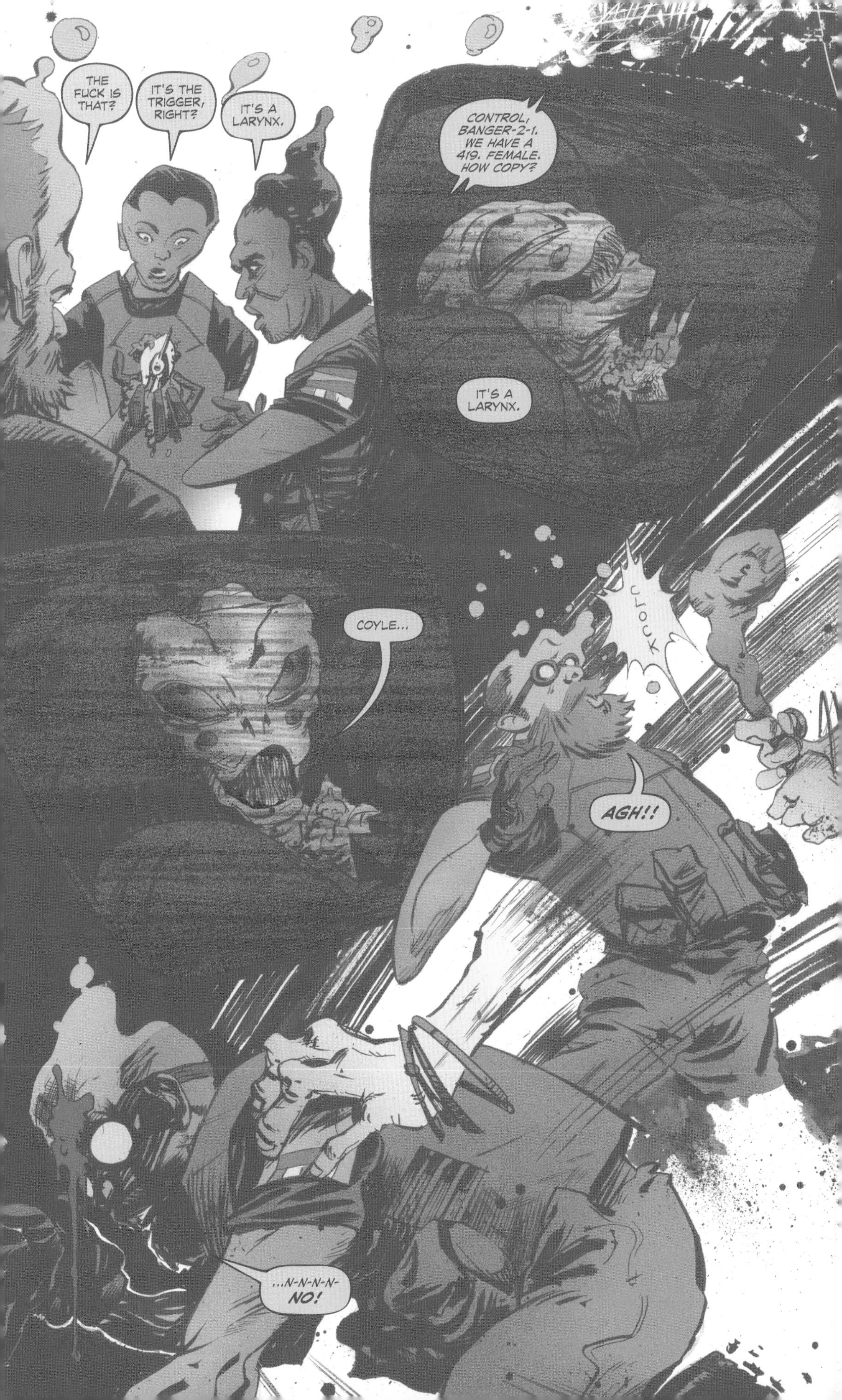

THE FUCK IS THAT?
IT'S THE TRIGGER, RIGHT?
IT'S A LARYNX.
CONTROL, BANGER-2-1. WE HAVE A 419. FEMALE. HOW COPY?
IT'S A LARYNX.
COYLE...
CLOCK
AGH!!
...N-N-N-N- NO!

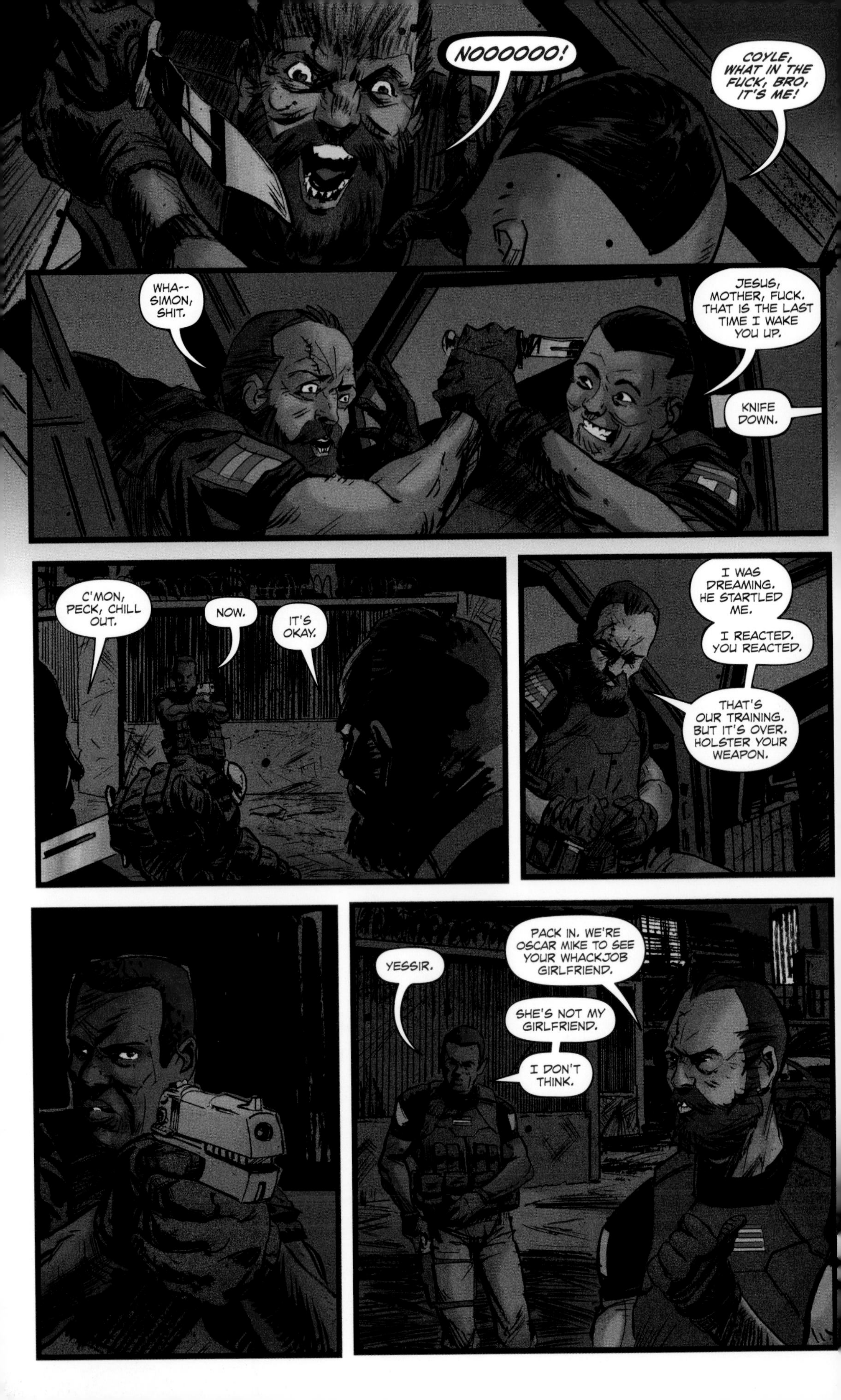
NOOOOOO!
COYLE, WHAT IN THE FUCK, BRO, IT'S ME!
WHA-- SIMON, SHIT.
JESUS, MOTHER, FUCK. THAT IS THE LAST TIME I WAKE YOU UP.
KNIFE DOWN.
C'MON, PECK, CHILL OUT.
NOW.
IT'S OKAY.
I WAS DREAMING. HE STARTLED ME.
I REACTED. YOU REACTED.
THAT'S OUR TRAINING. BUT IT'S OVER. HOLSTER YOUR WEAPON.
YESSIR.
PACK IN. WE'RE OSCAR MIKE TO SEE YOUR WHACKJOB GIRLFRIEND.
SHE'S NOT MY GIRLFRIEND.
I DON'T THINK.

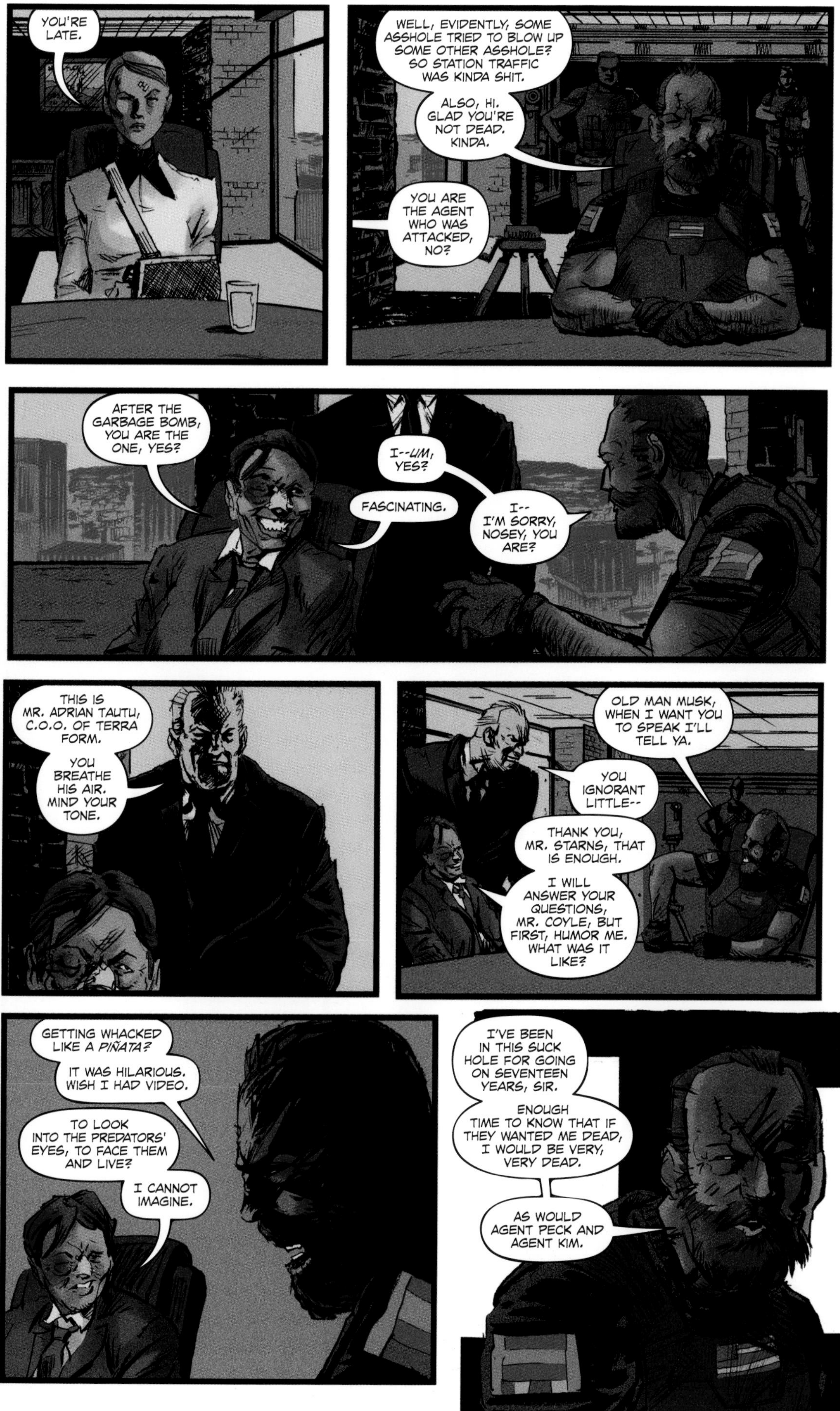
YOU'RE LATE.
WELL, EVIDENTLY, SOME ASSHOLE TRIED TO BLOW UP SOME OTHER ASSHOLE? SO STATION TRAFFIC WAS KINDA SHIT.
ALSO, HI. GLAD YOU'RE NOT DEAD. KINDA.
YOU ARE THE AGENT WHO WAS ATTACKED, NO?
AFTER THE GARBAGE BOMB, YOU ARE THE ONE, YES?
I--UM, YES?
FASCINATING.
I-- I'M SORRY, NOSEY, YOU ARE?
THIS IS MR. ADRIAN TAUTU, C.O.O. OF TERRA FORM.
YOU BREATHE HIS AIR. MIND YOUR TONE.
OLD MAN MUSK, WHEN I WANT YOU TO SPEAK I'LL TELL YA.
YOU IGNORANT LITTLE--
THANK YOU, MR. STARNS, THAT IS ENOUGH.
I WILL ANSWER YOUR QUESTIONS, MR. COYLE, BUT FIRST, HUMOR ME. WHAT WAS IT LIKE?
GETTING WHACKED LIKE A PIÑATA?
IT WAS HILARIOUS. WISH I HAD VIDEO.
TO LOOK INTO THE PREDATORS' EYES, TO FACE THEM AND LIVE?
I CANNOT IMAGINE.
I'VE BEEN IN THIS SUCK HOLE FOR GOING ON SEVENTEEN YEARS, SIR.
ENOUGH TIME TO KNOW THAT IF THEY WANTED ME DEAD, I WOULD BE VERY, VERY DEAD.
AS WOULD AGENT PECK AND AGENT KIM.

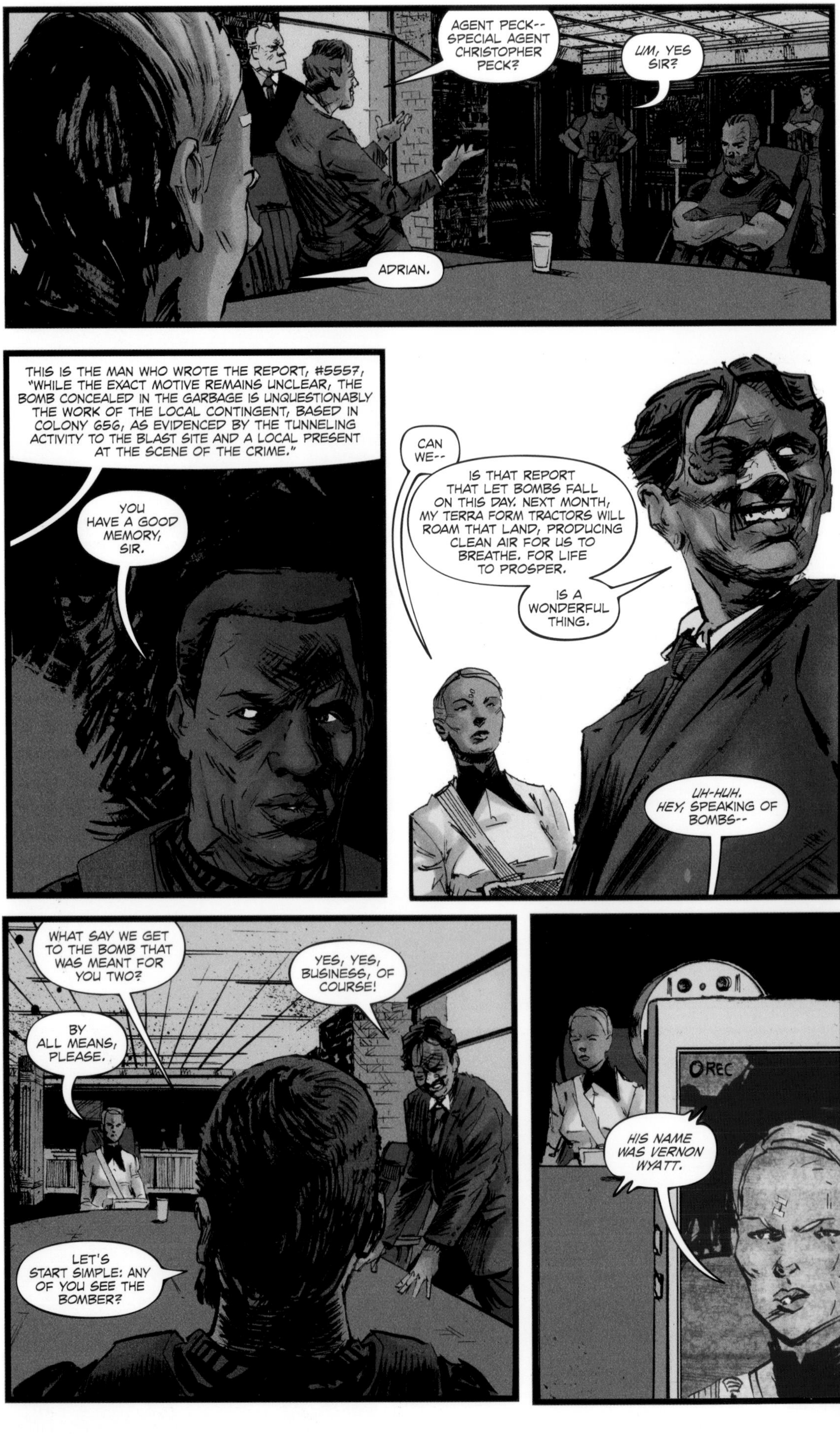
AGENT PECK-- SPECIAL AGENT CHRISTOPHER PECK?
UM, YES SIR?
ADRIAN.
THIS IS THE MAN WHO WROTE THE REPORT, #5557, "WHILE THE EXACT MOTIVE REMAINS UNCLEAR, THE BOMB CONCEALED IN THE GARBAGE IS UNQUESTIONABLY THE WORK OF THE LOCAL CONTINGENT, BASED IN COLONY 656, AS EVIDENCED BY THE TUNNELING ACTIVITY TO THE BLAST SITE AND A LOCAL PRESENT AT THE SCENE OF THE CRIME."
YOU HAVE A GOOD MEMORY, SIR.
CAN WE--
IS THAT REPORT THAT LET BOMBS FALL ON THIS DAY. NEXT MONTH, MY TERRA FORM TRACTORS WILL ROAM THAT LAND, PRODUCING CLEAN AIR FOR US TO BREATHE. FOR LIFE TO PROSPER.
IS A WONDERFUL THING.
UH-HUH. HEY, SPEAKING OF BOMBS--
WHAT SAY WE GET TO THE BOMB THAT WAS MEANT FOR YOU TWO?
YES, YES, BUSINESS, OF COURSE!
BY ALL MEANS, PLEASE.
LET'S START SIMPLE: ANY OF YOU SEE THE BOMBER?
REC
HIS NAME WAS VERNON WYATT.

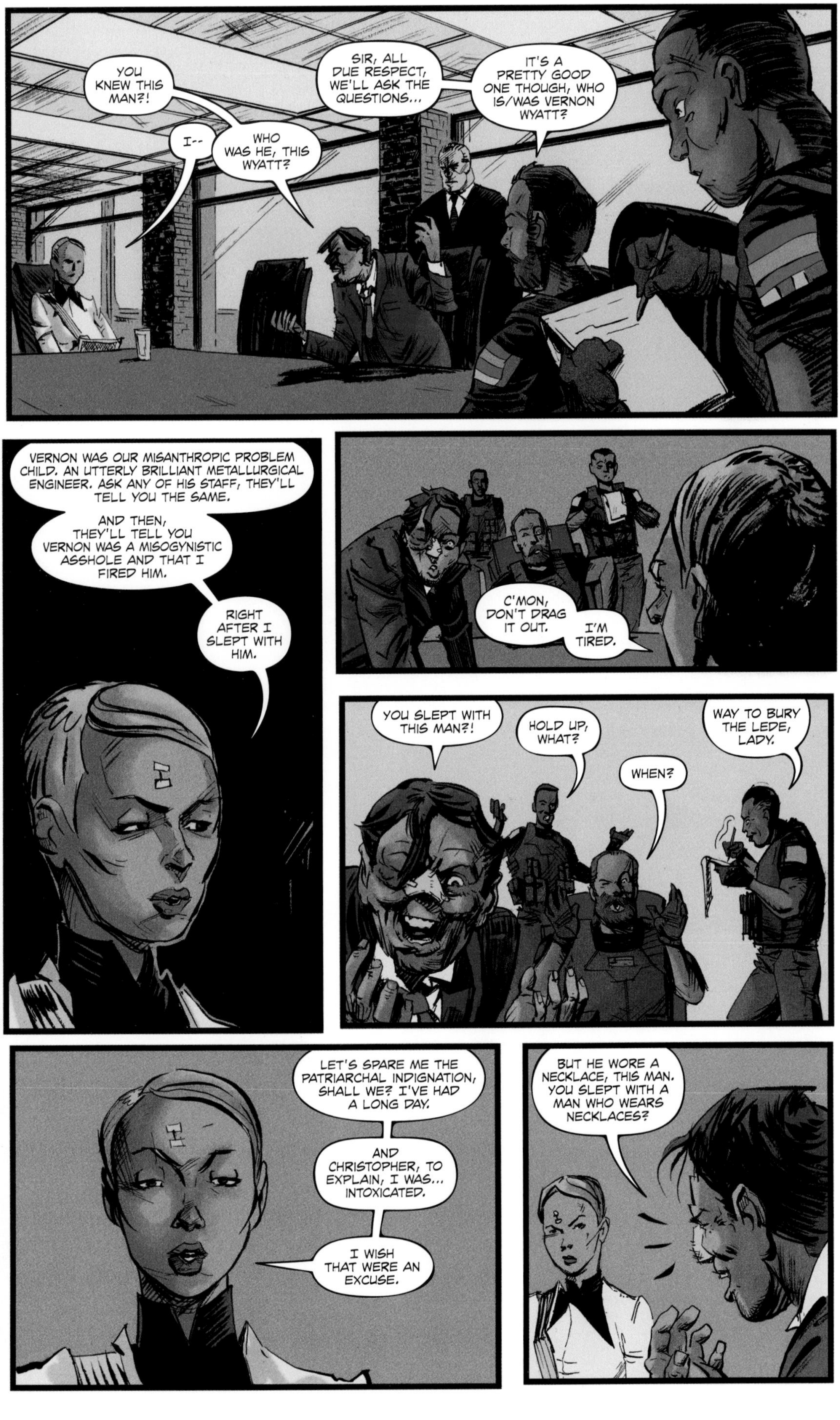
YOU KNEW THIS MAN?!
I--
WHO WAS HE, THIS WYATT?
SIR, ALL DUE RESPECT, WE'LL ASK THE QUESTIONS...
IT'S A PRETTY GOOD ONE THOUGH, WHO IS/WAS VERNON WYATT?
VERNON WAS OUR MISANTHROPIC PROBLEM CHILD. AN UTTERLY BRILLIANT METALLURGICAL ENGINEER. ASK ANY OF HIS STAFF, THEY'LL TELL YOU THE SAME.
AND THEN, THEY'LL TELL YOU VERNON WAS A MISOGYNISTIC ASSHOLE AND THAT I FIRED HIM.
RIGHT AFTER I SLEPT WITH HIM.
C'MON, DON'T DRAG IT OUT.
I'M TIRED.
YOU SLEPT WITH THIS MAN?!
HOLD UP, WHAT?
WHEN?
WAY TO BURY THE LEDE, LADY.
LET'S SPARE ME THE PATRIARCHAL INDIGNATION, SHALL WE? I'VE HAD A LONG DAY.
AND CHRISTOPHER, TO EXPLAIN, I WAS... INTOXICATED.
I WISH THAT WERE AN EXCUSE.
BUT HE WORE A NECKLACE, THIS MAN. YOU SLEPT WITH A MAN WHO WEARS NECKLACES?

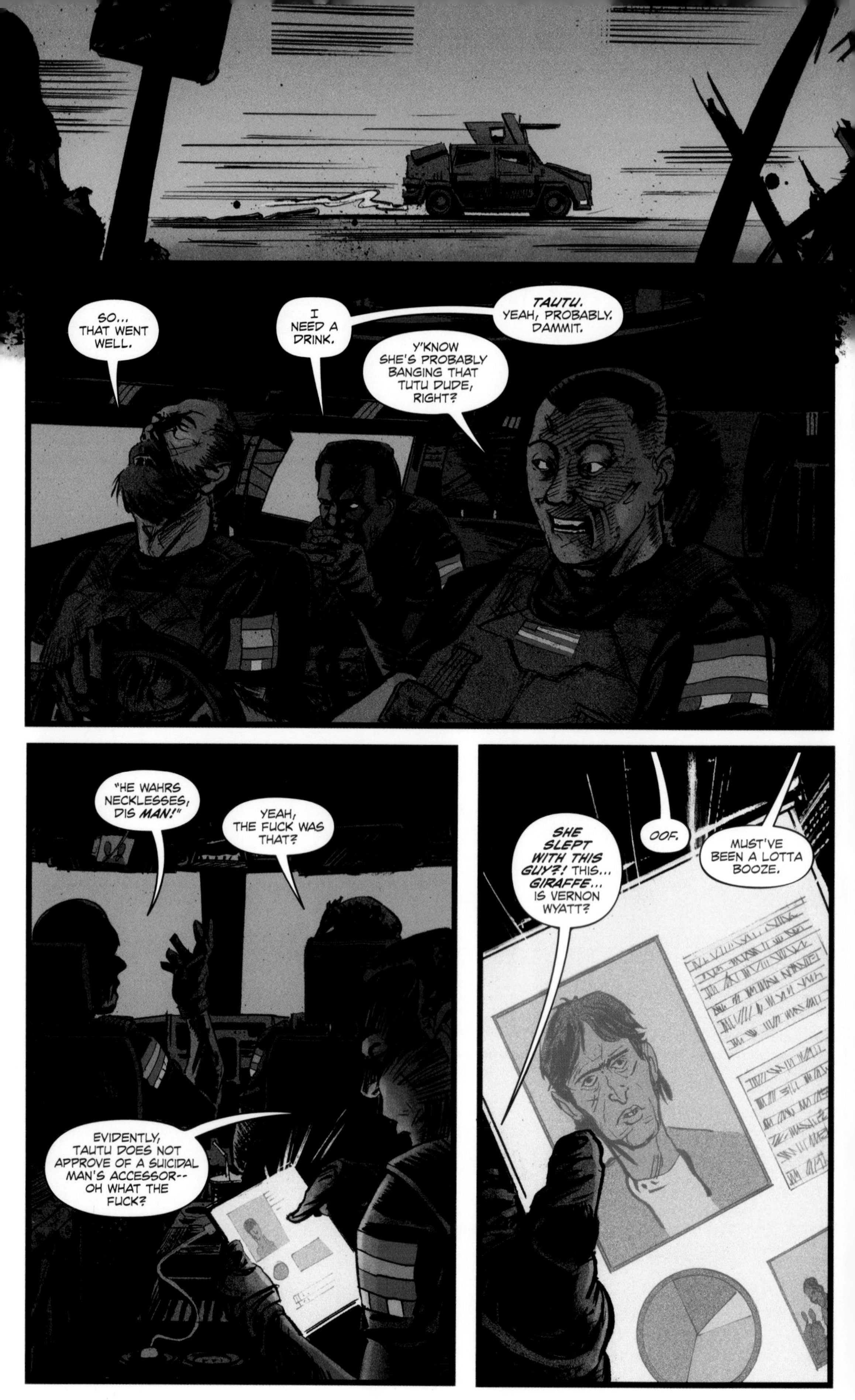
SO... THAT WENT WELL.
I NEED A DRINK.
Y'KNOW SHE'S PROBABLY BANGING THAT TUTU DUDE, RIGHT?
TAUTU. YEAH, PROBABLY. DAMMIT.
"HE WAHRS NECKLESSES, DIS MAN!"
YEAH, THE FUCK WAS THAT?
EVIDENTLY, TAUTU DOES NOT APPROVE OF A SUICIDAL MAN'S ACCESSOR-- OH WHAT THE FUCK?
SHE SLEPT WITH THIS GUY?! THIS... GIRAFFE... IS VERNON WYATT?
OOF.
MUST'VE BEEN A LOTTA BOOZE.

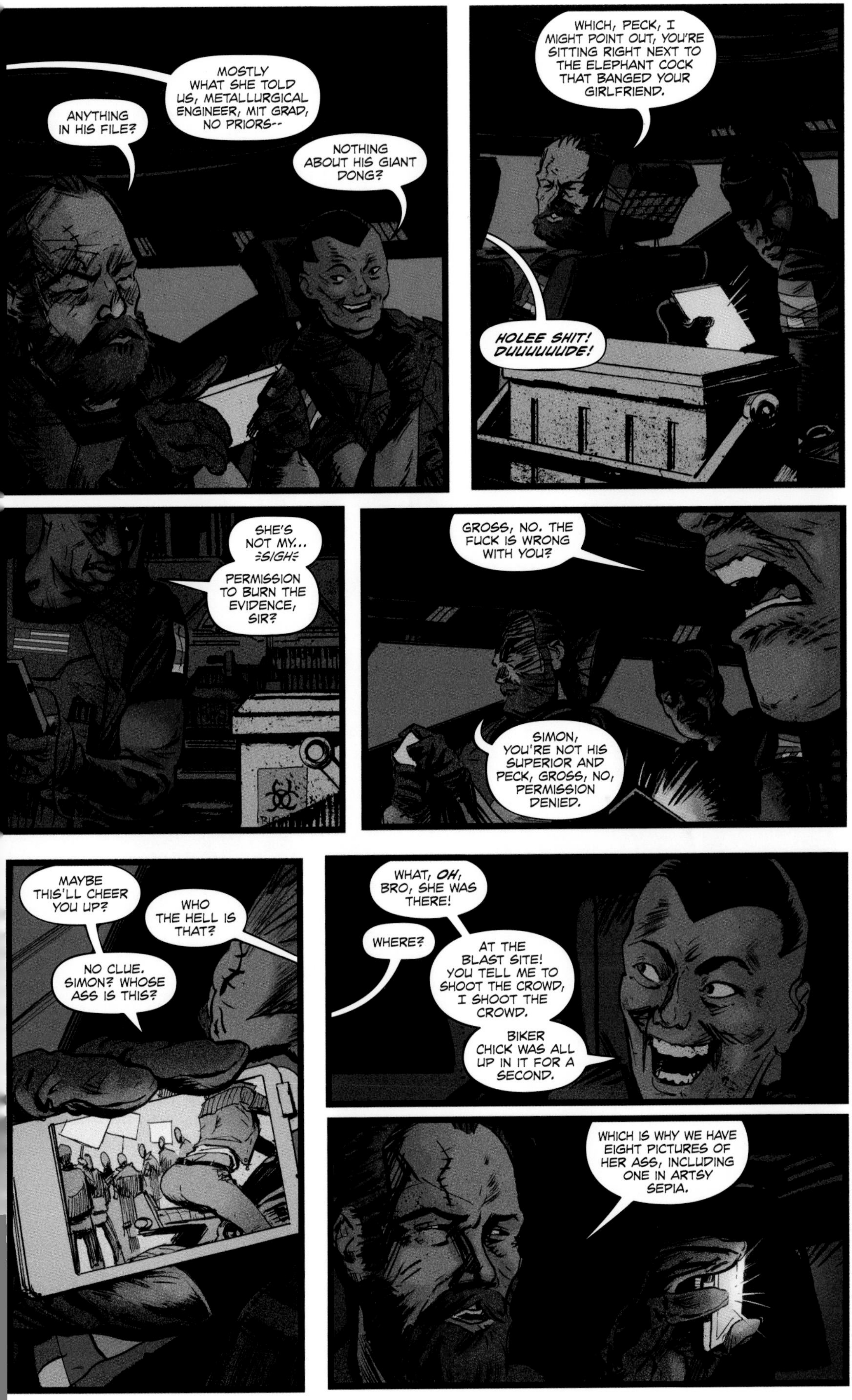
ANYTHING IN HIS FILE?
MOSTLY WHAT SHE TOLD US, METALLURGICAL ENGINEER, MIT GRAD, NO PRIORS--
NOTHING ABOUT HIS GIANT DONG?
WHICH, PECK, I MIGHT POINT OUT, YOU'RE SITTING RIGHT NEXT TO THE ELEPHANT COCK THAT BANGED YOUR GIRLFRIEND.
HOLEE SHIT! DUUUUUUDE!
SHE'S NOT MY... =SIGH=
PERMISSION TO BURN THE EVIDENCE, SIR?
GROSS, NO. THE FUCK IS WRONG WITH YOU?
SIMON, YOU'RE NOT HIS SUPERIOR AND PECK, GROSS, NO, PERMISSION DENIED.
MAYBE THIS'LL CHEER YOU UP?
WHO THE HELL IS THAT?
NO CLUE. SIMON? WHOSE ASS IS THIS?
WHAT, OH, BRO, SHE WAS THERE!
WHERE?
AT THE BLAST SITE! YOU TELL ME TO SHOOT THE CROWD, I SHOOT THE CROWD.
BIKER CHICK WAS ALL UP IN IT FOR A SECOND.
WHICH IS WHY WE HAVE EIGHT PICTURES OF HER ASS, INCLUDING ONE IN ARTSY SEPIA.

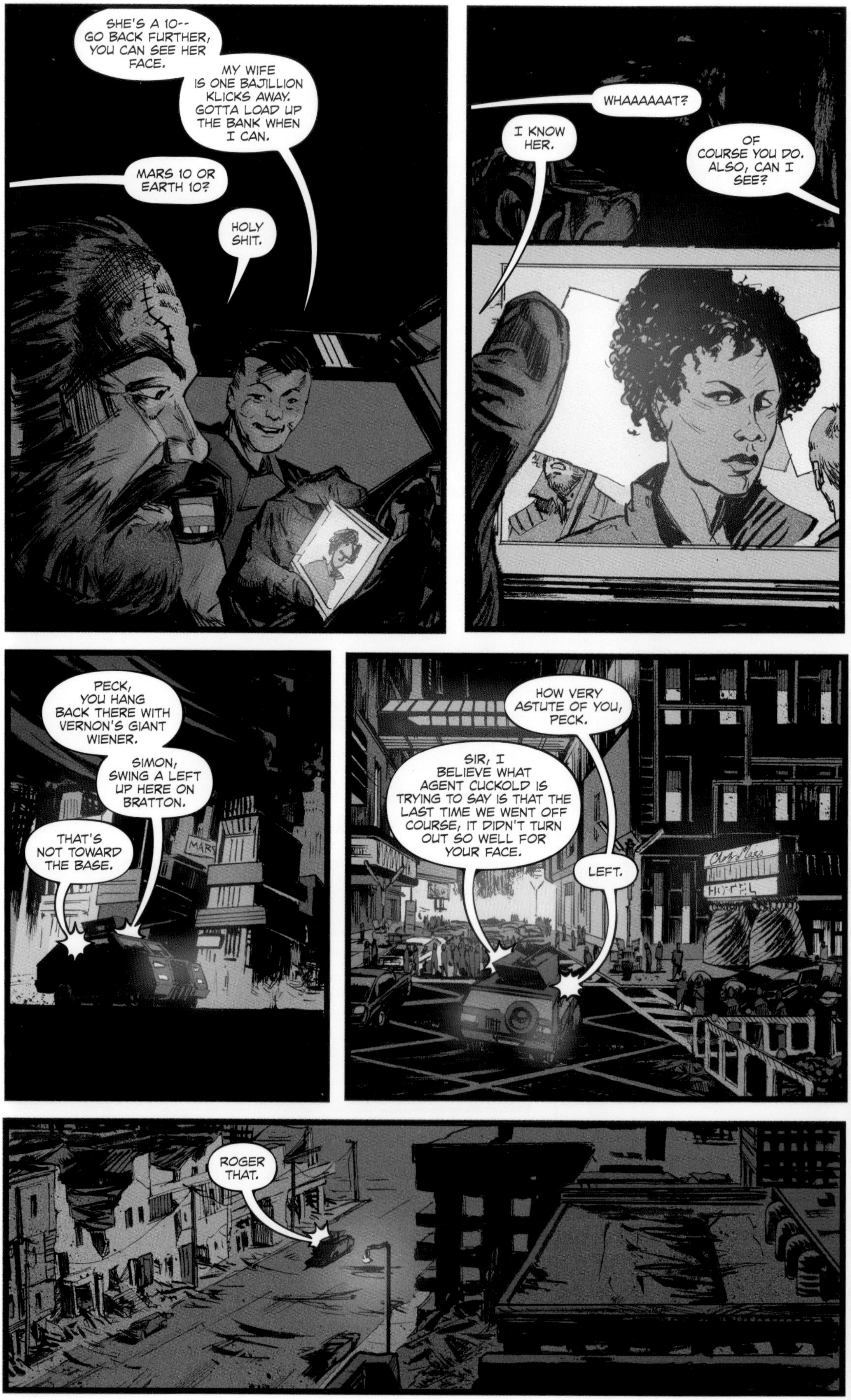
SHE'S A 10-- GO BACK FURTHER, YOU CAN SEE HER FACE.
MY WIFE IS ONE BAJILLION KLICKS AWAY. GOTTA LOAD UP THE BANK WHEN I CAN.
MARS 10 OR EARTH 10?
HOLY SHIT.
WHAAAAAAT?
I KNOW HER.
OF COURSE YOU DO. ALSO, CAN I SEE?
PECK, YOU HANG BACK THERE WITH VERNON'S GIANT WIENER.
SIMON, SWING A LEFT UP HERE ON BRATTON.
THAT'S NOT TOWARD THE BASE.
HOW VERY ASTUTE OF YOU, PECK.
SIR, I BELIEVE WHAT AGENT CUCKOLD IS TRYING TO SAY IS THAT THE LAST TIME WE WENT OFF COURSE, IT DIDN'T TURN OUT SO WELL FOR YOUR FACE.
LEFT.
ROGER THAT.

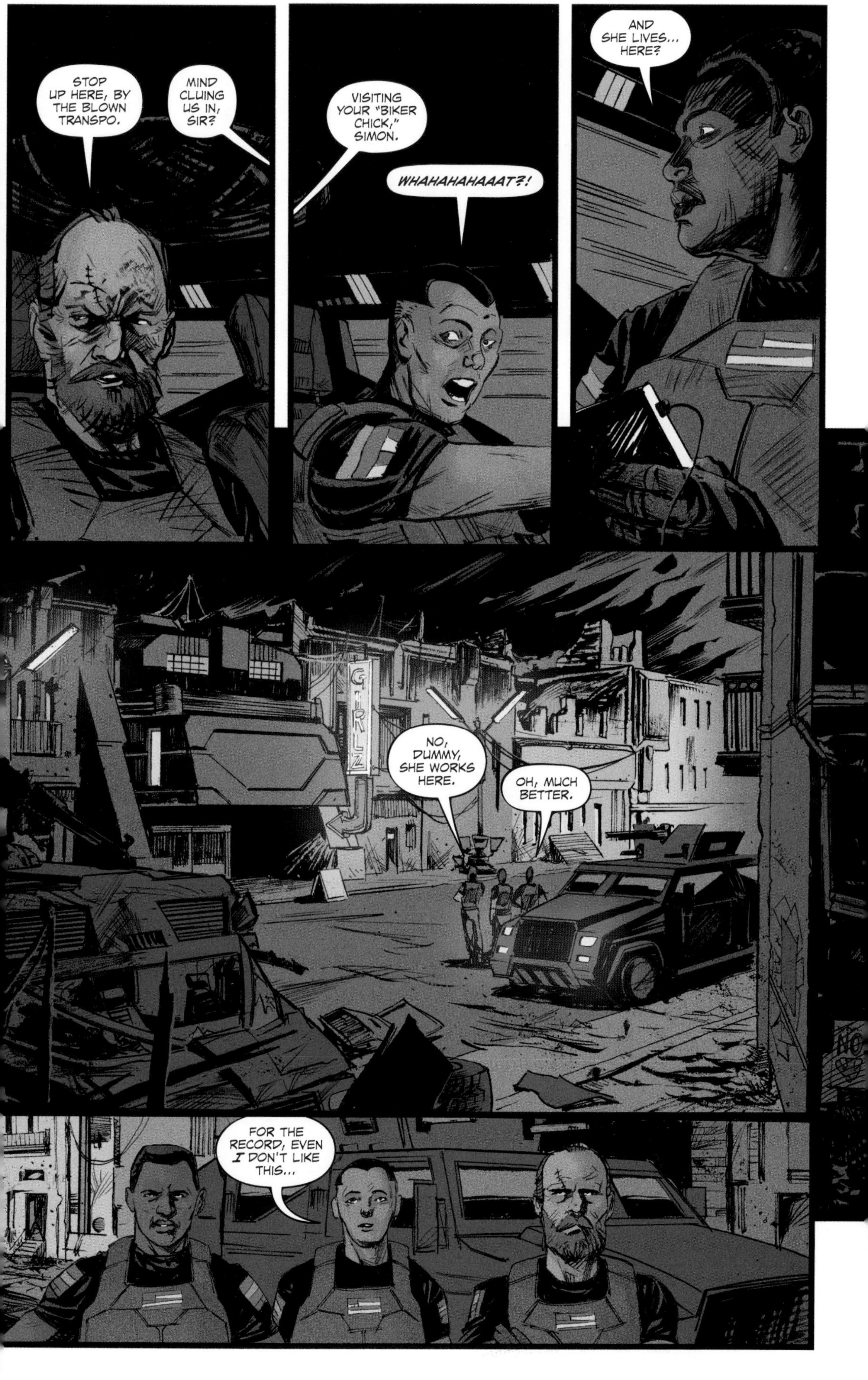
STOP UP HERE, BY THE BLOWN TRANSPO.
MIND CLUING US IN, SIR?
VISITING YOUR "BIKER CHICK," SIMON.
WHAHAHAHAAAT?!
AND SHE LIVES... HERE?
GIRLZ
NO, DUMMY, SHE WORKS HERE.
OH, MUCH BETTER.
FOR THE RECORD, EVEN I DON'T LIKE THIS...

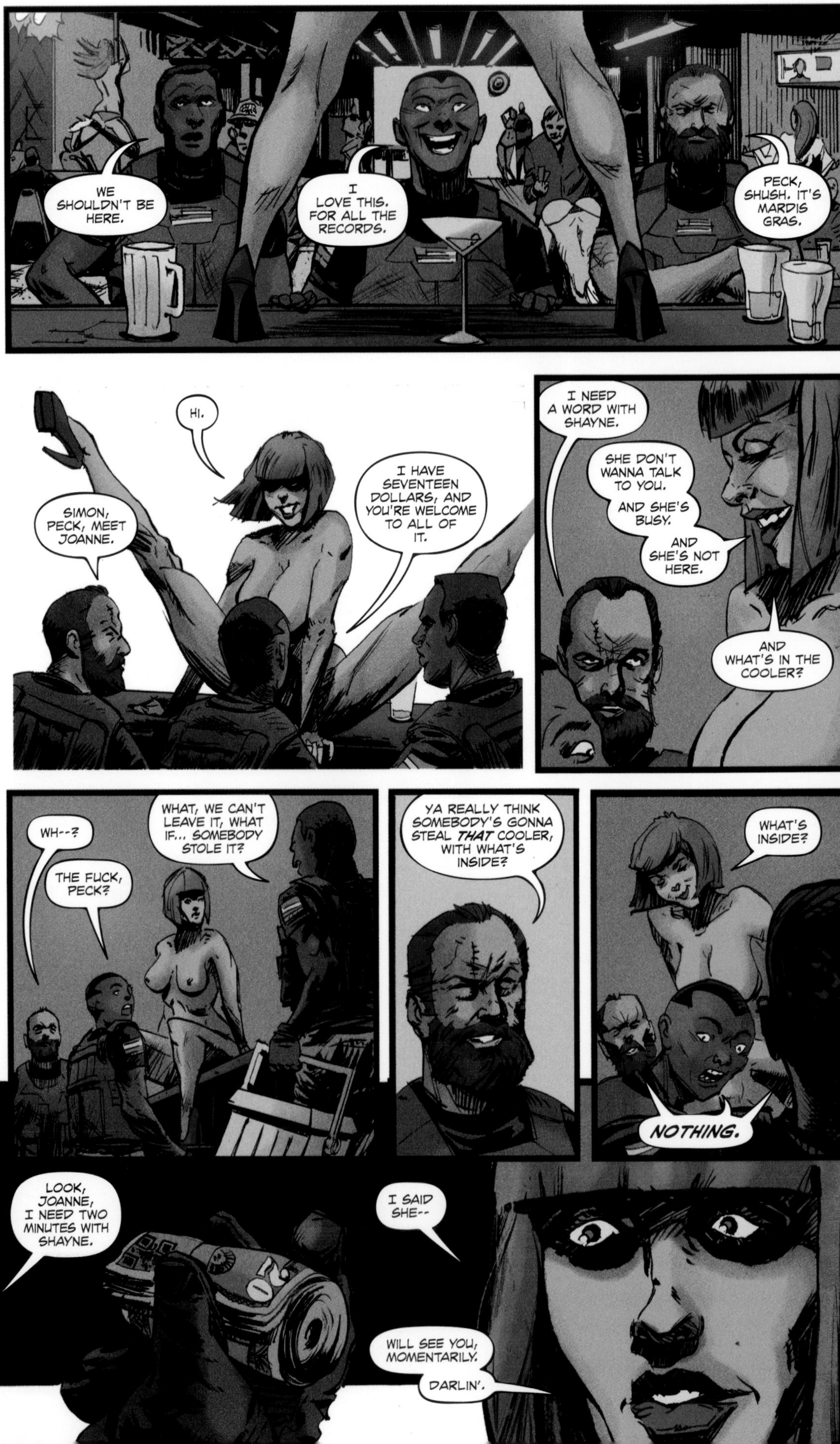

WE SHOULDN'T BE HERE.
I LOVE THIS. FOR ALL THE RECORDS.
PECK, SHUSH. IT'S MARDIS GRAS.
HI.
SIMON, PECK, MEET JOANNE.
I HAVE SEVENTEEN DOLLARS, AND YOU'RE WELCOME TO ALL OF IT.
I NEED A WORD WITH SHAYNE.
SHE DON'T WANNA TALK TO YOU.
AND SHE'S BUSY.
AND SHE'S NOT HERE.
AND WHAT'S IN THE COOLER?
WH--?
THE FUCK, PECK?
WHAT, WE CAN'T LEAVE IT, WHAT IF... SOMEBODY STOLE IT?
YA REALLY THINK SOMEBODY'S GONNA STEAL *THAT* COOLER, WITH WHAT'S INSIDE?
WHAT'S INSIDE?
NOTHING.
LOOK, JOANNE, I NEED TWO MINUTES WITH SHAYNE.
I SAID SHE--
WILL SEE YOU, MOMENTARILY.
DARLIN'.

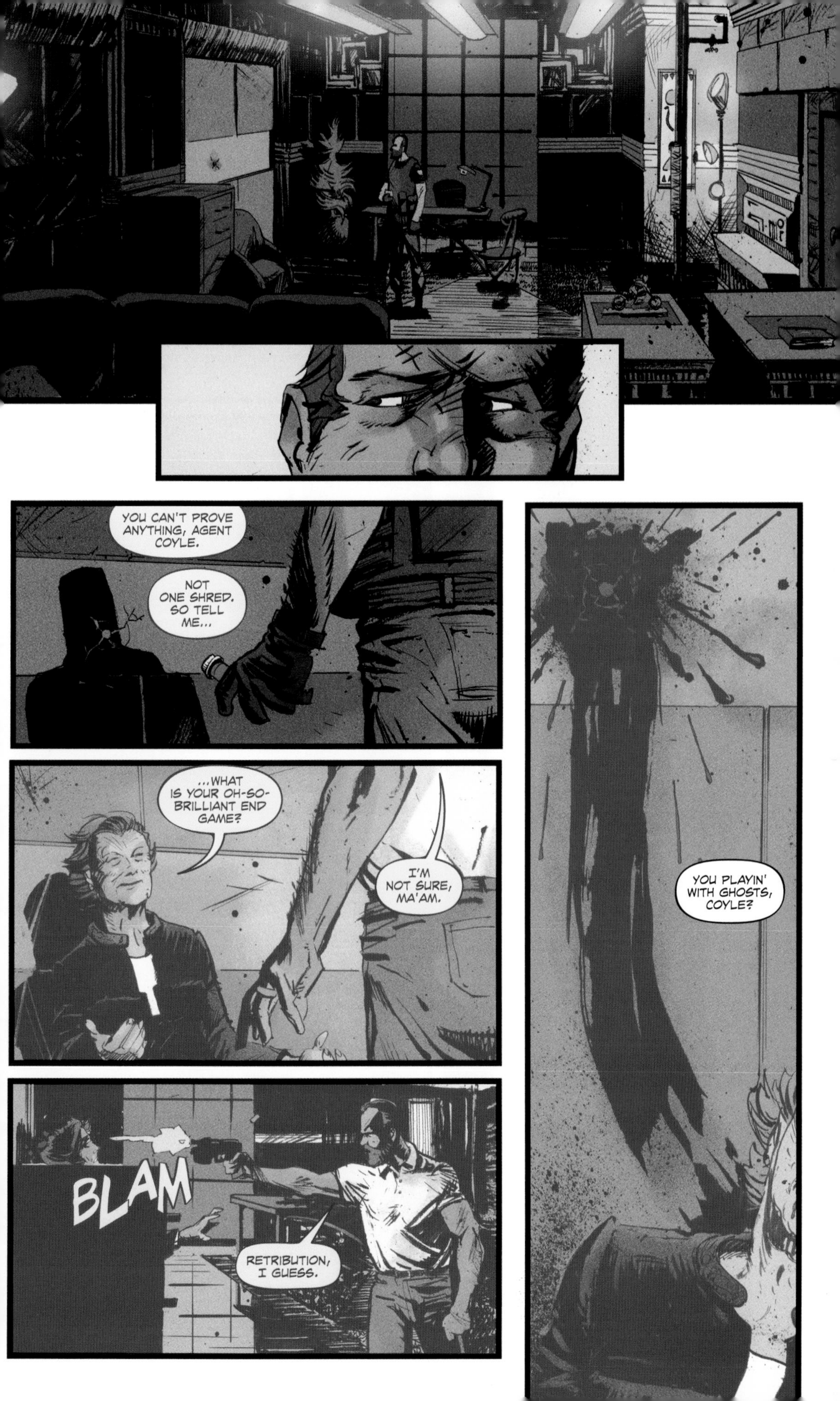

YOU CAN'T PROVE ANYTHING, AGENT COYLE.
NOT ONE SHRED. SO TELL ME...
...WHAT IS YOUR OH-SO-BRILLIANT END GAME?
I'M NOT SURE, MA'AM.
BLAM
RETRIBUTION, I GUESS.
YOU PLAYIN' WITH GHOSTS, COYLE?

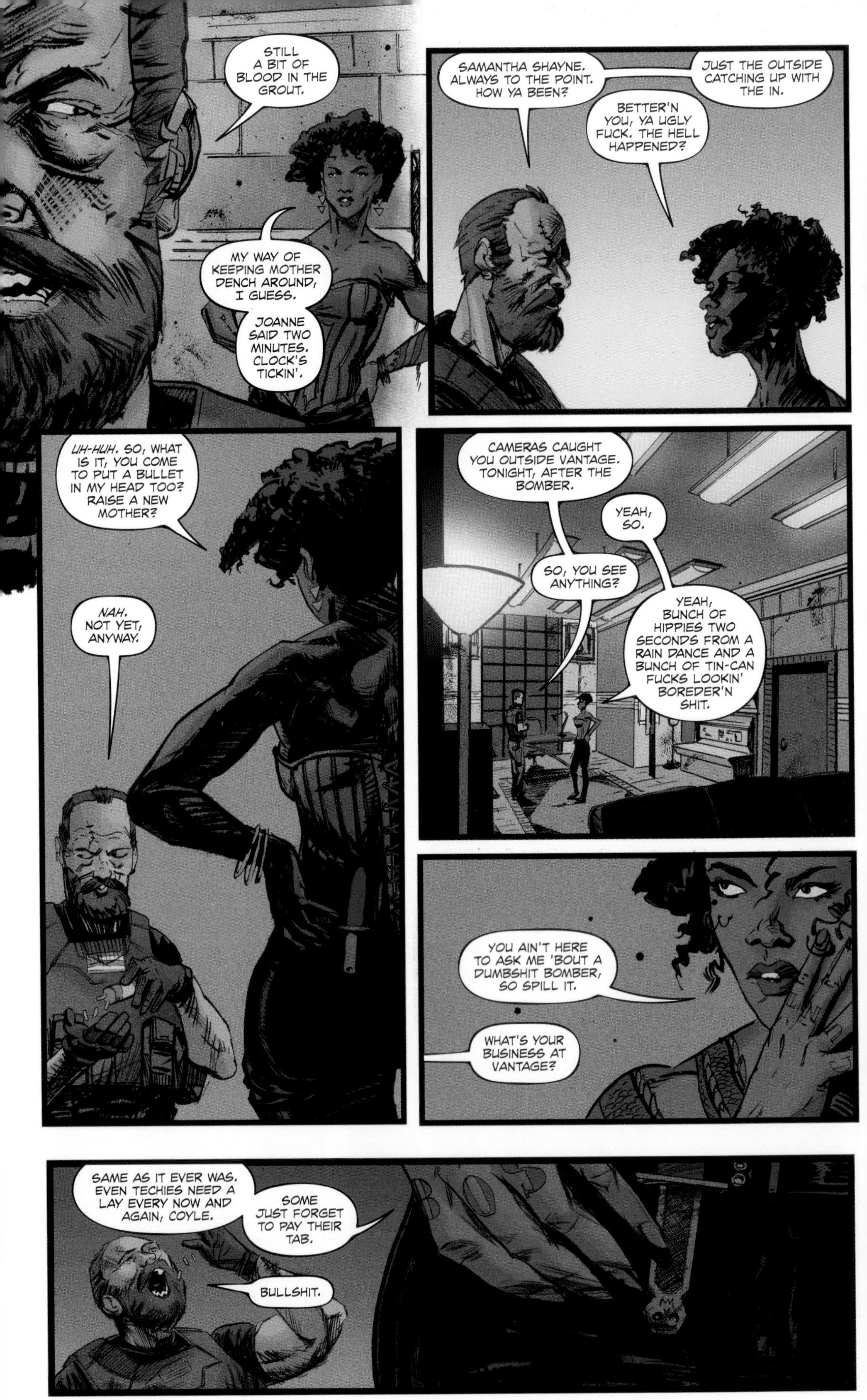

STILL A BIT OF BLOOD IN THE GROUT.
MY WAY OF KEEPING MOTHER DENCH AROUND, I GUESS.
JOANNE SAID TWO MINUTES. CLOCK'S TICKIN'.
SAMANTHA SHAYNE. ALWAYS TO THE POINT. HOW YA BEEN?
JUST THE OUTSIDE CATCHING UP WITH THE IN.
BETTER'N YOU, YA UGLY FUCK. THE HELL HAPPENED?
UH-HUH. SO, WHAT IS IT, YOU COME TO PUT A BULLET IN MY HEAD TOO? RAISE A NEW MOTHER?
NAH. NOT YET, ANYWAY.
CAMERAS CAUGHT YOU OUTSIDE VANTAGE. TONIGHT, AFTER THE BOMBER.
YEAH, SO.
SO, YOU SEE ANYTHING?
YEAH, BUNCH OF HIPPIES TWO SECONDS FROM A RAIN DANCE AND A BUNCH OF TIN-CAN FUCKS LOOKIN' BOREDER'N SHIT.
YOU AIN'T HERE TO ASK ME 'BOUT A DUMBSHIT BOMBER, SO SPILL IT.
WHAT'S YOUR BUSINESS AT VANTAGE?
SAME AS IT EVER WAS. EVEN TECHIES NEED A LAY EVERY NOW AND AGAIN, COYLE.
SOME JUST FORGET TO PAY THEIR TAB.
BULLSHIT.

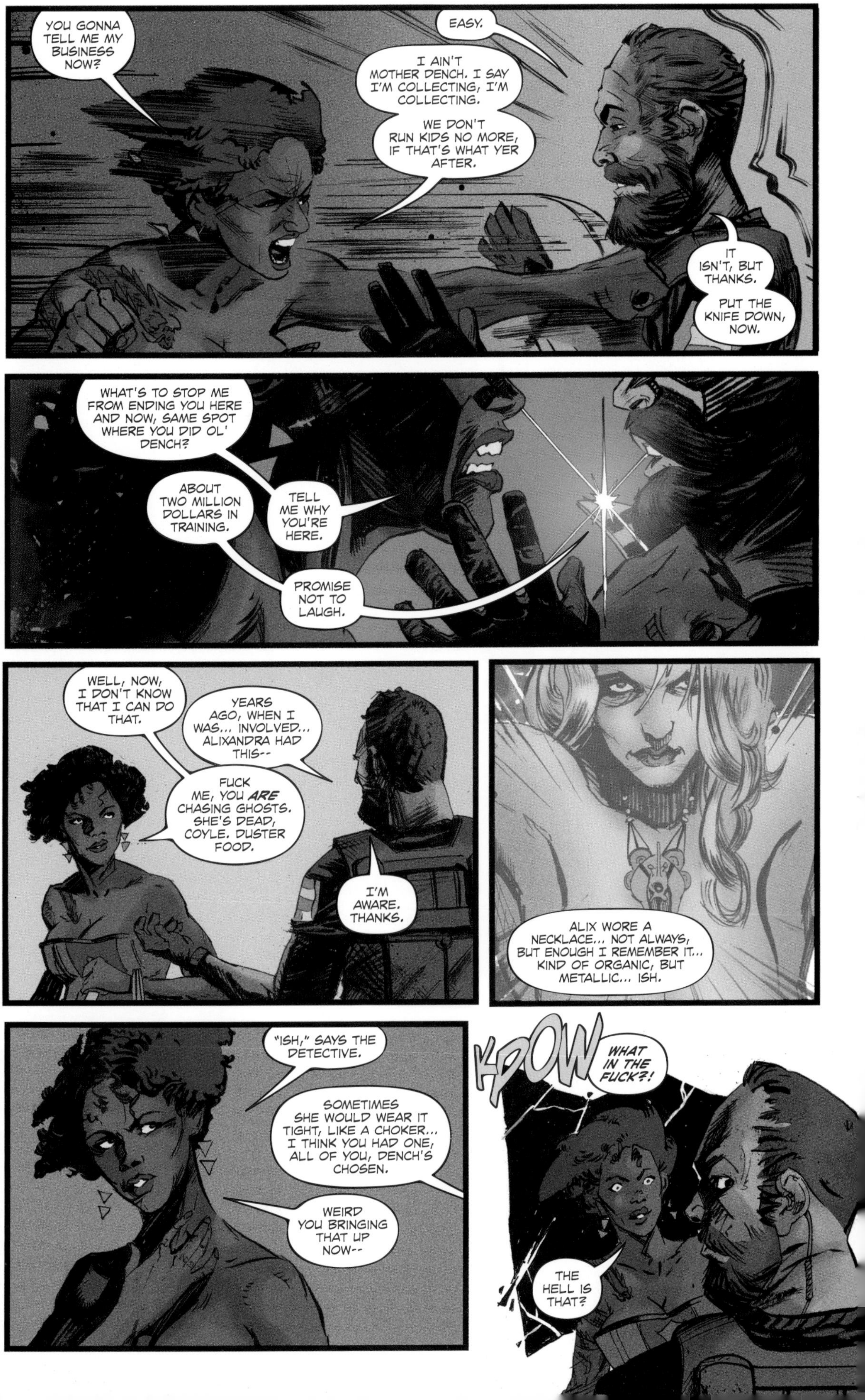
YOU GONNA TELL ME MY BUSINESS NOW?
EASY.
I AIN'T MOTHER DENCH. I SAY I'M COLLECTING, I'M COLLECTING.
WE DON'T RUN KIDS NO MORE, IF THAT'S WHAT YER AFTER.
IT ISN'T, BUT THANKS.
PUT THE KNIFE DOWN, NOW.
WHAT'S TO STOP ME FROM ENDING YOU HERE AND NOW, SAME SPOT WHERE YOU DID OL' DENCH?
ABOUT TWO MILLION DOLLARS IN TRAINING.
TELL ME WHY YOU'RE HERE.
PROMISE NOT TO LAUGH.
WELL, NOW, I DON'T KNOW THAT I CAN DO THAT.
YEARS AGO, WHEN I WAS... INVOLVED... ALIXANDRA HAD THIS--
FUCK ME, YOU *ARE* CHASING GHOSTS. SHE'S DEAD, COYLE. DUSTER FOOD.
I'M AWARE. THANKS.
ALIX WORE A NECKLACE... NOT ALWAYS, BUT ENOUGH I REMEMBER IT... KIND OF ORGANIC, BUT METALLIC... ISH.
"ISH," SAYS THE DETECTIVE.
SOMETIMES SHE WOULD WEAR IT TIGHT, LIKE A CHOKER... I THINK YOU HAD ONE, ALL OF YOU, DENCH'S CHOSEN.
WEIRD YOU BRINGING THAT UP NOW--
KDOW
WHAT IN THE FUCK?!
THE HELL IS THAT?

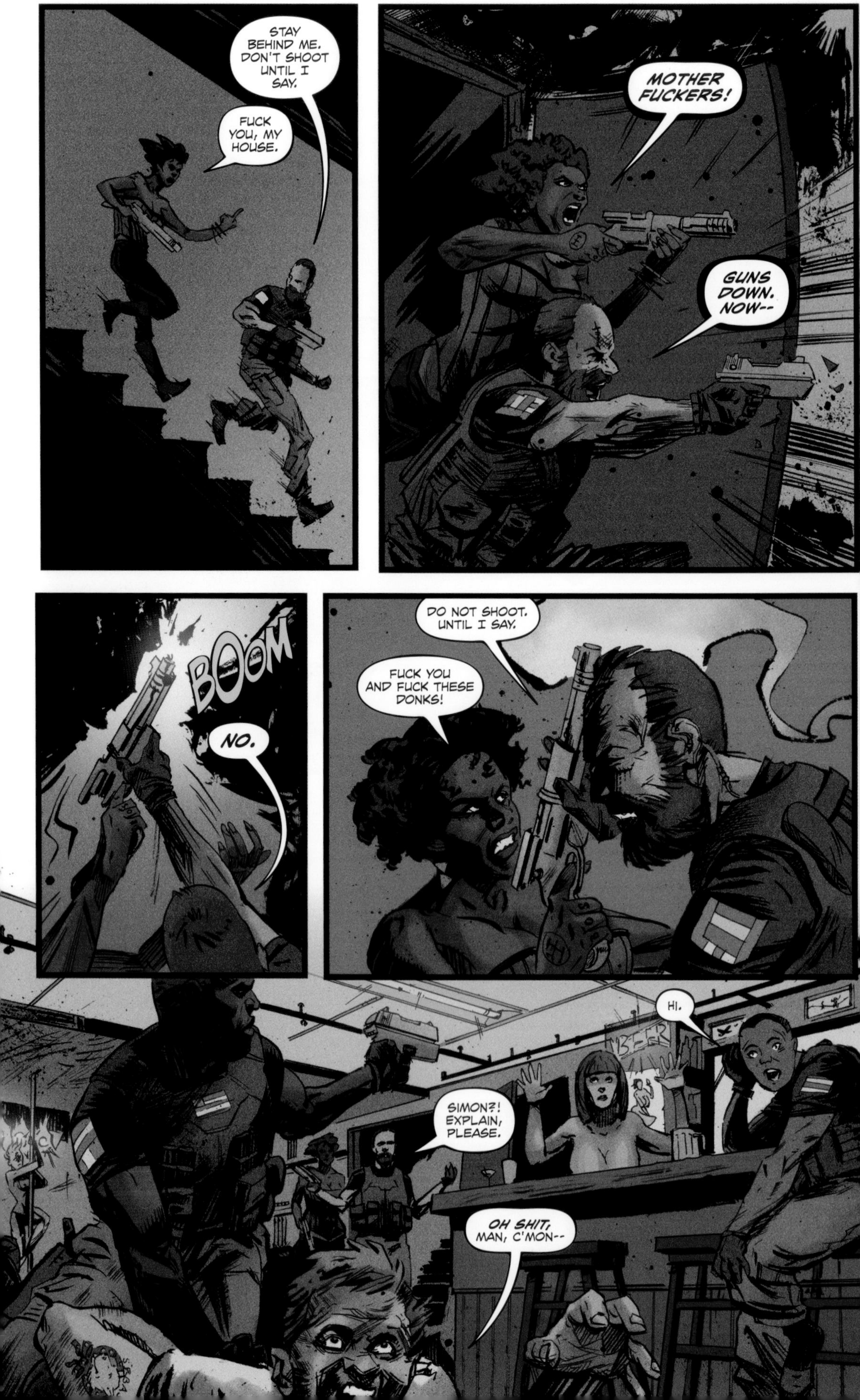
STAY BEHIND ME. DON'T SHOOT UNTIL I SAY.
FUCK YOU, MY HOUSE.
MOTHER FUCKERS!
GUNS DOWN. NOW--
BOOM
NO.
DO NOT SHOOT. UNTIL I SAY.
FUCK YOU AND FUCK THESE DONKS!
HI.
SIMON?! EXPLAIN, PLEASE.
OH SHIT, MAN, C'MON--

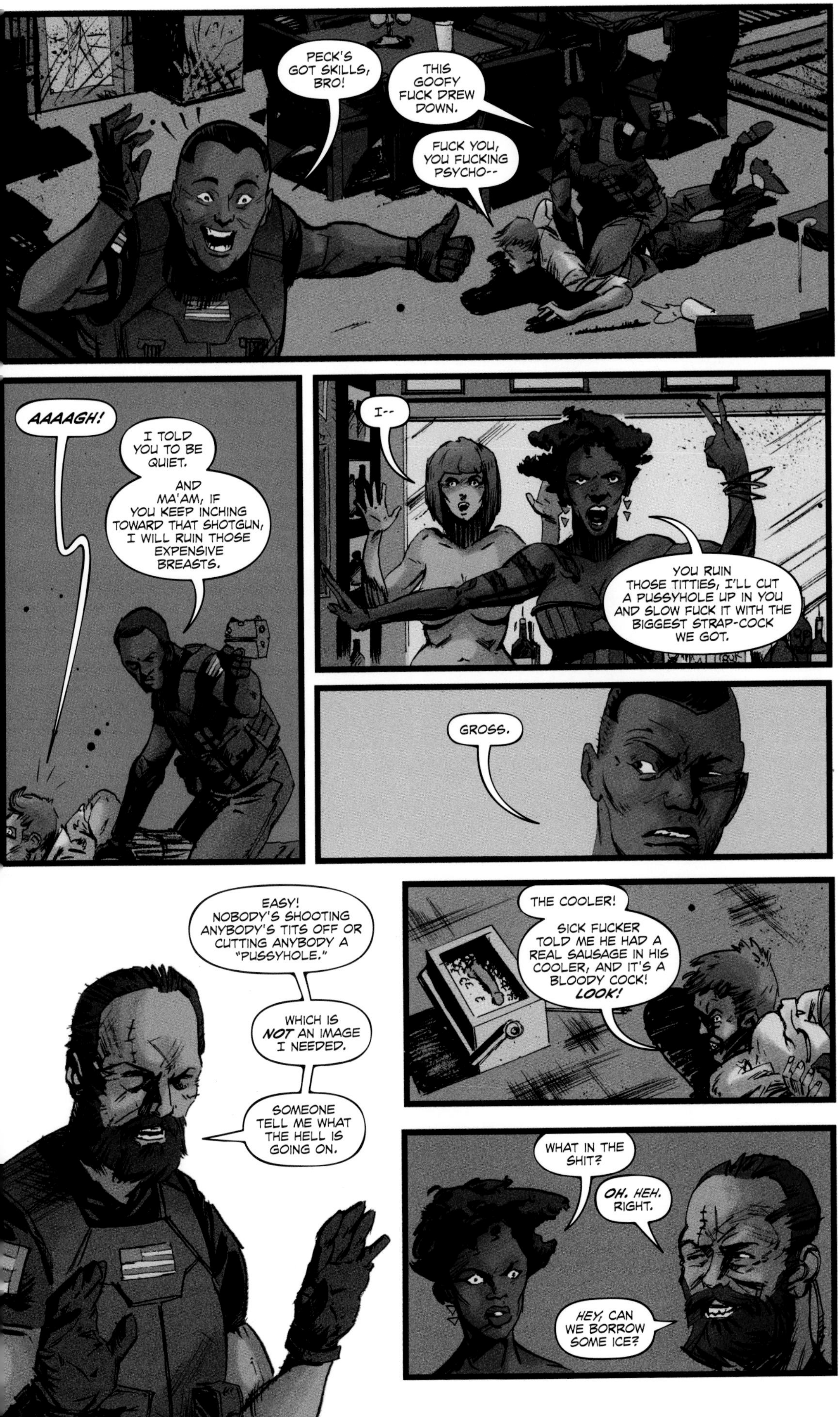
PECK'S GOT SKILLS, BRO!
THIS GOOFY FUCK DREW DOWN.
FUCK YOU, YOU FUCKING PSYCHO--
AAAAGH!
I TOLD YOU TO BE QUIET.
AND MA'AM, IF YOU KEEP INCHING TOWARD THAT SHOTGUN, I WILL RUIN THOSE EXPENSIVE BREASTS.
I--
YOU RUIN THOSE TITTIES, I'LL CUT A PUSSYHOLE UP IN YOU AND SLOW FUCK IT WITH THE BIGGEST STRAP-COCK WE GOT.
GROSS.
EASY! NOBODY'S SHOOTING ANYBODY'S TITS OFF OR CUTTING ANYBODY A "PUSSYHOLE."
WHICH IS NOT AN IMAGE I NEEDED.
SOMEONE TELL ME WHAT THE HELL IS GOING ON.
THE COOLER!
SICK FUCKER TOLD ME HE HAD A REAL SAUSAGE IN HIS COOLER, AND IT'S A BLOODY COCK! LOOK!
WHAT IN THE SHIT?
OH. HEH. RIGHT.
HEY, CAN WE BORROW SOME ICE?

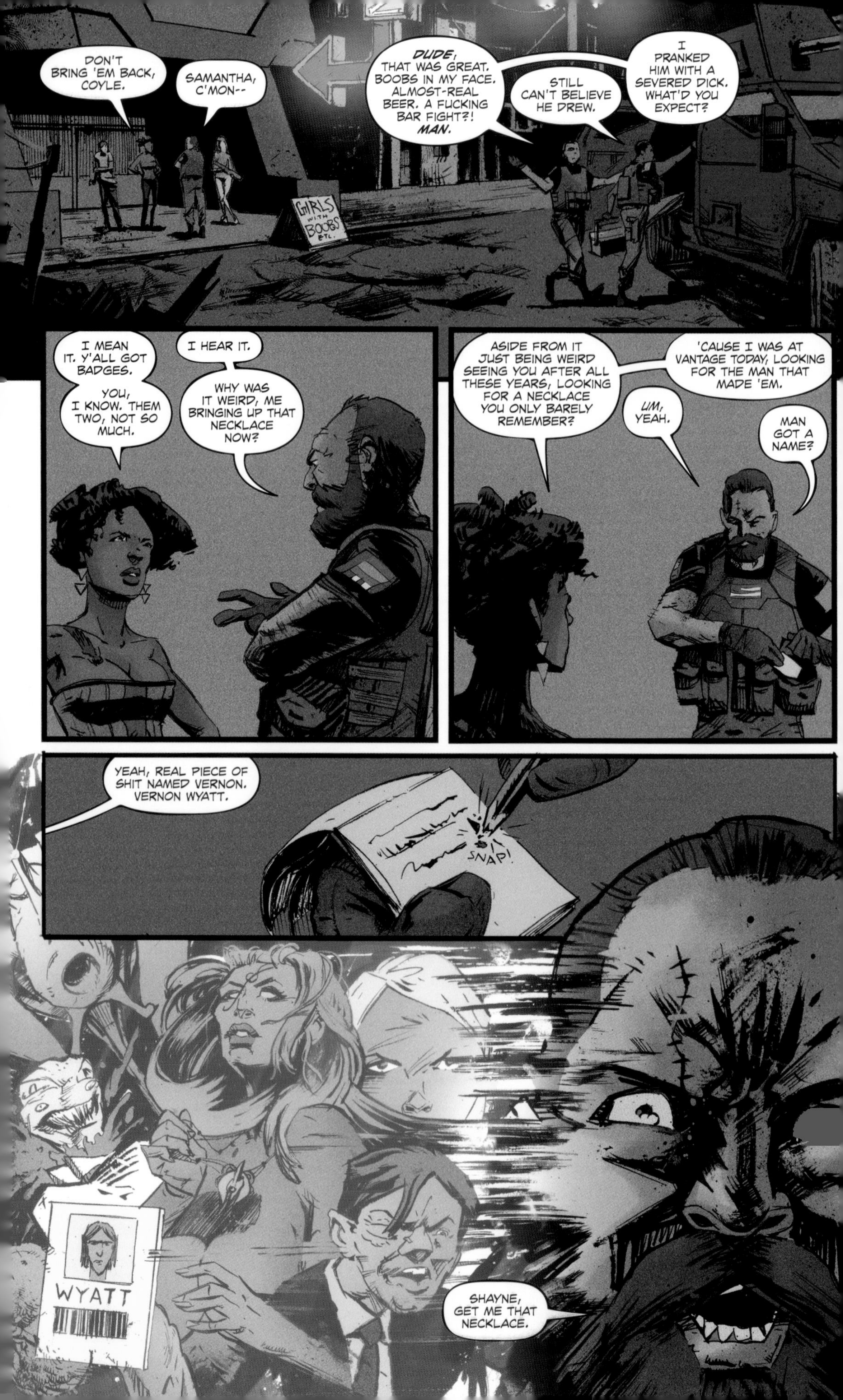
DON'T BRING 'EM BACK, COYLE.
SAMANTHA, C'MON--
GIRLS WITH BOOBS ETC.
DUDE, THAT WAS GREAT. BOOBS IN MY FACE. ALMOST-REAL BEER. A FUCKING BAR FIGHT?! MAN.
STILL CAN'T BELIEVE HE DREW.
I PRANKED HIM WITH A SEVERED DICK. WHAT'D YOU EXPECT?
I MEAN IT. Y'ALL GOT BADGES.
YOU, I KNOW. THEM TWO, NOT SO MUCH.
I HEAR IT.
WHY WAS IT WEIRD, ME BRINGING UP THAT NECKLACE NOW?
ASIDE FROM IT JUST BEING WEIRD SEEING YOU AFTER ALL THESE YEARS, LOOKING FOR A NECKLACE YOU ONLY BARELY REMEMBER?
'CAUSE I WAS AT VANTAGE TODAY, LOOKING FOR THE MAN THAT MADE 'EM.
UM, YEAH.
MAN GOT A NAME?
YEAH, REAL PIECE OF SHIT NAMED VERNON. VERNON WYATT.
SNAP!
WYATT
SHAYNE, GET ME THAT NECKLACE.

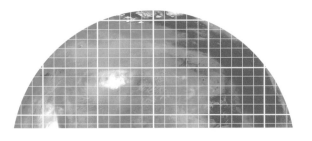

CHAPTER 03

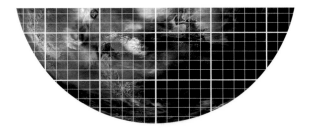

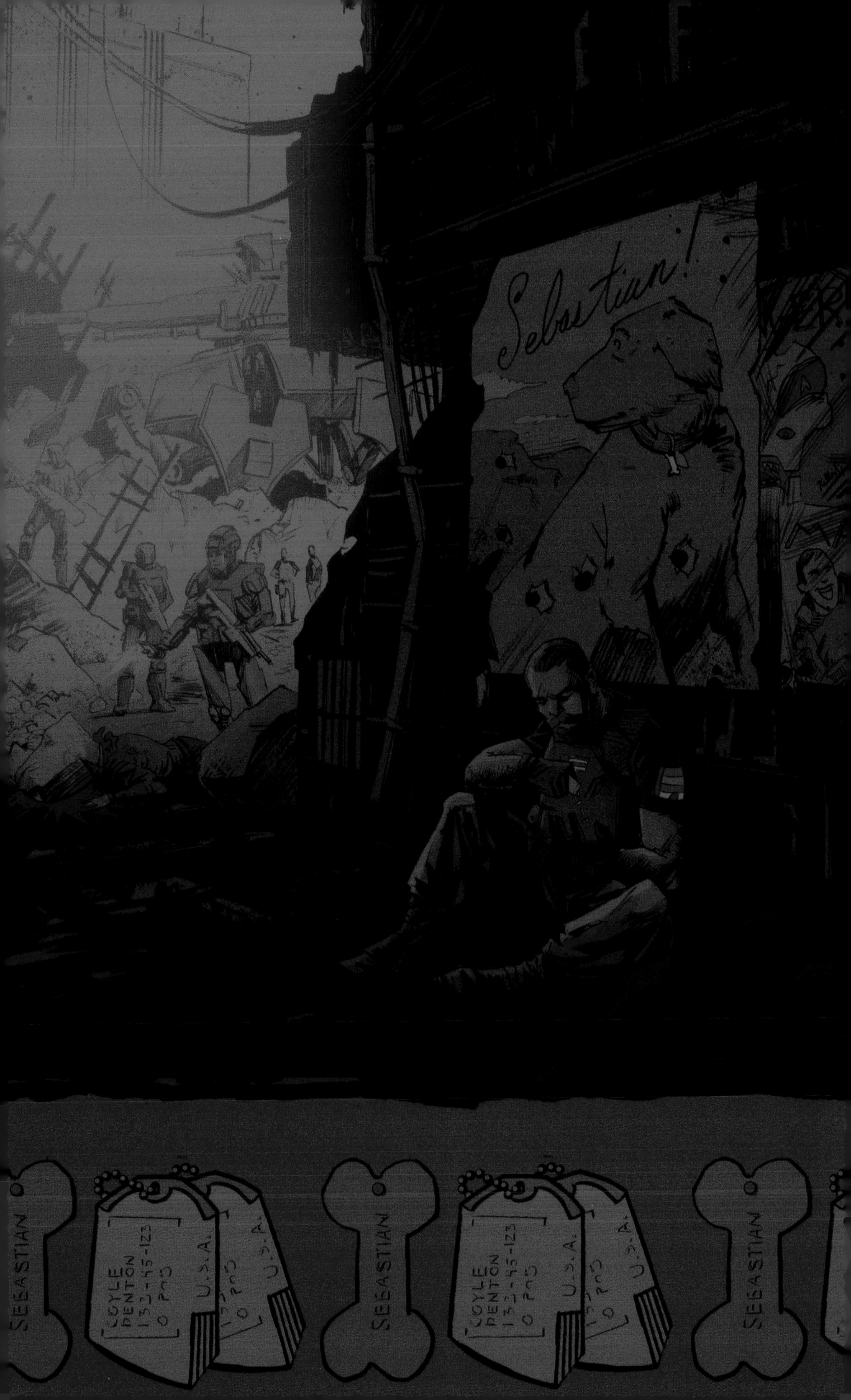
Sebastian!
SEBASTIAN
COYLE
DENTON
132-45-123
O POS
U.S.A.

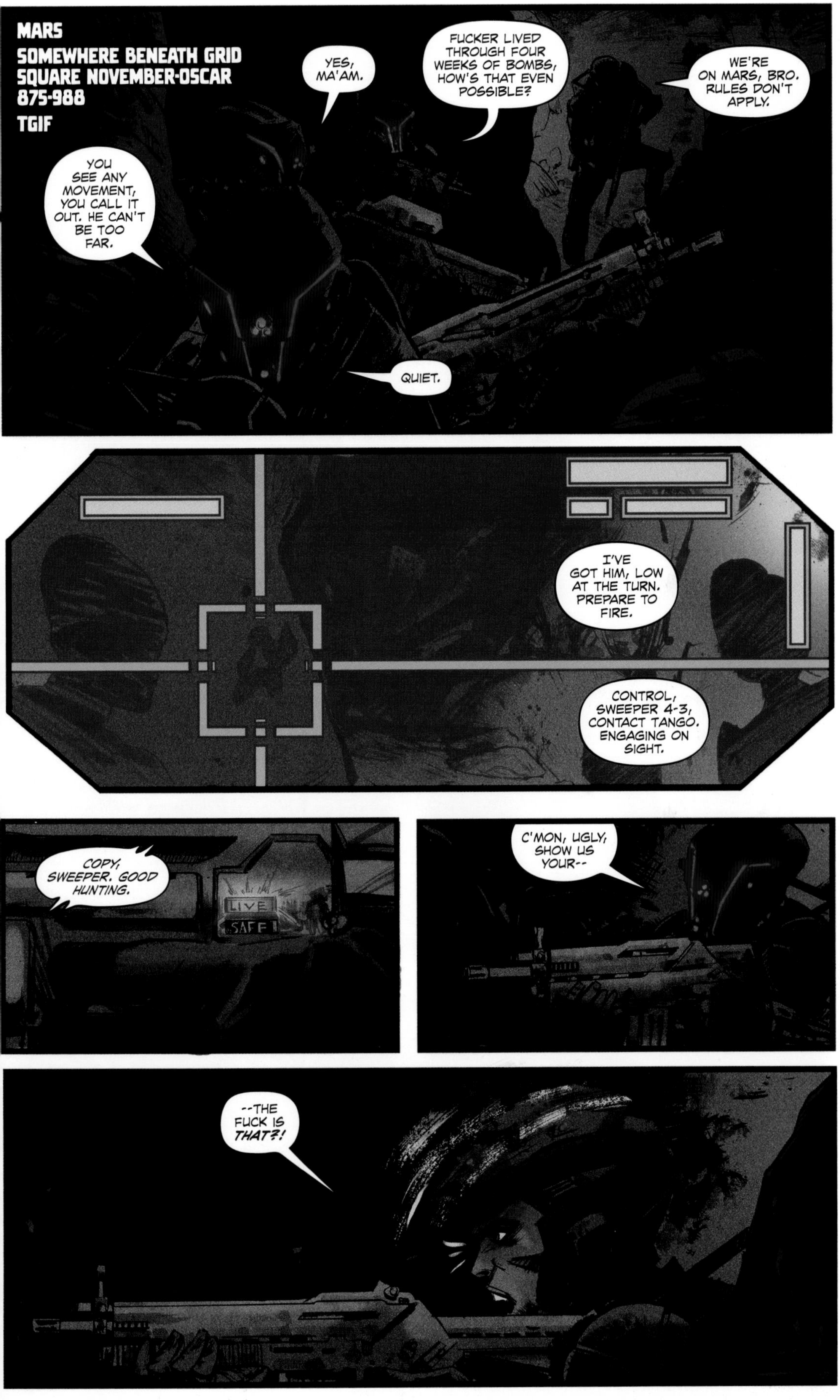
MARS
SOMEWHERE BENEATH GRID SQUARE NOVEMBER-OSCAR 875-988
TGIF
YOU SEE ANY MOVEMENT, YOU CALL IT OUT. HE CAN'T BE TOO FAR.
YES, MA'AM.
FUCKER LIVED THROUGH FOUR WEEKS OF BOMBS, HOW'S THAT EVEN POSSIBLE?
WE'RE ON MARS, BRO. RULES DON'T APPLY.
QUIET.
I'VE GOT HIM, LOW AT THE TURN. PREPARE TO FIRE.
CONTROL, SWEEPER 4-3, CONTACT TANGO. ENGAGING ON SIGHT.
COPY, SWEEPER. GOOD HUNTING.
LIVE
SAFE
C'MON, UGLY, SHOW US YOUR--
--THE FUCK IS *THAT?!*

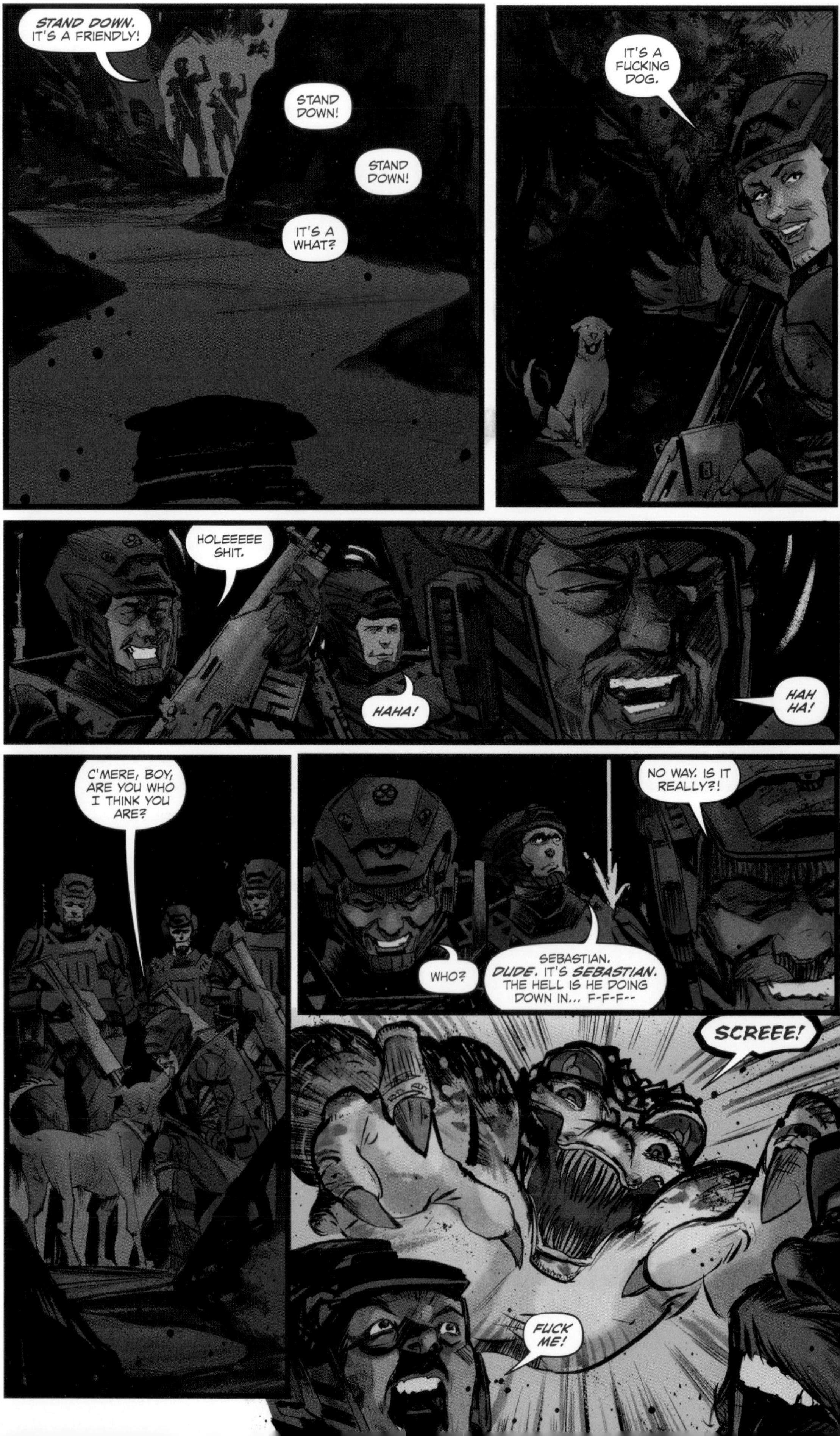
STAND DOWN. IT'S A FRIENDLY!
STAND DOWN!
STAND DOWN!
IT'S A WHAT?
IT'S A FUCKING DOG.
HOLEEEEE SHIT.
HAHA!
HAH HA!
C'MERE, BOY, ARE YOU WHO I THINK YOU ARE?
NO WAY. IS IT REALLY?!
WHO?
SEBASTIAN. DUDE. IT'S SEBASTIAN. THE HELL IS HE DOING DOWN IN... F-F-F--
SCREEE!
FUCK ME!

CONTA--
CKKK--
JEEZUS CHRIST--
CONTACT TANGO, CONTACT--
DISTURBING FOOTAGE THIS MORNING...
...WITH FOUR MARINES DEAD, AMBUSHED WHILE CLEARING THE LOCAL COLONY NEAR HARRISON STATION.
IT'S A SAD REMINDER THAT THOUGH THE WAR HAS WANED, THE AMERICAN LOSSES STILL CONTINUE.
THERE IS ONE GLIMMER OF HOPE, HOWEVER, AS YOU SAW IN THE FOOTAGE: SEBASTIAN, THE FIRST DOG ON MARS AND THE PLUCKIEST DOG IN THE COSMOS... IS STILL ALIVE.
ALL THIS AND MORE ON "YOUR MARS MORNING, TODAY!" STAY WITH US.
EXCUSE ME, SIR.
YES?
TURN THAT SHIT OFF.
ANTAGE

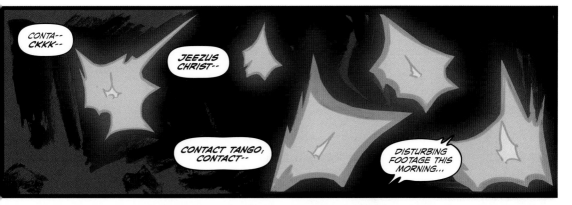

CHAPTER 03

The creatures outside looked from pig to man, and from man to pig, and from pig to man again; but already it was impossible to say which was which.

George Orwell, Animal Farm

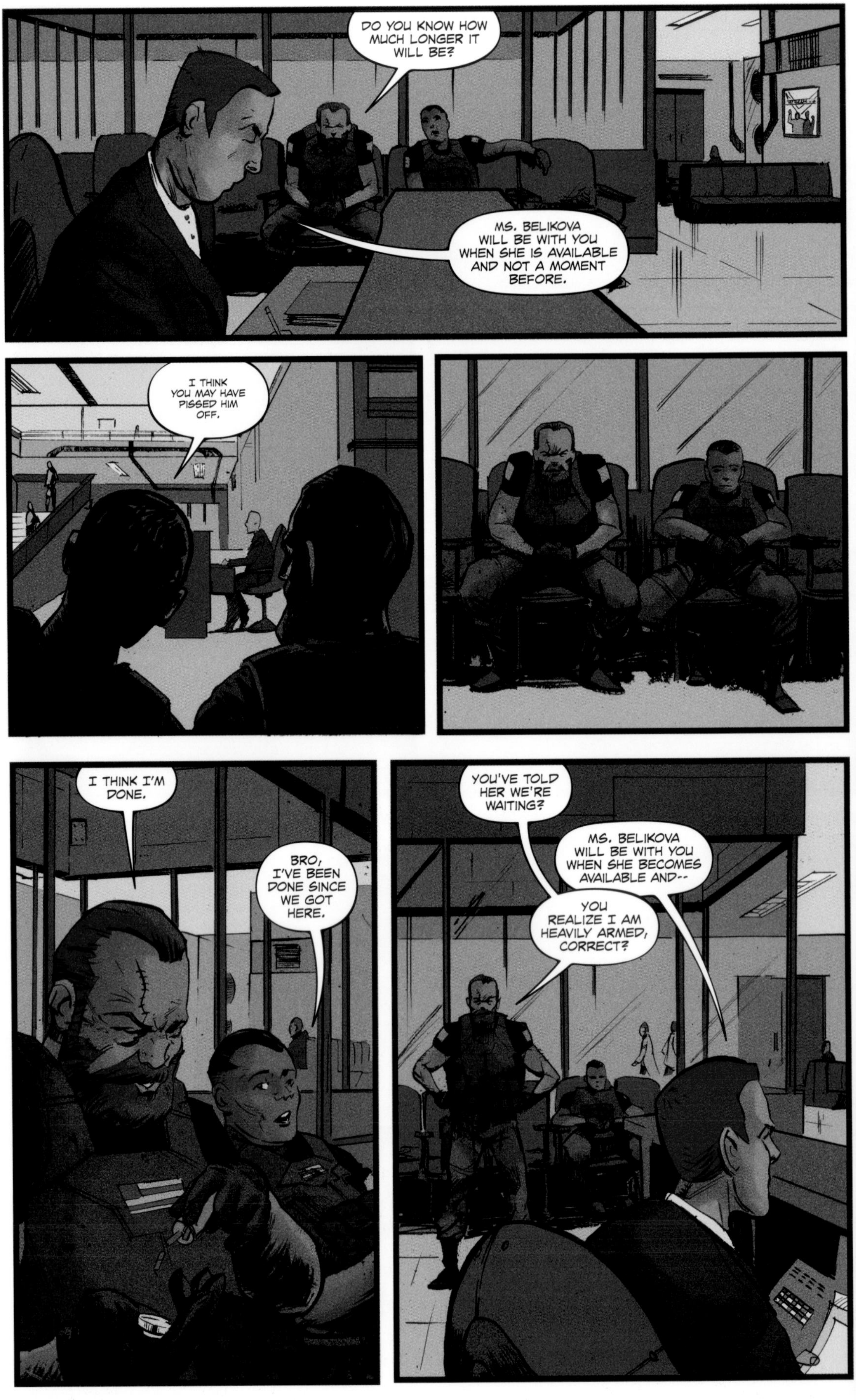
DO YOU KNOW HOW MUCH LONGER IT WILL BE?
MS. BELIKOVA WILL BE WITH YOU WHEN SHE IS AVAILABLE AND NOT A MOMENT BEFORE.
I THINK YOU MAY HAVE PISSED HIM OFF.
I THINK I'M DONE.
BRO, I'VE BEEN DONE SINCE WE GOT HERE.
YOU'VE TOLD HER WE'RE WAITING?
MS. BELIKOVA WILL BE WITH YOU WHEN SHE BECOMES AVAILABLE AND--
YOU REALIZE I AM HEAVILY ARMED, CORRECT?

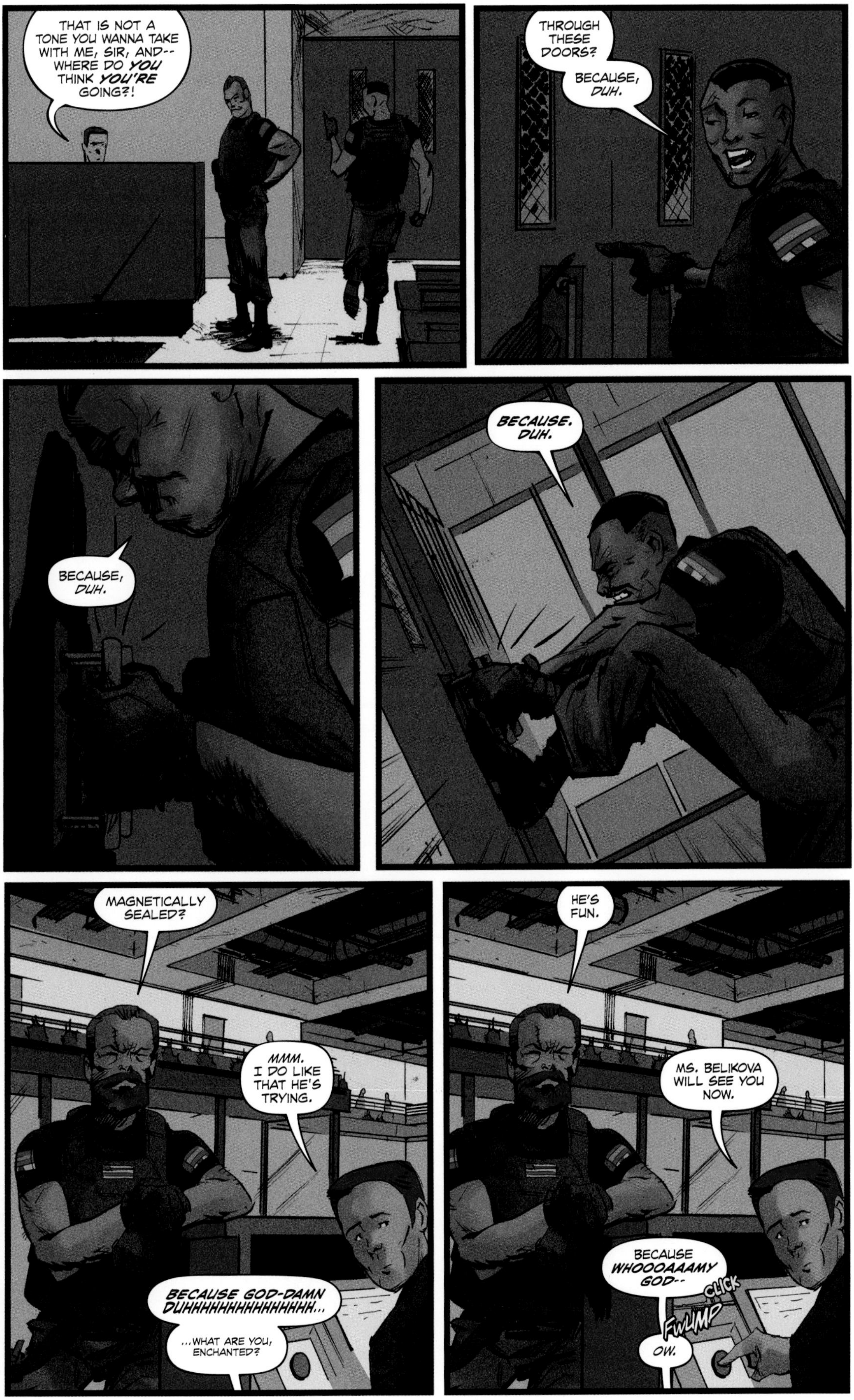
THAT IS NOT A TONE YOU WANNA TAKE WITH ME, SIR, AND-- WHERE DO *YOU* THINK *YOU'RE* GOING?!
THROUGH THESE DOORS?
BECAUSE, *DUH.*
BECAUSE, *DUH.*
BECAUSE. DUH.
MAGNETICALLY SEALED?
MMM. I DO LIKE THAT HE'S TRYING.
BECAUSE GOD-DAMN DUHHHHHHHHHHHHHHHH...
...WHAT ARE YOU, ENCHANTED?
HE'S FUN.
MS. BELIKOVA WILL SEE YOU NOW.
BECAUSE *WHOOOAAAMY GOD--*
CLICK
FWUMP
OW.

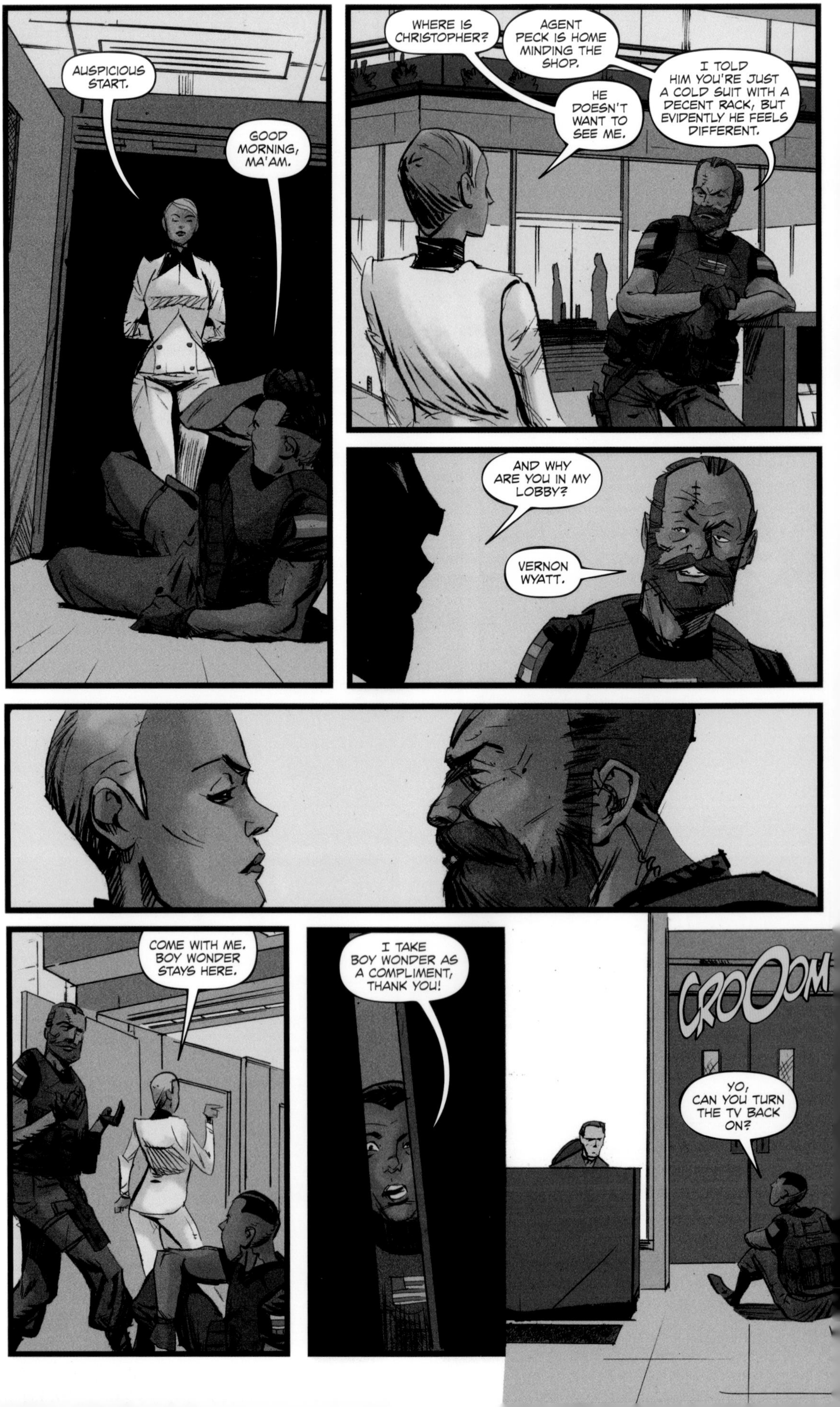
AUSPICIOUS START.
GOOD MORNING, MA'AM.
WHERE IS CHRISTOPHER?
AGENT PECK IS HOME MINDING THE SHOP.
HE DOESN'T WANT TO SEE ME.
I TOLD HIM YOU'RE JUST A COLD SUIT WITH A DECENT RACK, BUT EVIDENTLY HE FEELS DIFFERENT.
AND WHY ARE YOU IN MY LOBBY?
VERNON WYATT.
COME WITH ME. BOY WONDER STAYS HERE.
I TAKE BOY WONDER AS A COMPLIMENT, THANK YOU!
CROOOM
YO, CAN YOU TURN THE TV BACK ON?

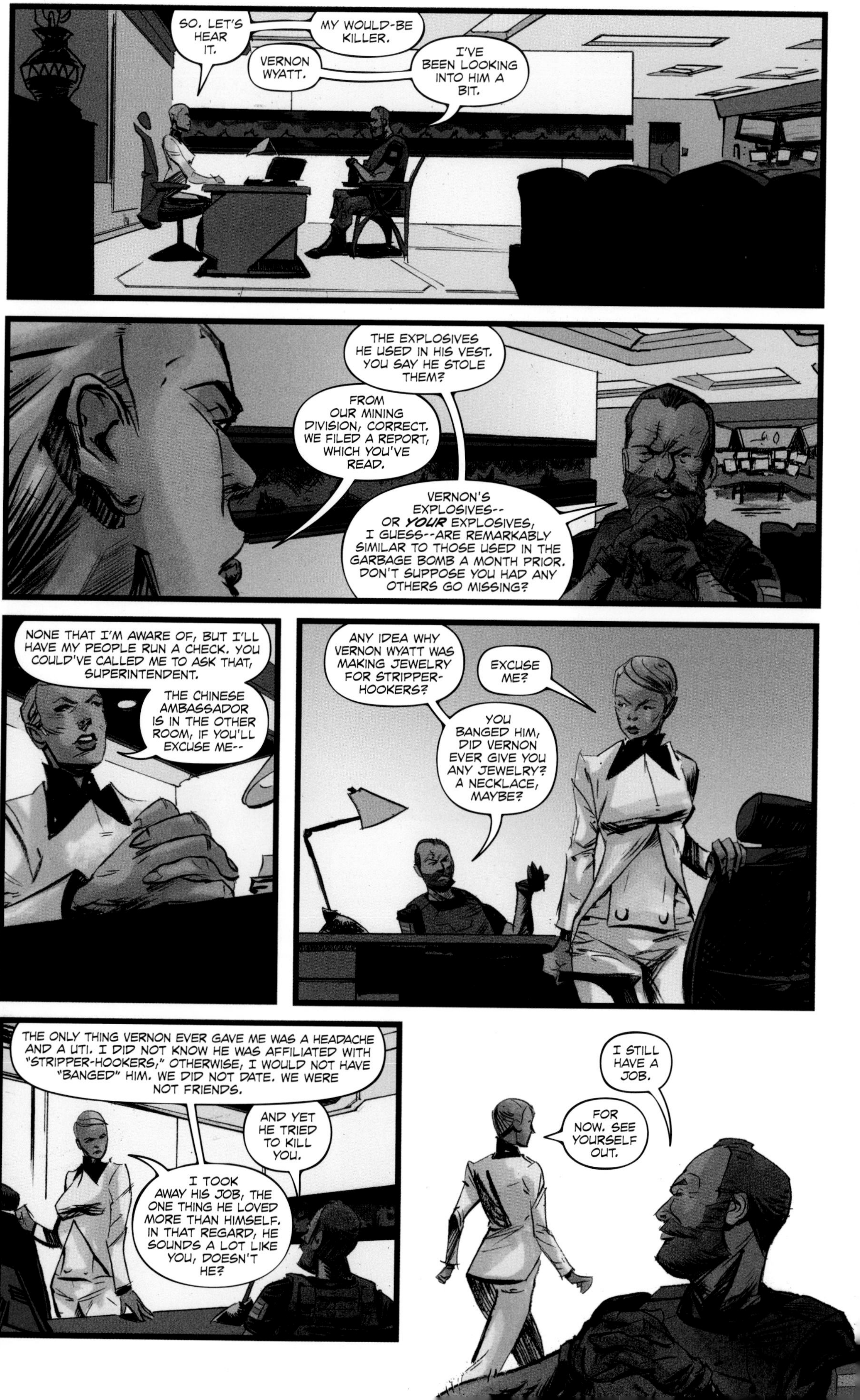
SO. LET'S HEAR IT.
MY WOULD-BE KILLER.
VERNON WYATT.
I'VE BEEN LOOKING INTO HIM A BIT.
THE EXPLOSIVES HE USED IN HIS VEST. YOU SAY HE STOLE THEM?
FROM OUR MINING DIVISION, CORRECT. WE FILED A REPORT, WHICH YOU'VE READ.
VERNON'S EXPLOSIVES-- OR *YOUR* EXPLOSIVES, I GUESS--ARE REMARKABLY SIMILAR TO THOSE USED IN THE GARBAGE BOMB A MONTH PRIOR. DON'T SUPPOSE YOU HAD ANY OTHERS GO MISSING?
NONE THAT I'M AWARE OF, BUT I'LL HAVE MY PEOPLE RUN A CHECK. YOU COULD'VE CALLED ME TO ASK THAT, SUPERINTENDENT.
THE CHINESE AMBASSADOR IS IN THE OTHER ROOM, IF YOU'LL EXCUSE ME--
ANY IDEA WHY VERNON WYATT WAS MAKING JEWELRY FOR STRIPPER-HOOKERS?
EXCUSE ME?
YOU BANGED HIM, DID VERNON EVER GIVE YOU ANY JEWELRY? A NECKLACE, MAYBE?
THE ONLY THING VERNON EVER GAVE ME WAS A HEADACHE AND A UTI. I DID NOT KNOW HE WAS AFFILIATED WITH "STRIPPER-HOOKERS," OTHERWISE, I WOULD NOT HAVE "BANGED" HIM. WE DID NOT DATE. WE WERE NOT FRIENDS.
AND YET HE TRIED TO KILL YOU.
I TOOK AWAY HIS JOB, THE ONE THING HE LOVED MORE THAN HIMSELF. IN THAT REGARD, HE SOUNDS A LOT LIKE YOU, DOESN'T HE?
I STILL HAVE A JOB.
FOR NOW. SEE YOURSELF OUT.

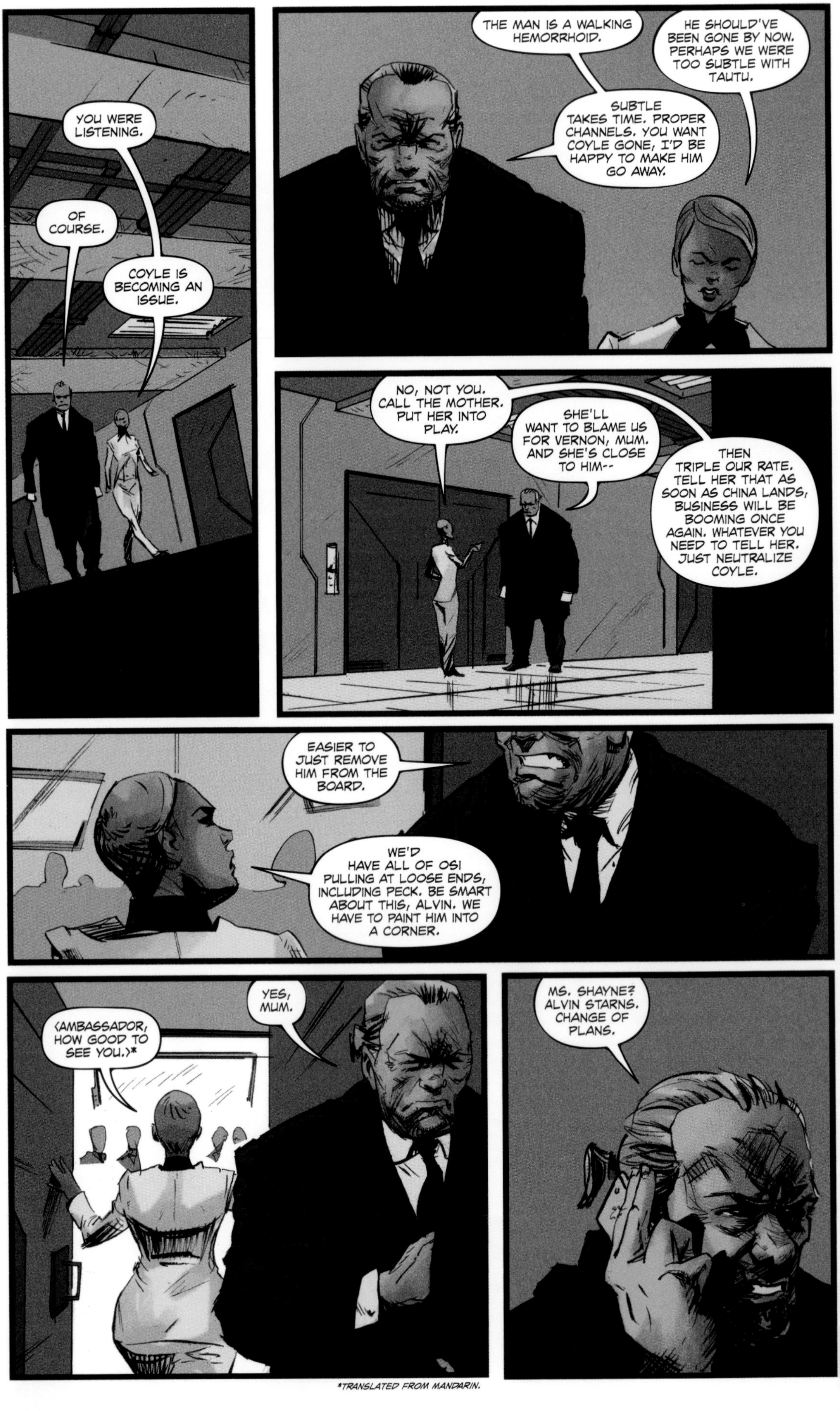
YOU WERE LISTENING.
OF COURSE.
COYLE IS BECOMING AN ISSUE.
THE MAN IS A WALKING HEMORRHOID.
HE SHOULD'VE BEEN GONE BY NOW. PERHAPS WE WERE TOO SUBTLE WITH TAUTU.
SUBTLE TAKES TIME. PROPER CHANNELS. YOU WANT COYLE GONE, I'D BE HAPPY TO MAKE HIM GO AWAY.
NO, NOT YOU. CALL THE MOTHER. PUT HER INTO PLAY.
SHE'LL WANT TO BLAME US FOR VERNON, MUM. AND SHE'S CLOSE TO HIM--
THEN TRIPLE OUR RATE. TELL HER THAT AS SOON AS CHINA LANDS, BUSINESS WILL BE BOOMING ONCE AGAIN. WHATEVER YOU NEED TO TELL HER. JUST NEUTRALIZE COYLE.
EASIER TO JUST REMOVE HIM FROM THE BOARD.
WE'D HAVE ALL OF OSI PULLING AT LOOSE ENDS, INCLUDING PECK. BE SMART ABOUT THIS, ALVIN. WE HAVE TO PAINT HIM INTO A CORNER.
YES, MUM.
<AMBASSADOR, HOW GOOD TO SEE YOU.>*
MS. SHAYNE? ALVIN STARNS. CHANGE OF PLANS.

*TRANSLATED FROM MANDARIN.

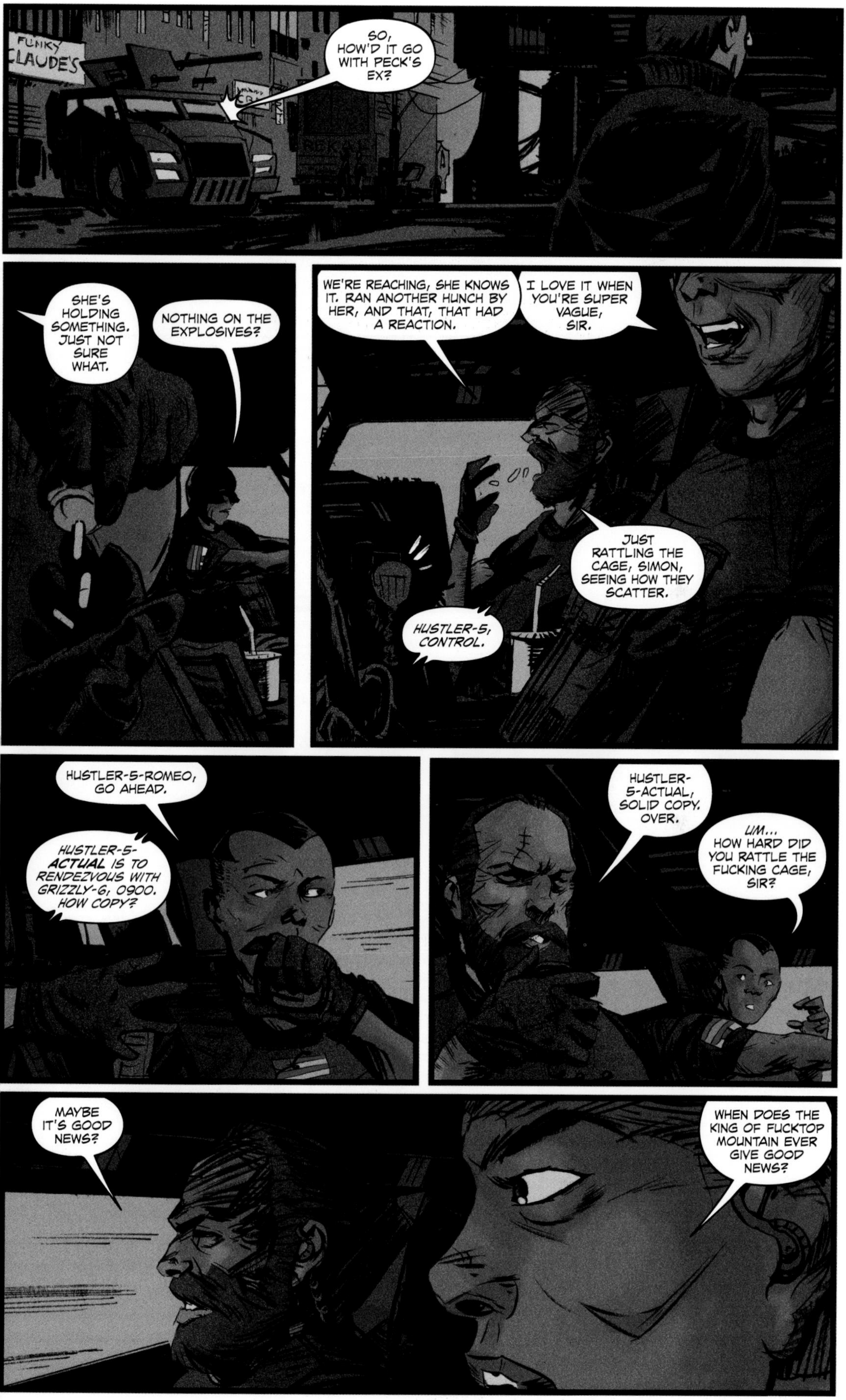
FUNKY CLAUDE'S
SO, HOW'D IT GO WITH PECK'S EX?
SHE'S HOLDING SOMETHING. JUST NOT SURE WHAT.
NOTHING ON THE EXPLOSIVES?
WE'RE REACHING, SHE KNOWS IT. RAN ANOTHER HUNCH BY HER, AND THAT, THAT HAD A REACTION.
I LOVE IT WHEN YOU'RE SUPER VAGUE, SIR.
JUST RATTLING THE CAGE, SIMON, SEEING HOW THEY SCATTER.
HUSTLER-5, CONTROL.
HUSTLER-5-ROMEO, GO AHEAD.
HUSTLER-5-ACTUAL IS TO RENDEZVOUS WITH GRIZZLY-6, 0900. HOW COPY?
HUSTLER-5-ACTUAL, SOLID COPY. OVER.
UM... HOW HARD DID YOU RATTLE THE FUCKING CAGE, SIR?
MAYBE IT'S GOOD NEWS?
WHEN DOES THE KING OF FUCKTOP MOUNTAIN EVER GIVE GOOD NEWS?

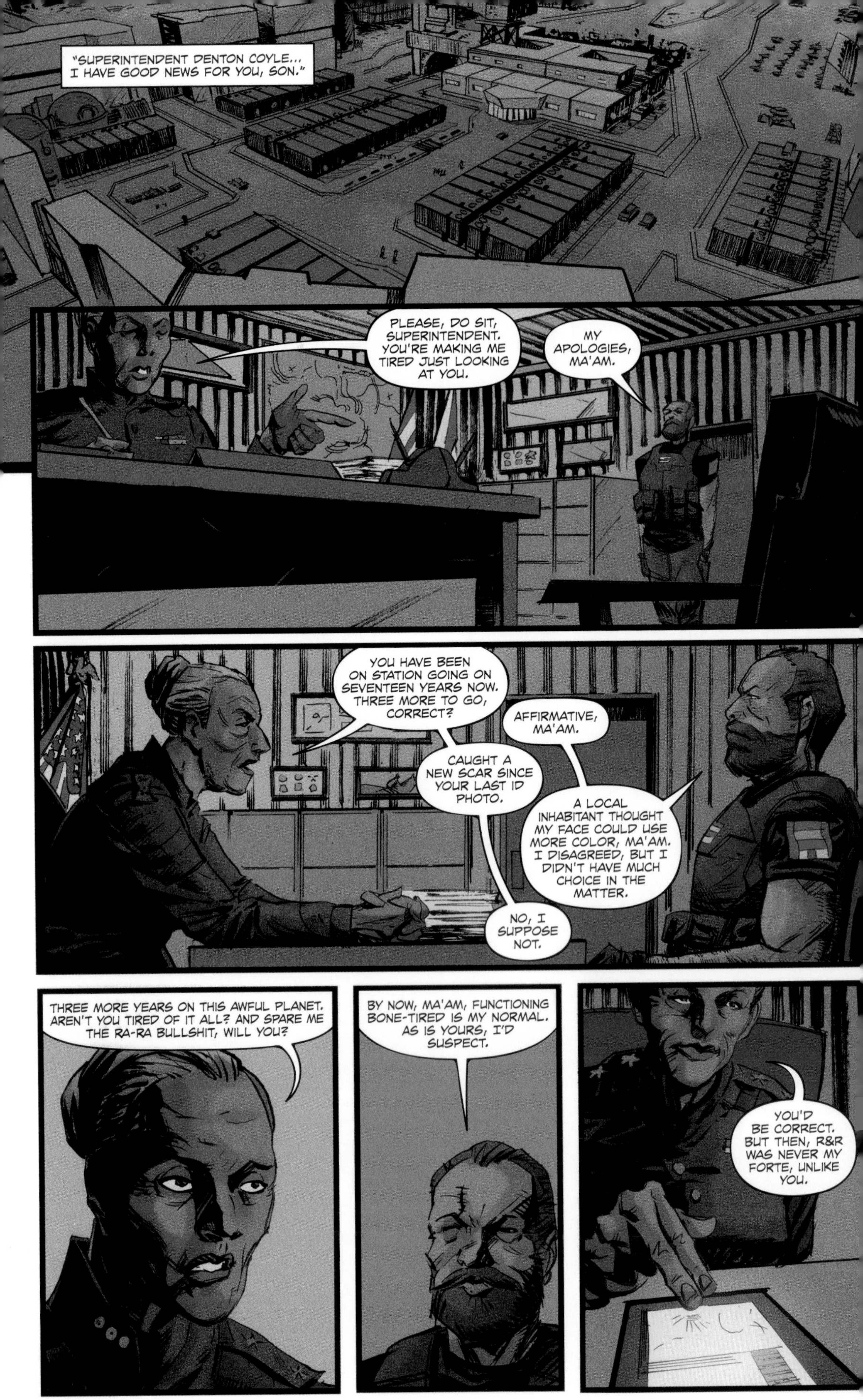
"SUPERINTENDENT DENTON COYLE... I HAVE GOOD NEWS FOR YOU, SON."
PLEASE, DO SIT, SUPERINTENDENT. YOU'RE MAKING ME TIRED JUST LOOKING AT YOU.
MY APOLOGIES, MA'AM.
YOU HAVE BEEN ON STATION GOING ON SEVENTEEN YEARS NOW. THREE MORE TO GO, CORRECT?
AFFIRMATIVE, MA'AM.
CAUGHT A NEW SCAR SINCE YOUR LAST ID PHOTO.
A LOCAL INHABITANT THOUGHT MY FACE COULD USE MORE COLOR, MA'AM. I DISAGREED, BUT I DIDN'T HAVE MUCH CHOICE IN THE MATTER.
NO, I SUPPOSE NOT.
THREE MORE YEARS ON THIS AWFUL PLANET. AREN'T YOU TIRED OF IT ALL? AND SPARE ME THE RA-RA BULLSHIT, WILL YOU?
BY NOW, MA'AM, FUNCTIONING BONE-TIRED IS MY NORMAL. AS IS YOURS, I'D SUSPECT.
YOU'D BE CORRECT. BUT THEN, R&R WAS NEVER MY FORTE, UNLIKE YOU.

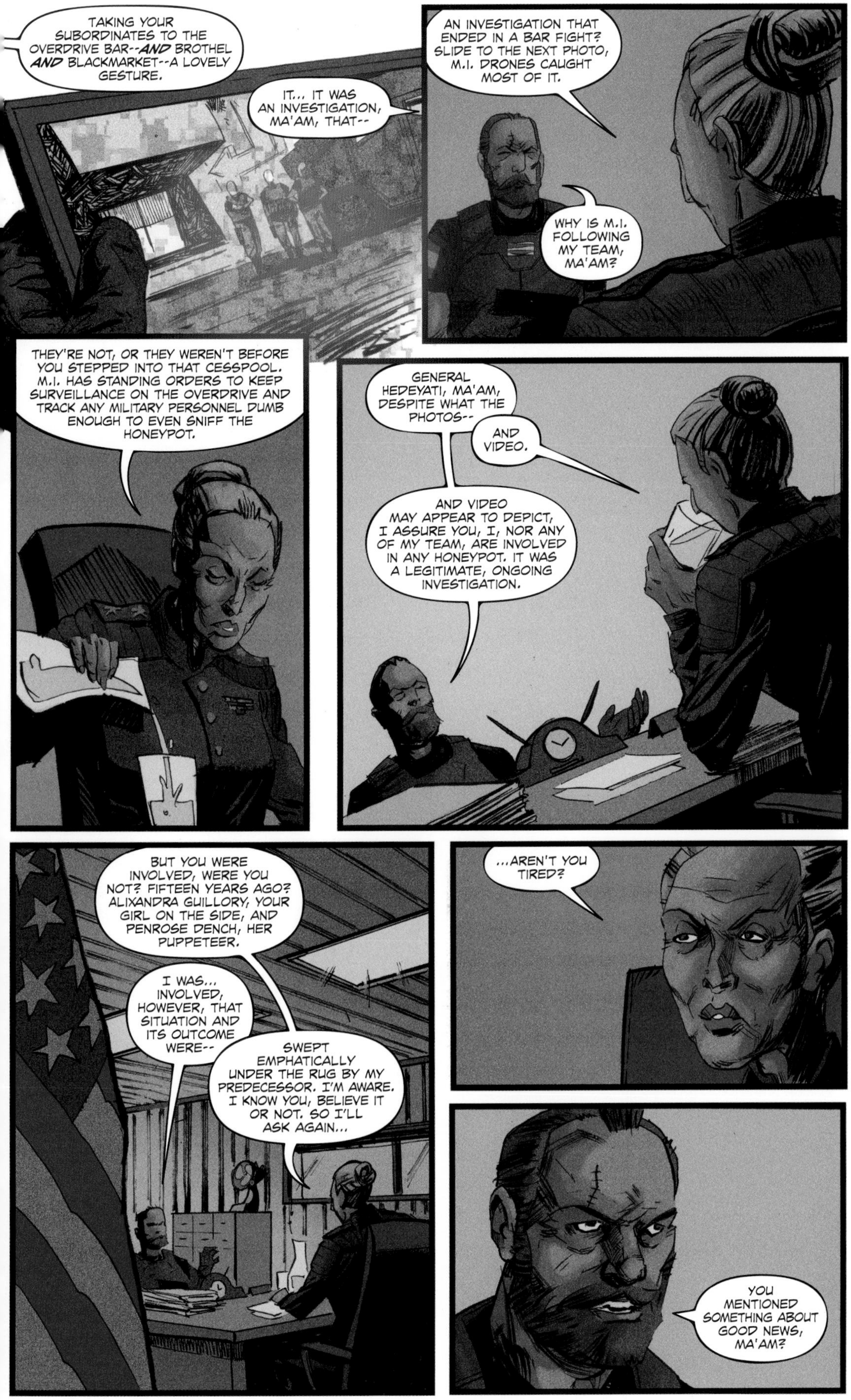
TAKING YOUR SUBORDINATES TO THE OVERDRIVE BAR--*AND* BROTHEL *AND* BLACKMARKET--A LOVELY GESTURE.
IT... IT WAS AN INVESTIGATION, MA'AM, THAT--
AN INVESTIGATION THAT ENDED IN A BAR FIGHT? SLIDE TO THE NEXT PHOTO, M.I. DRONES CAUGHT MOST OF IT.
WHY IS M.I. FOLLOWING MY TEAM, MA'AM?
THEY'RE NOT, OR THEY WEREN'T BEFORE YOU STEPPED INTO THAT CESSPOOL. M.I. HAS STANDING ORDERS TO KEEP SURVEILLANCE ON THE OVERDRIVE AND TRACK ANY MILITARY PERSONNEL DUMB ENOUGH TO EVEN SNIFF THE HONEYPOT.
GENERAL HEDEYATI, MA'AM, DESPITE WHAT THE PHOTOS--
AND VIDEO.
AND VIDEO MAY APPEAR TO DEPICT, I ASSURE YOU, I, NOR ANY OF MY TEAM, ARE INVOLVED IN ANY HONEYPOT. IT WAS A LEGITIMATE, ONGOING INVESTIGATION.
BUT YOU WERE INVOLVED, WERE YOU NOT? FIFTEEN YEARS AGO? ALIXANDRA GUILLORY, YOUR GIRL ON THE SIDE, AND PENROSE DENCH, HER PUPPETEER.
I WAS... INVOLVED, HOWEVER, THAT SITUATION AND ITS OUTCOME WERE--
SWEPT EMPHATICALLY UNDER THE RUG BY MY PREDECESSOR. I'M AWARE. I KNOW YOU, BELIEVE IT OR NOT. SO I'LL ASK AGAIN...
...AREN'T YOU TIRED?
YOU MENTIONED SOMETHING ABOUT GOOD NEWS, MA'AM?

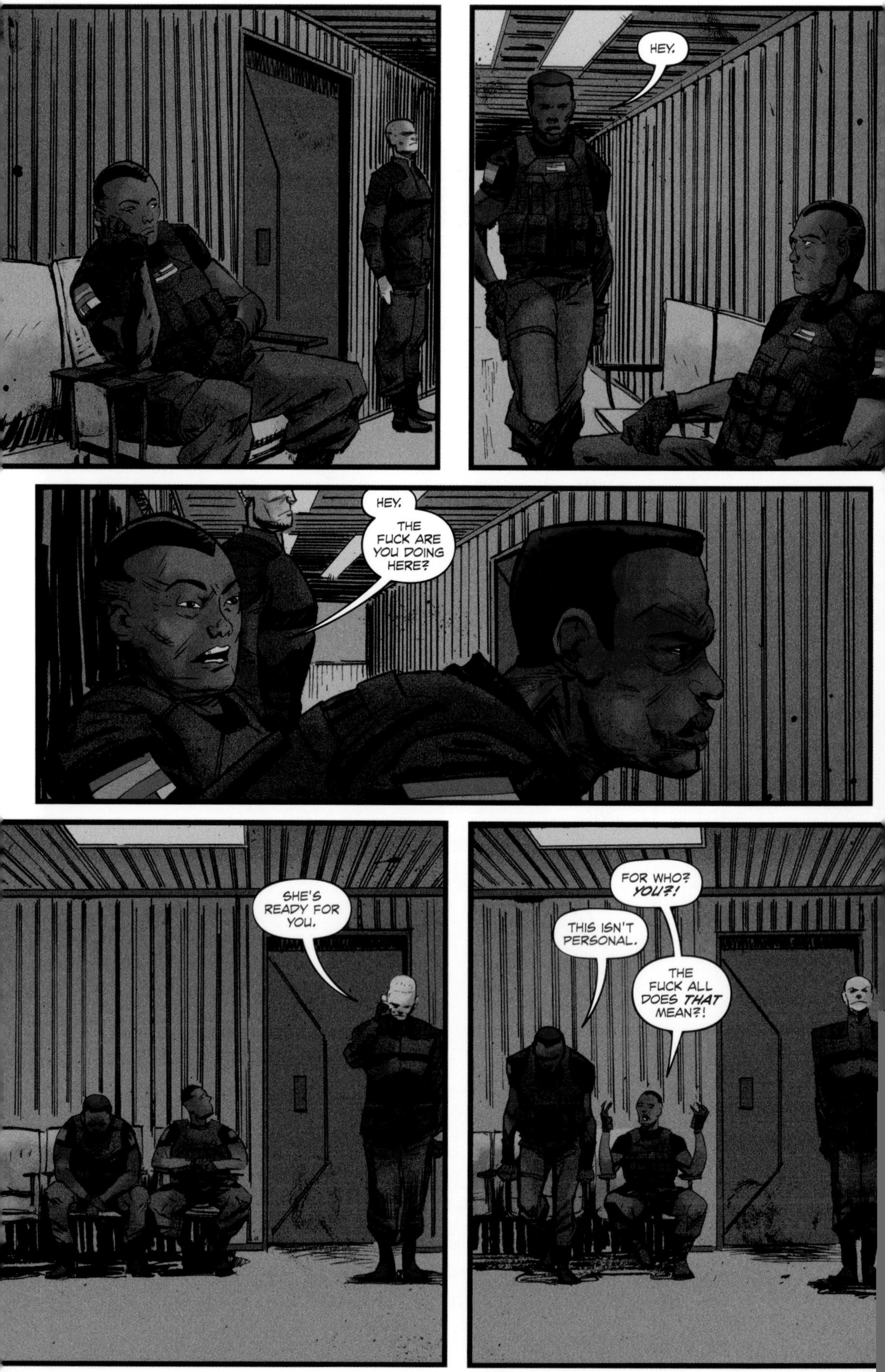
HEY.
HEY.
THE FUCK ARE YOU DOING HERE?
SHE'S READY FOR YOU.
THIS ISN'T PERSONAL.
FOR WHO? YOU?!
THE FUCK ALL DOES THAT MEAN?!

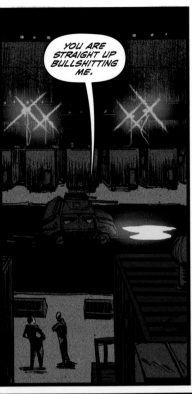

YOU ARE STRAIGHT UP BULLSHITTING ME.

IT'S DONE.

CAN'T BE DONE, DUDE. NO WAY. LETS GO BACK--

IT'S DONE, SIMON.

YOU'RE A SHORT TIMER, NOW?!

TWO MONTHS. I'M ON THE FIRST BUCKET OUT.

AND THIS FUCKING GUY BACK HERE, THIS FUCKING FUCK FUCK GUY--

IT'S NOT PERSONAL.

EVERYTIME YOU SAY THAT, IT SOUNDS MORE AND MORE LIKE IT IS PERSONAL, PECK!! YOU FUCKING SHITBIRD!

SIMON, HE'S YOUR CO.

NO, FUCK THAT! HE'S NOT MY CO *NOW*. HE'S A SHITBIRD. IN TWO MONTHS, WHEN YOU'RE SLUGGING REAL BOOZE, UP TO YOUR EARS IN NOT-MARS, *THEN* HE'S MY FUCKING CO--

IT'S NOT PERS--

DON'T FUCKING SAY IT, SHITBIRD!

I DIDN'T ASK FOR THIS. YOU'RE OUT IN TWO YEARS; THEY NEED SOMEONE THAT'S ALREADY IN COUNTRY, WHO'S HERE FOR THE LONG HAUL. THAT LEAVES ME.

SUPER-INTENDENT SHITBIRD!

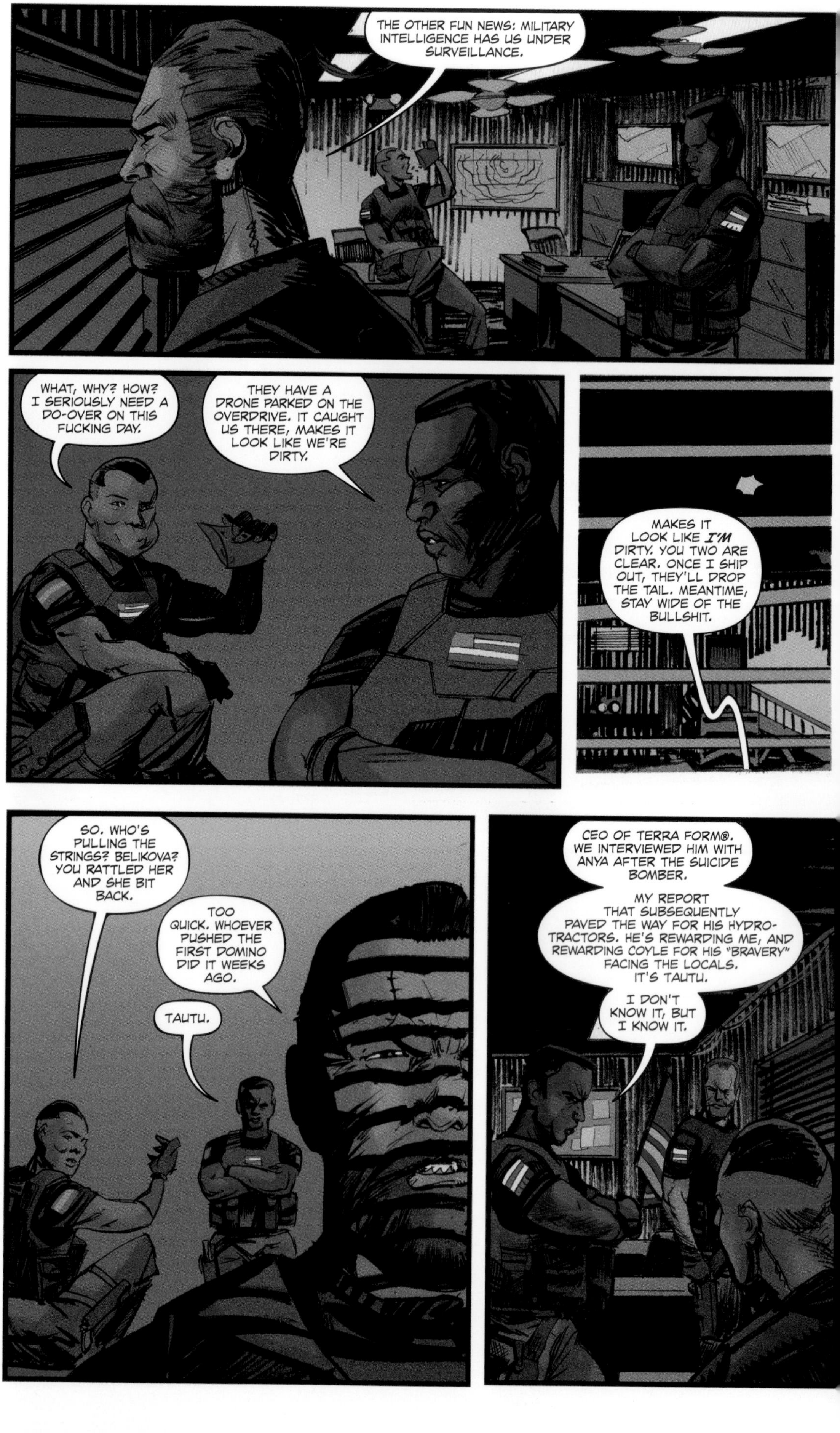
THE OTHER FUN NEWS: MILITARY INTELLIGENCE HAS US UNDER SURVEILLANCE.
WHAT, WHY? HOW? I SERIOUSLY NEED A DO-OVER ON THIS FUCKING DAY.
THEY HAVE A DRONE PARKED ON THE OVERDRIVE. IT CAUGHT US THERE, MAKES IT LOOK LIKE WE'RE DIRTY.
MAKES IT LOOK LIKE I'M DIRTY. YOU TWO ARE CLEAR. ONCE I SHIP OUT, THEY'LL DROP THE TAIL. MEANTIME, STAY WIDE OF THE BULLSHIT.
SO. WHO'S PULLING THE STRINGS? BELIKOVA? YOU RATTLED HER AND SHE BIT BACK.
TOO QUICK. WHOEVER PUSHED THE FIRST DOMINO DID IT WEEKS AGO.
TAUTU.
CEO OF TERRA FORM®. WE INTERVIEWED HIM WITH ANYA AFTER THE SUICIDE BOMBER.
MY REPORT THAT SUBSEQUENTLY PAVED THE WAY FOR HIS HYDRO-TRACTORS. HE'S REWARDING ME, AND REWARDING COYLE FOR HIS "BRAVERY" FACING THE LOCALS. IT'S TAUTU.
I DON'T KNOW IT, BUT I KNOW IT.

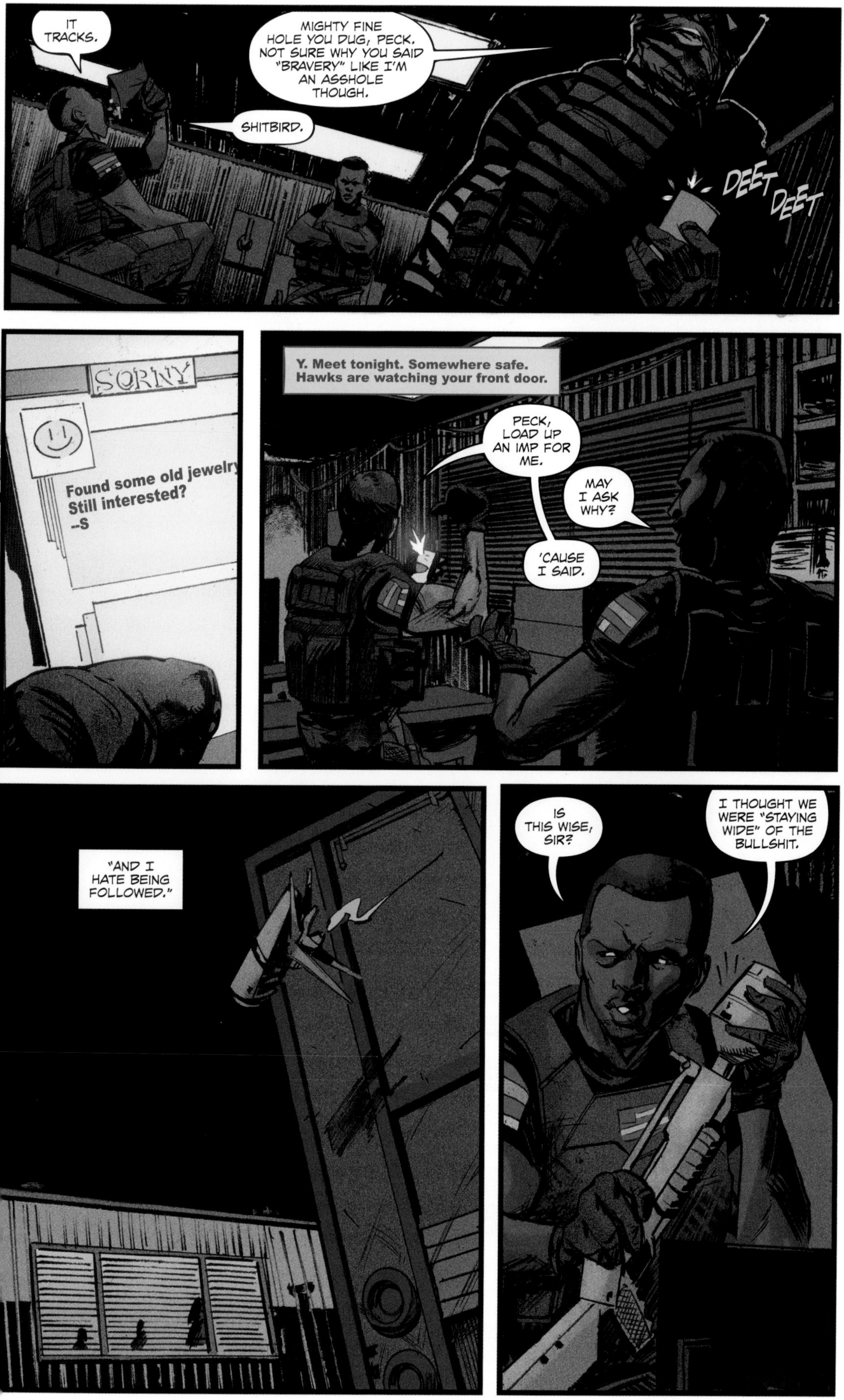
IT TRACKS.
MIGHTY FINE HOLE YOU DUG, PECK. NOT SURE WHY YOU SAID "BRAVERY" LIKE I'M AN ASSHOLE THOUGH.
SHITBIRD.
DEET DEET
SORNY
Found some old jewelry
Still interested?
--S
Y. Meet tonight. Somewhere safe.
Hawks are watching your front door.
PECK, LOAD UP AN IMP FOR ME.
MAY I ASK WHY?
'CAUSE I SAID.
"AND I HATE BEING FOLLOWED."
IS THIS WISE, SIR?
I THOUGHT WE WERE "STAYING WIDE" OF THE BULLSHIT.

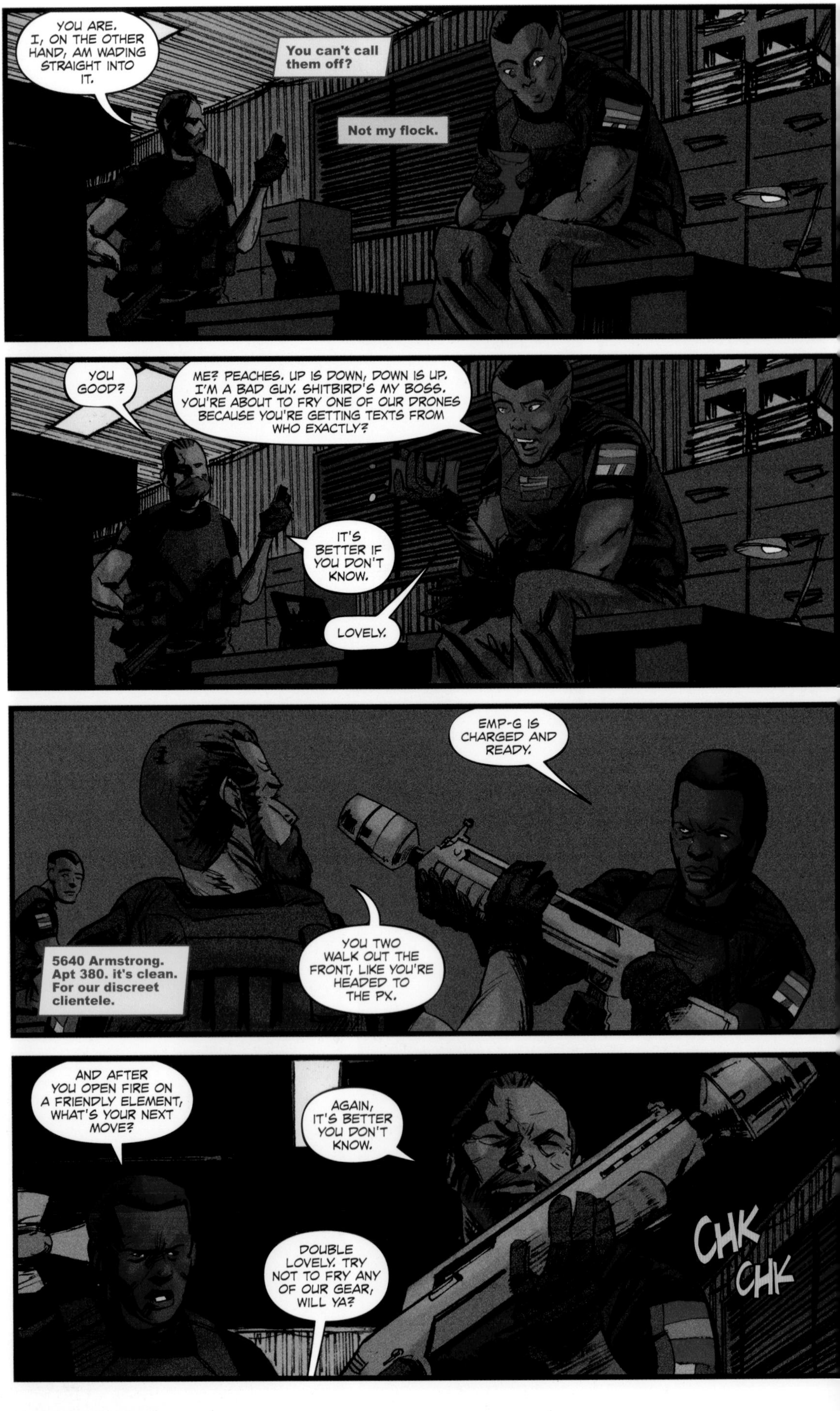
YOU ARE. I, ON THE OTHER HAND, AM WADING STRAIGHT INTO IT.
You can't call them off?
Not my flock.
YOU GOOD?
ME? PEACHES. UP IS DOWN, DOWN IS UP. I'M A BAD GUY. SHITBIRD'S MY BOSS. YOU'RE ABOUT TO FRY ONE OF OUR DRONES BECAUSE YOU'RE GETTING TEXTS FROM WHO EXACTLY?
IT'S BETTER IF YOU DON'T KNOW.
LOVELY.
EMP-G IS CHARGED AND READY.
5640 Armstrong. Apt 380. it's clean. For our discreet clientele.
YOU TWO WALK OUT THE FRONT, LIKE YOU'RE HEADED TO THE PX.
AND AFTER YOU OPEN FIRE ON A FRIENDLY ELEMENT, WHAT'S YOUR NEXT MOVE?
AGAIN, IT'S BETTER YOU DON'T KNOW.
DOUBLE LOVELY. TRY NOT TO FRY ANY OF OUR GEAR, WILL YA?
CHK
CHK

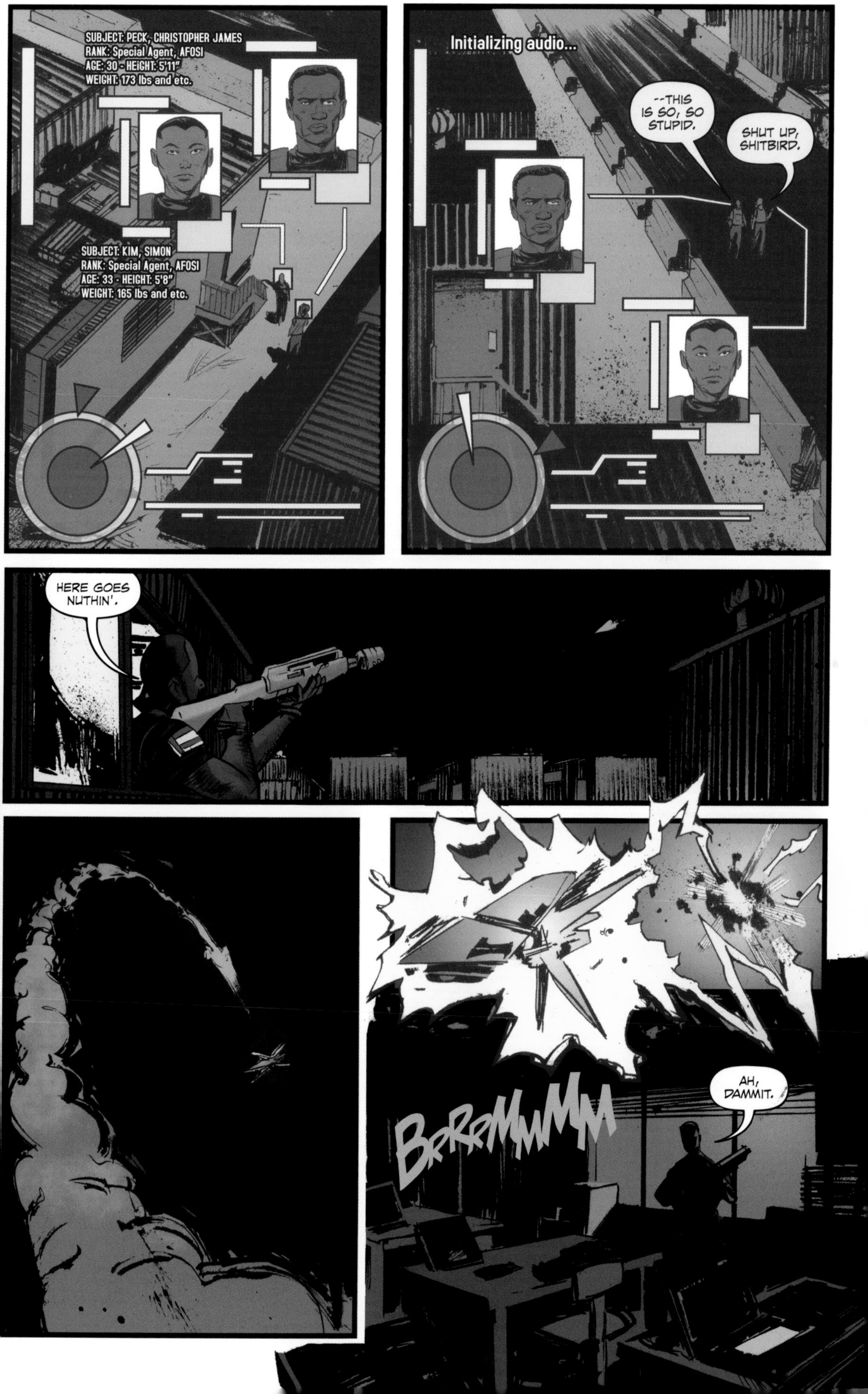
SUBJECT: PECK, CHRISTOPHER JAMES
RANK: Special Agent, AFOSI
AGE: 30 - HEIGHT: 5'11"
WEIGHT: 173 lbs and etc.
SUBJECT: KIM, SIMON
RANK: Special Agent, AFOSI
AGE: 33 - HEIGHT: 5'8"
WEIGHT: 165 lbs and etc.
Initializing audio...
--THIS IS SO, SO STUPID.
SHUT UP, SHITBIRD.
HERE GOES NUTHIN'.
BRRRMMMM
AH, DAMMIT.

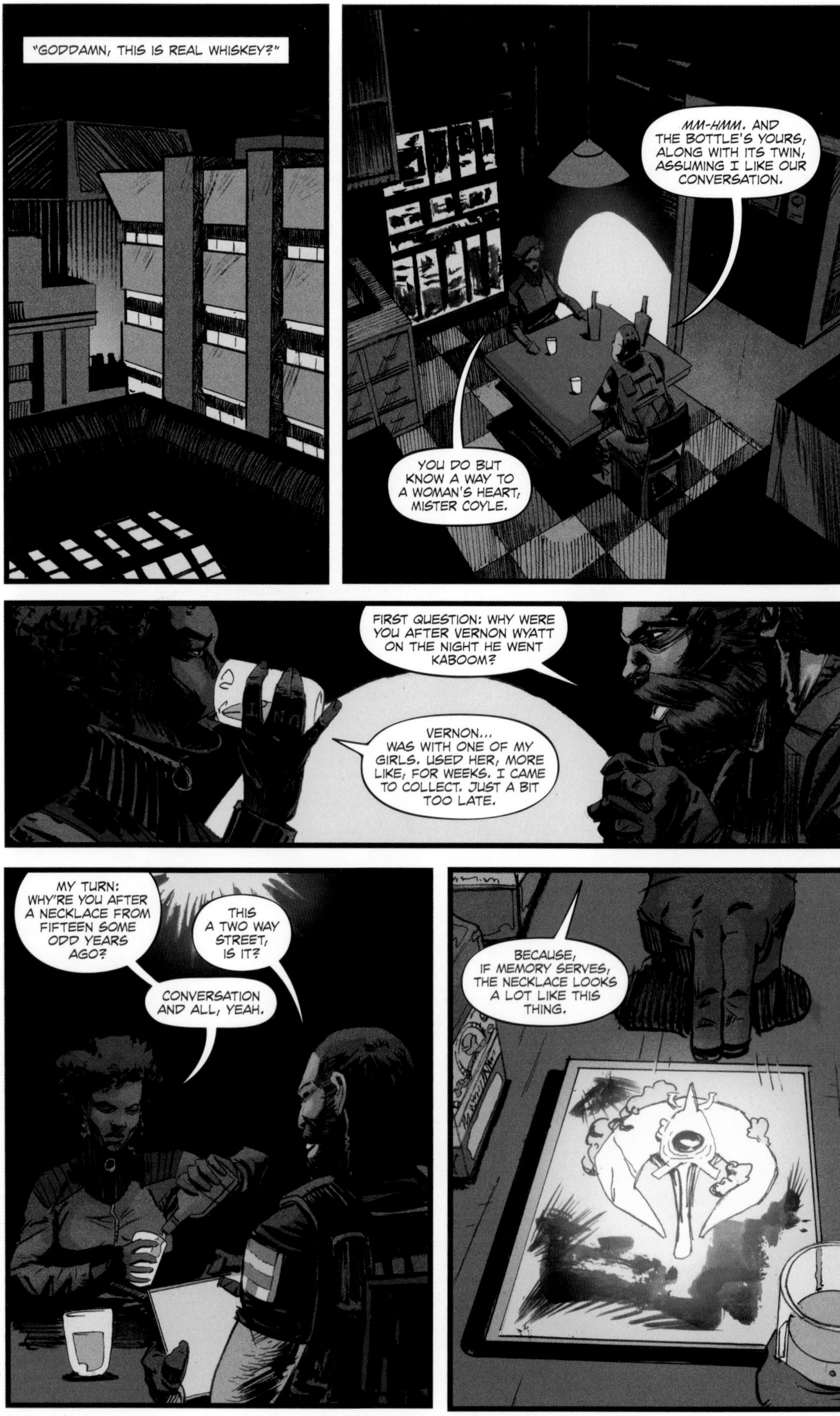

"GODDAMN, THIS IS REAL WHISKEY?"
MM-HMM. AND THE BOTTLE'S YOURS, ALONG WITH ITS TWIN, ASSUMING I LIKE OUR CONVERSATION.
YOU DO BUT KNOW A WAY TO A WOMAN'S HEART, MISTER COYLE.
FIRST QUESTION: WHY WERE YOU AFTER VERNON WYATT ON THE NIGHT HE WENT KABOOM?
VERNON... WAS WITH ONE OF MY GIRLS. USED HER, MORE LIKE, FOR WEEKS. I CAME TO COLLECT. JUST A BIT TOO LATE.
MY TURN: WHY'RE YOU AFTER A NECKLACE FROM FIFTEEN SOME ODD YEARS AGO?
THIS A TWO WAY STREET, IS IT?
CONVERSATION AND ALL, YEAH.
BECAUSE, IF MEMORY SERVES, THE NECKLACE LOOKS A LOT LIKE THIS THING.

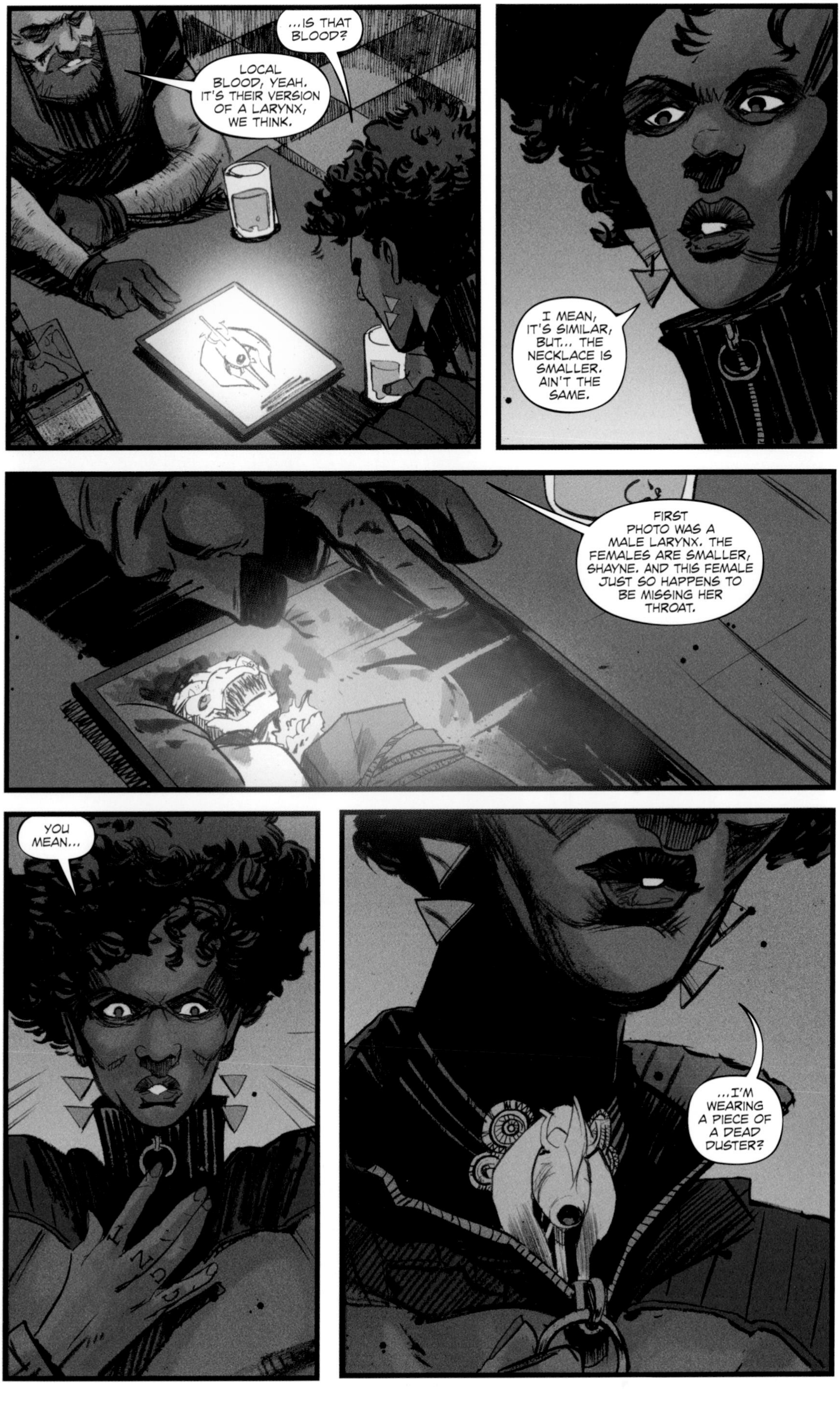

...IS THAT BLOOD?
LOCAL BLOOD, YEAH. IT'S THEIR VERSION OF A LARYNX, WE THINK.
I MEAN, IT'S SIMILAR, BUT... THE NECKLACE IS SMALLER. AIN'T THE SAME.
FIRST PHOTO WAS A MALE LARYNX. THE FEMALES ARE SMALLER, SHAYNE. AND THIS FEMALE JUST SO HAPPENS TO BE MISSING HER THROAT.
YOU MEAN...
...I'M WEARING A PIECE OF A DEAD DUSTER?

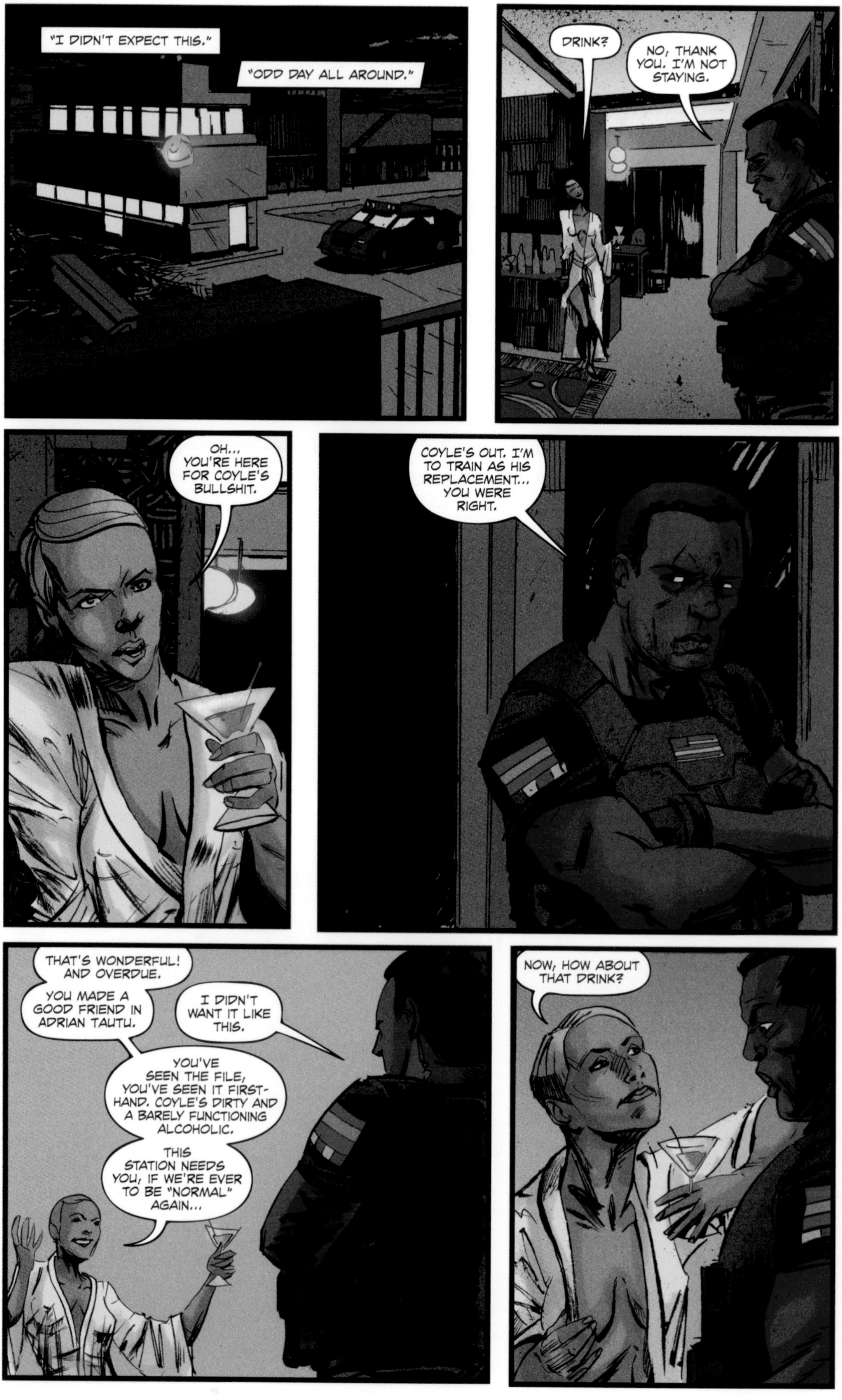
"I DIDN'T EXPECT THIS."
"ODD DAY ALL AROUND."
DRINK?
NO, THANK YOU. I'M NOT STAYING.
OH... YOU'RE HERE FOR COYLE'S BULLSHIT.
COYLE'S OUT. I'M TO TRAIN AS HIS REPLACEMENT... YOU WERE RIGHT.
THAT'S WONDERFUL! AND OVERDUE.
YOU MADE A GOOD FRIEND IN ADRIAN TAUTU.
I DIDN'T WANT IT LIKE THIS.
YOU'VE SEEN THE FILE, YOU'VE SEEN IT FIRST-HAND. COYLE'S DIRTY AND A BARELY FUNCTIONING ALCOHOLIC.
THIS STATION NEEDS YOU, IF WE'RE EVER TO BE "NORMAL" AGAIN...
NOW, HOW ABOUT THAT DRINK?

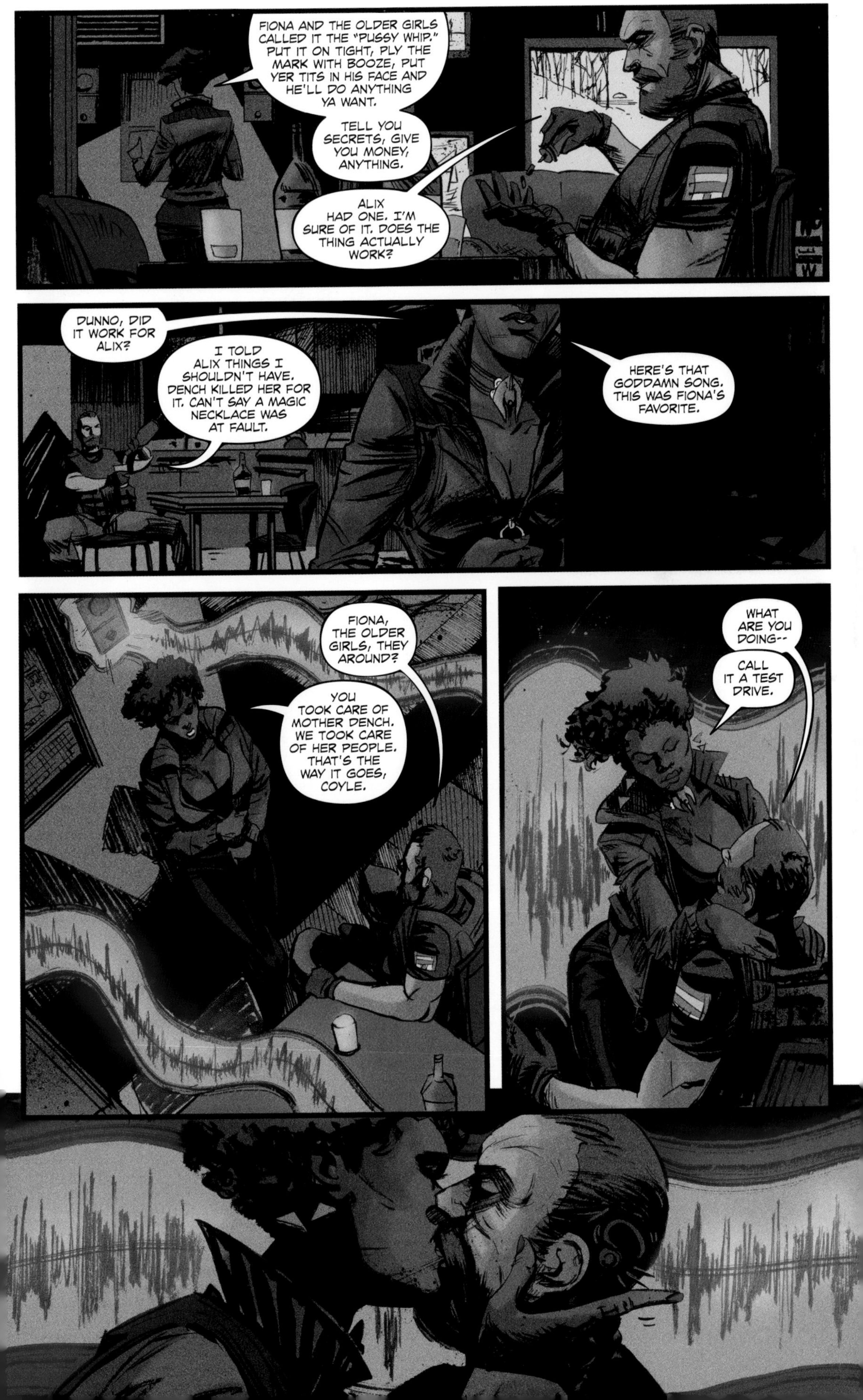
FIONA AND THE OLDER GIRLS CALLED IT THE "PUSSY WHIP." PUT IT ON TIGHT, PLY THE MARK WITH BOOZE, PUT YER TITS IN HIS FACE AND HE'LL DO ANYTHING YA WANT.
TELL YOU SECRETS, GIVE YOU MONEY, ANYTHING.
ALIX HAD ONE. I'M SURE OF IT. DOES THE THING ACTUALLY WORK?
DUNNO, DID IT WORK FOR ALIX?
I TOLD ALIX THINGS I SHOULDN'T HAVE. DENCH KILLED HER FOR IT. CAN'T SAY A MAGIC NECKLACE WAS AT FAULT.
HERE'S THAT GODDAMN SONG. THIS WAS FIONA'S FAVORITE.
FIONA, THE OLDER GIRLS, THEY AROUND?
YOU TOOK CARE OF MOTHER DENCH. WE TOOK CARE OF HER PEOPLE. THAT'S THE WAY IT GOES, COYLE.
WHAT ARE YOU DOING--
CALL IT A TEST DRIVE.

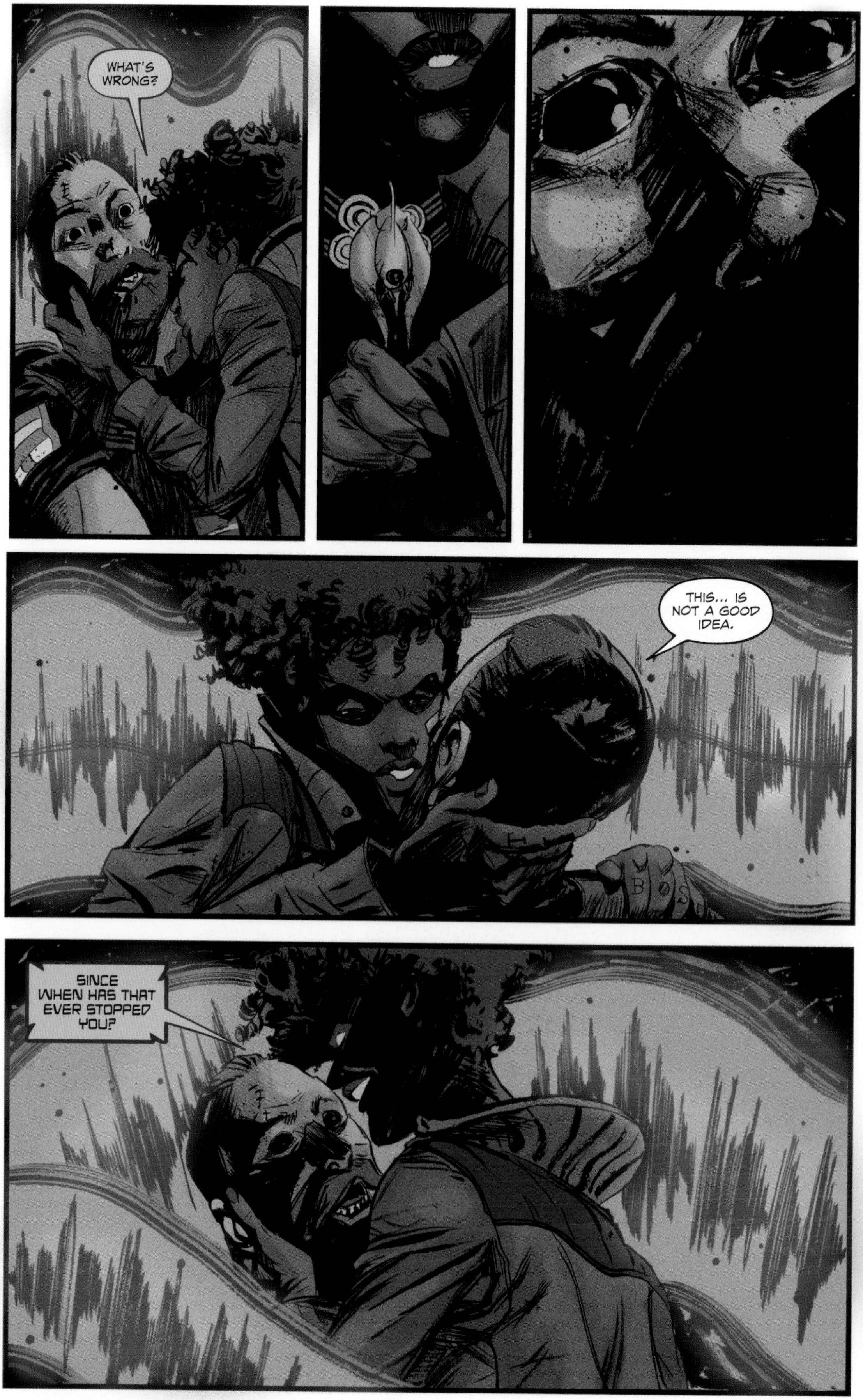
WHAT'S WRONG?
THIS... IS NOT A GOOD IDEA.
SINCE WHEN HAS THAT EVER STOPPED YOU?

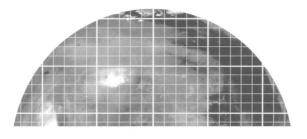

CHAPTER 04

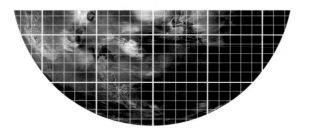

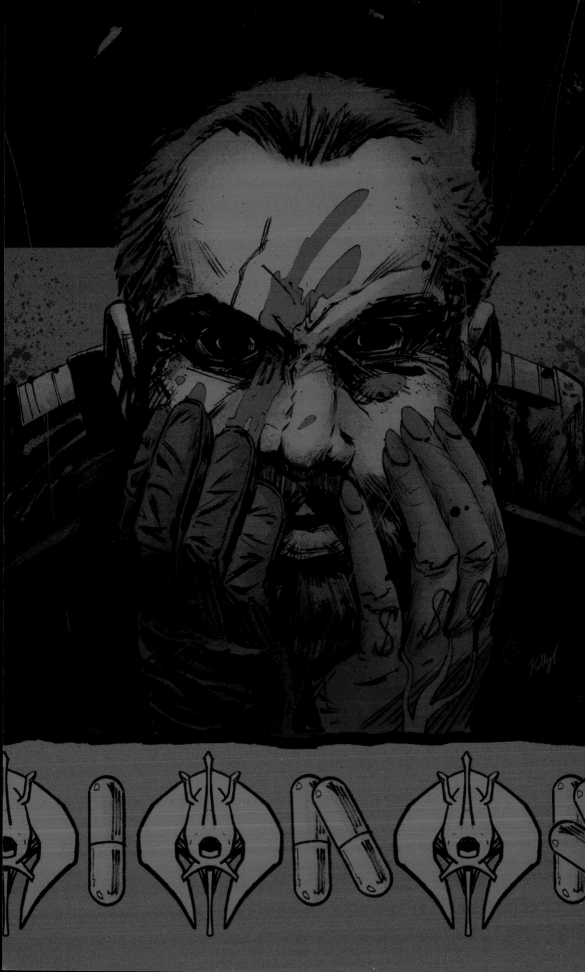

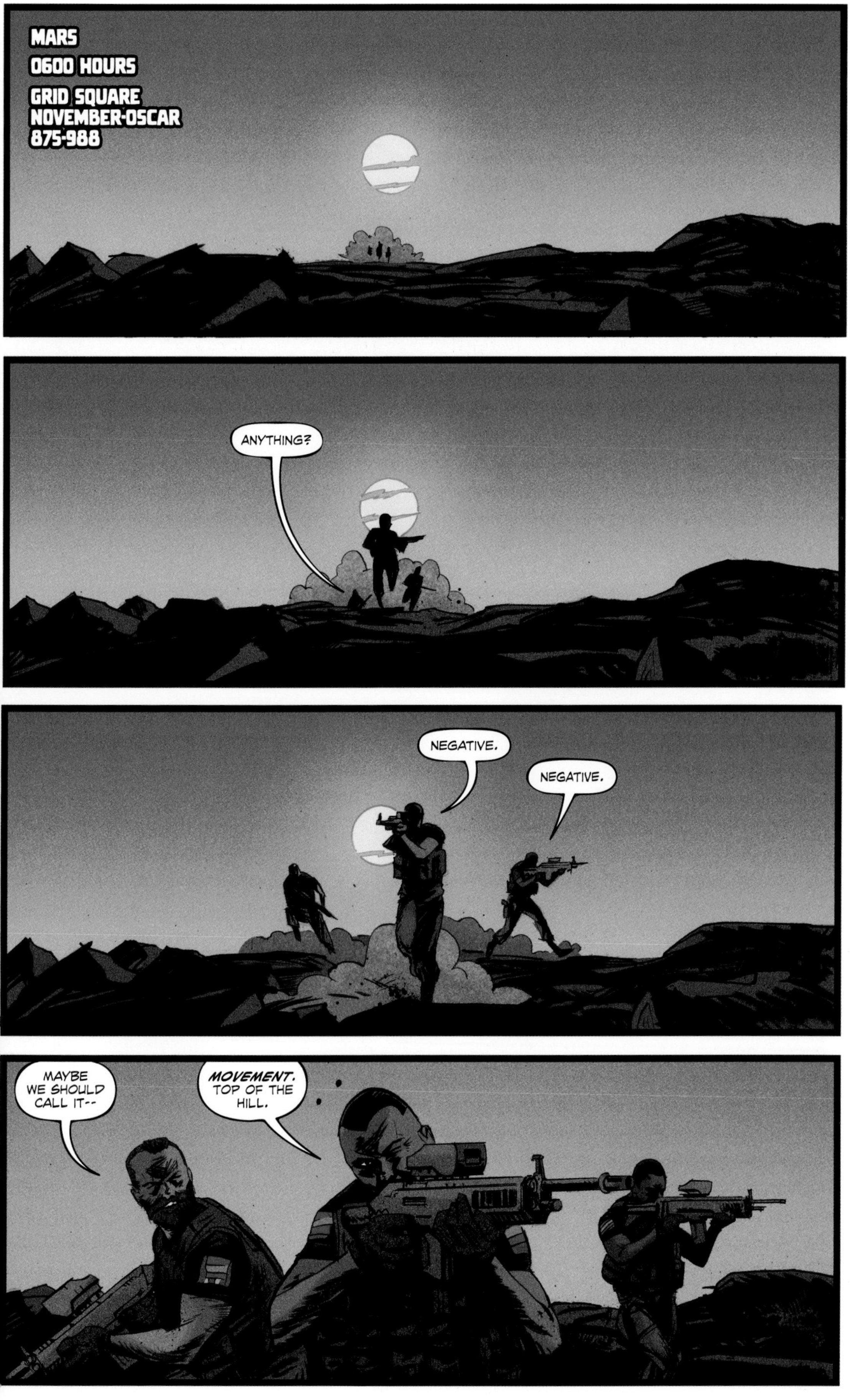
MARS
0600 HOURS
GRID SQUARE NOVEMBER-OSCAR 875-988
ANYTHING?
NEGATIVE.
NEGATIVE.
MAYBE WE SHOULD CALL IT--
MOVEMENT. TOP OF THE HILL.

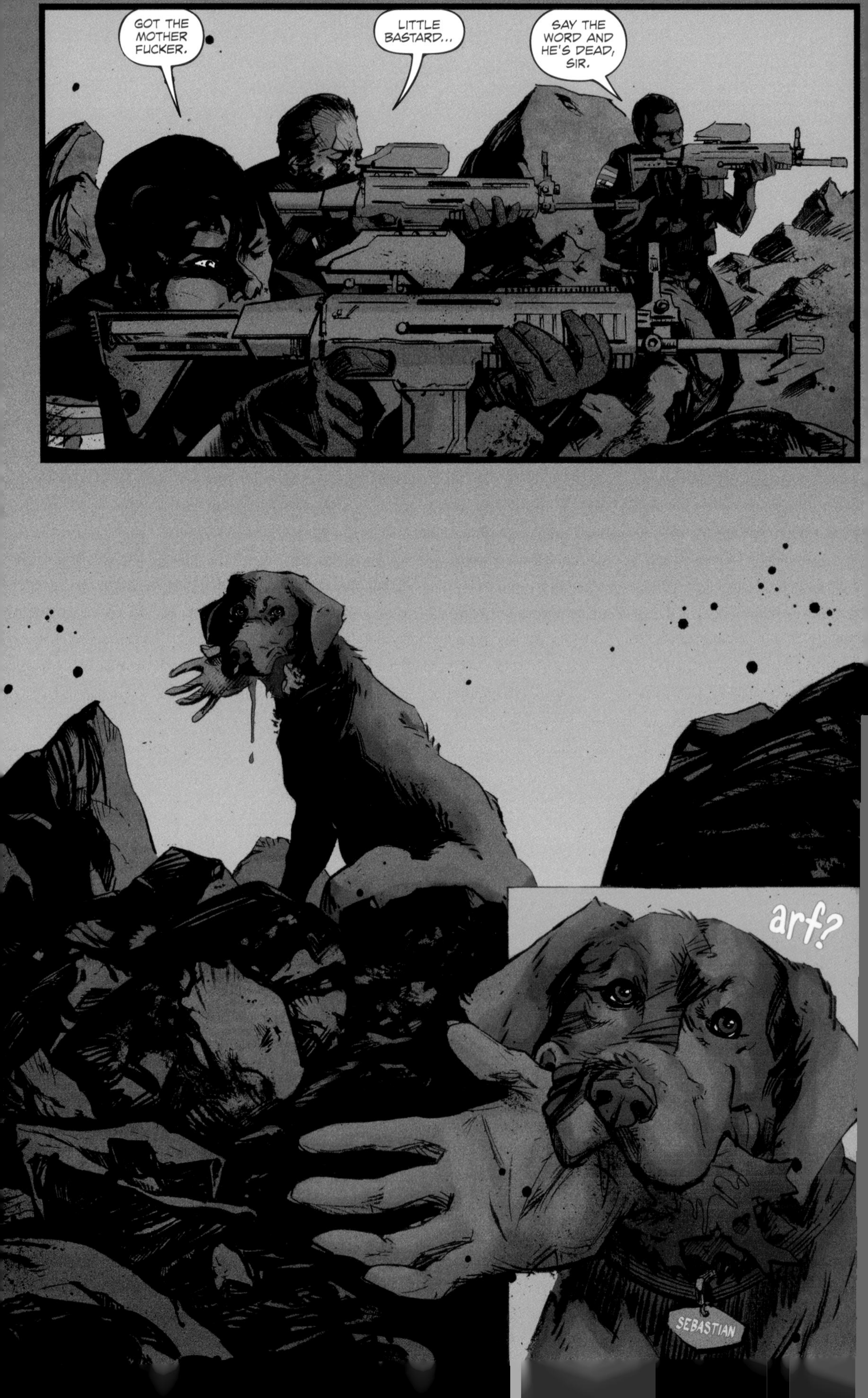
GOT THE MOTHER FUCKER.
LITTLE BASTARD...
SAY THE WORD AND HE'S DEAD, SIR.
arf?
SEBASTIAN

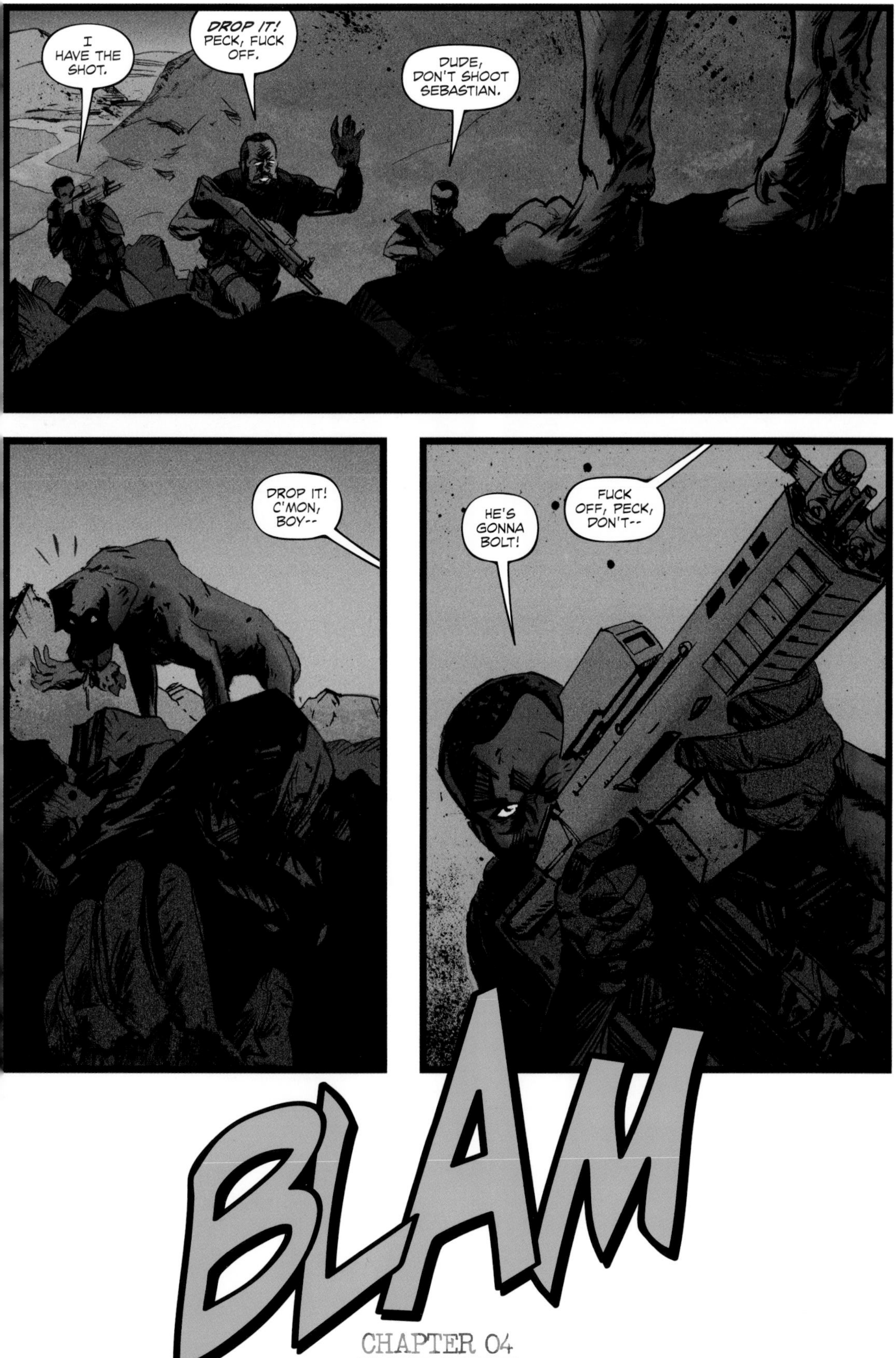
I HAVE THE SHOT.
DROP IT! PECK, FUCK OFF.
DUDE, DON'T SHOOT SEBASTIAN.
DROP IT! C'MON, BOY--
HE'S GONNA BOLT!
FUCK OFF, PECK, DON'T--
BLAM

CHAPTER 04

The past beats inside me, like a second heart

John Banville, *The Sea*

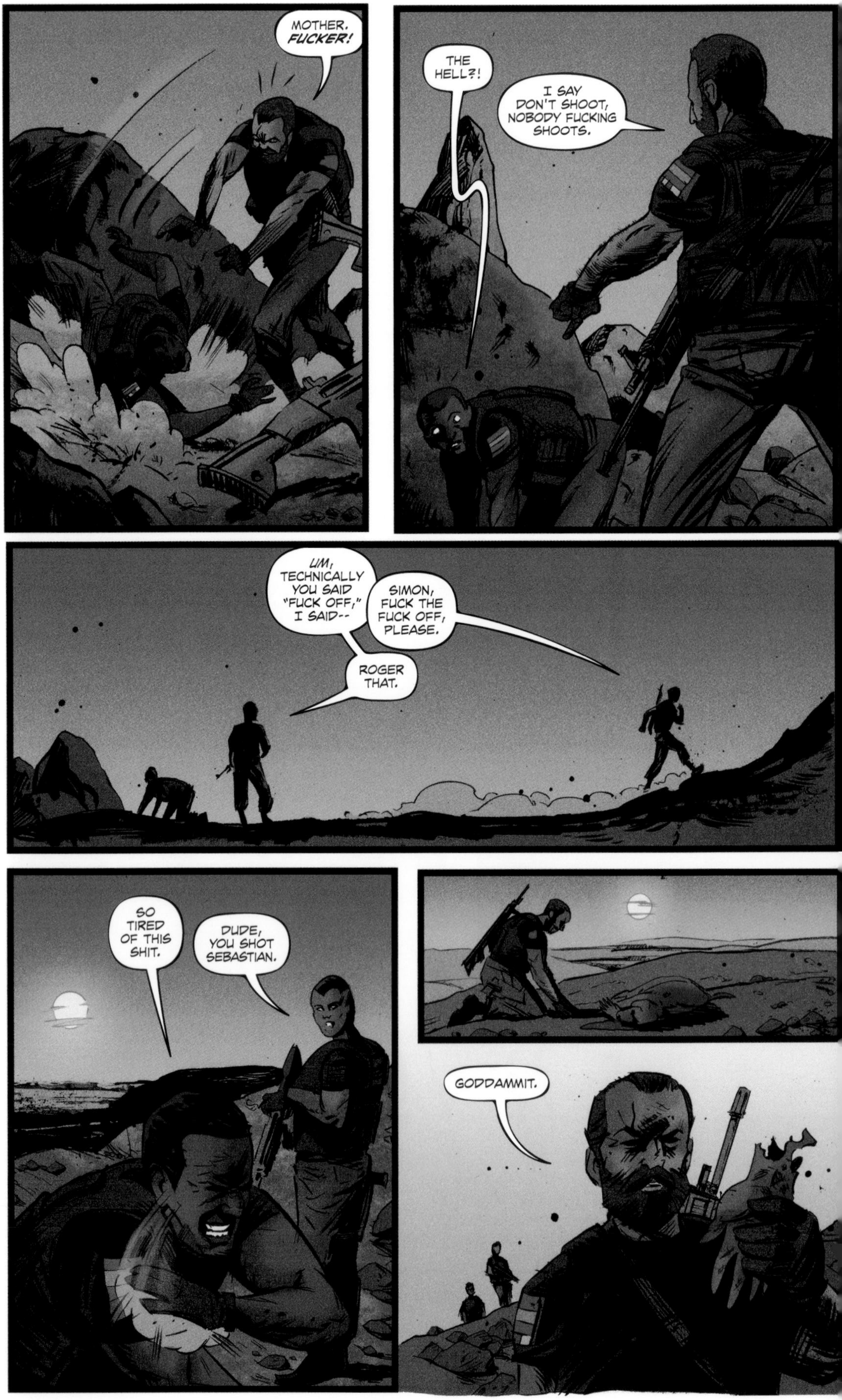
MOTHER. *FUCKER!*
THE HELL?!
I SAY DON'T SHOOT, NOBODY FUCKING SHOOTS.
UM, TECHNICALLY YOU SAID "FUCK OFF," I SAID--
SIMON, FUCK THE FUCK OFF, PLEASE.
ROGER THAT.
SO TIRED OF THIS SHIT.
DUDE, YOU SHOT SEBASTIAN.
GODDAMMIT.

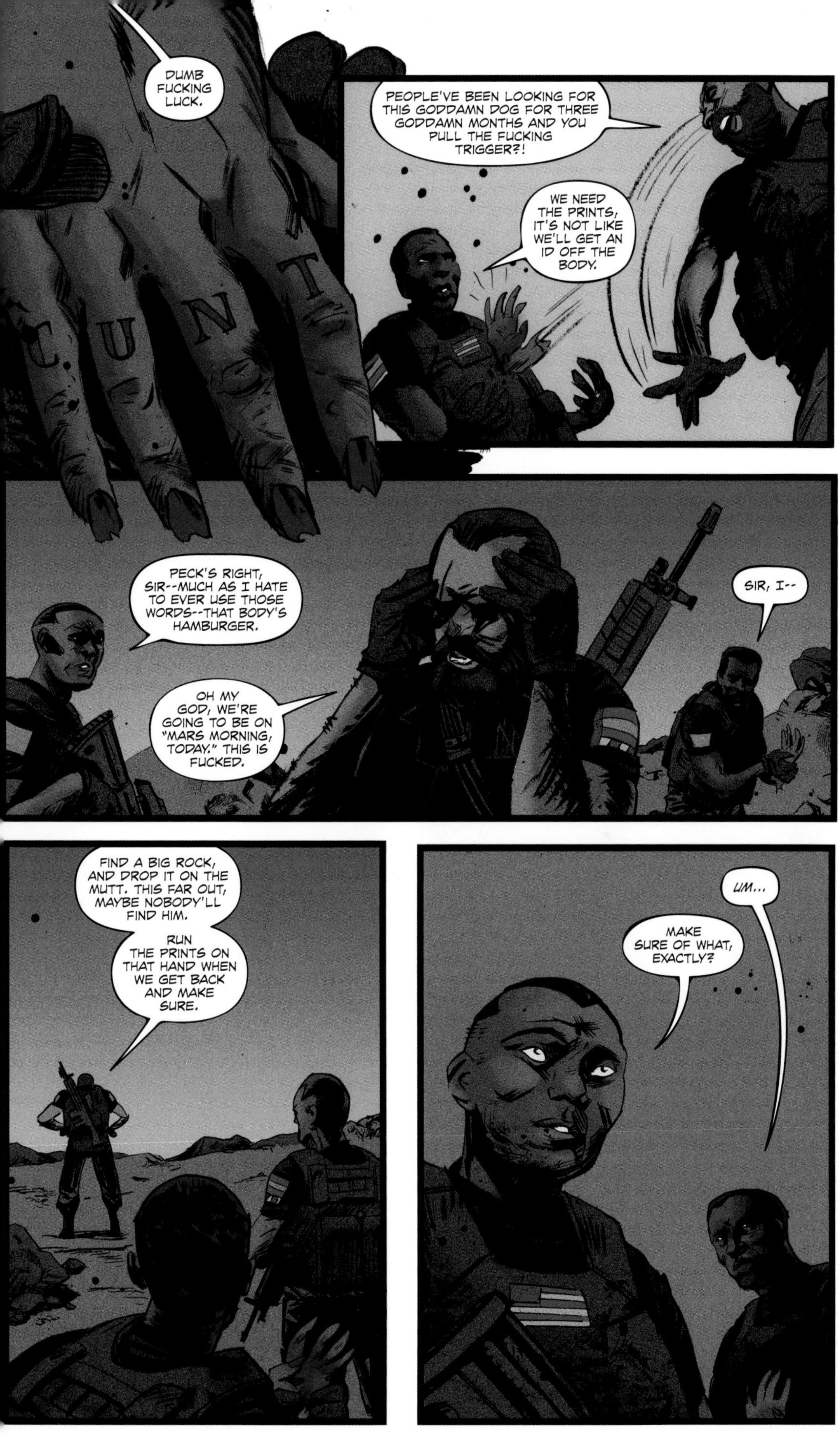

DUMB FUCKING LUCK.
C U N T
PEOPLE'VE BEEN LOOKING FOR THIS GODDAMN DOG FOR THREE GODDAMN MONTHS AND YOU PULL THE FUCKING TRIGGER?!
WE NEED THE PRINTS, IT'S NOT LIKE WE'LL GET AN ID OFF THE BODY.
PECK'S RIGHT, SIR--MUCH AS I HATE TO EVER USE THOSE WORDS--THAT BODY'S HAMBURGER.
OH MY GOD, WE'RE GOING TO BE ON "MARS MORNING, TODAY." THIS IS FUCKED.
SIR, I--
FIND A BIG ROCK, AND DROP IT ON THE MUTT. THIS FAR OUT, MAYBE NOBODY'LL FIND HIM.
RUN THE PRINTS ON THAT HAND WHEN WE GET BACK AND MAKE SURE.
UM...
MAKE SURE OF WHAT, EXACTLY?

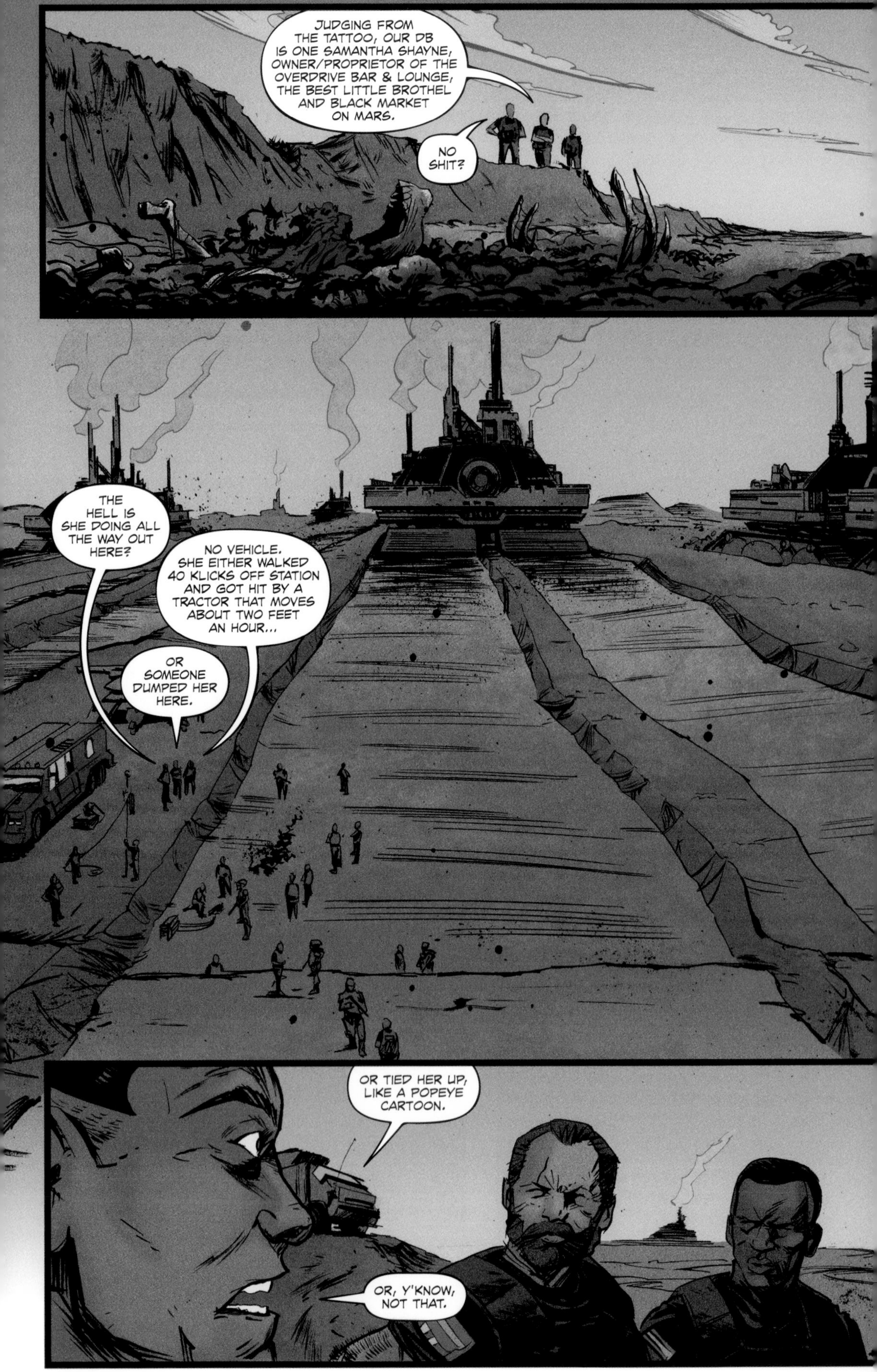
JUDGING FROM THE TATTOO, OUR DB IS ONE SAMANTHA SHAYNE, OWNER/PROPRIETOR OF THE OVERDRIVE BAR & LOUNGE, THE BEST LITTLE BROTHEL AND BLACK MARKET ON MARS.
NO SHIT?
THE HELL IS SHE DOING ALL THE WAY OUT HERE?
NO VEHICLE. SHE EITHER WALKED 40 KLICKS OFF STATION AND GOT HIT BY A TRACTOR THAT MOVES ABOUT TWO FEET AN HOUR...
OR SOMEONE DUMPED HER HERE.
OR TIED HER UP, LIKE A POPEYE CARTOON.
OR, Y'KNOW, NOT THAT.

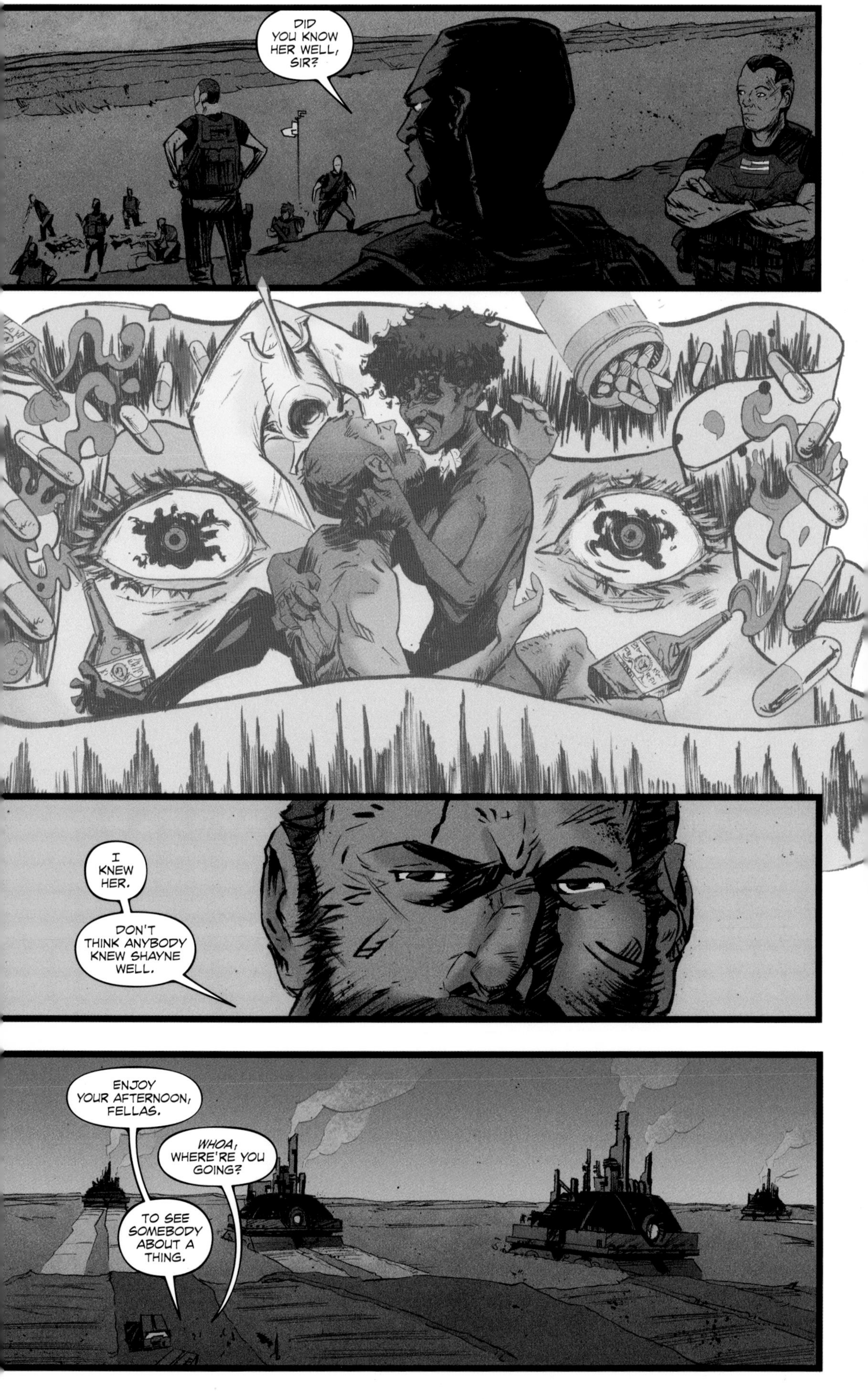
DID YOU KNOW HER WELL, SIR?
I KNEW HER.
DON'T THINK ANYBODY KNEW SHAYNE WELL.
ENJOY YOUR AFTERNOON, FELLAS.
WHOA, WHERE'RE YOU GOING?
TO SEE SOMEBODY ABOUT A THING.

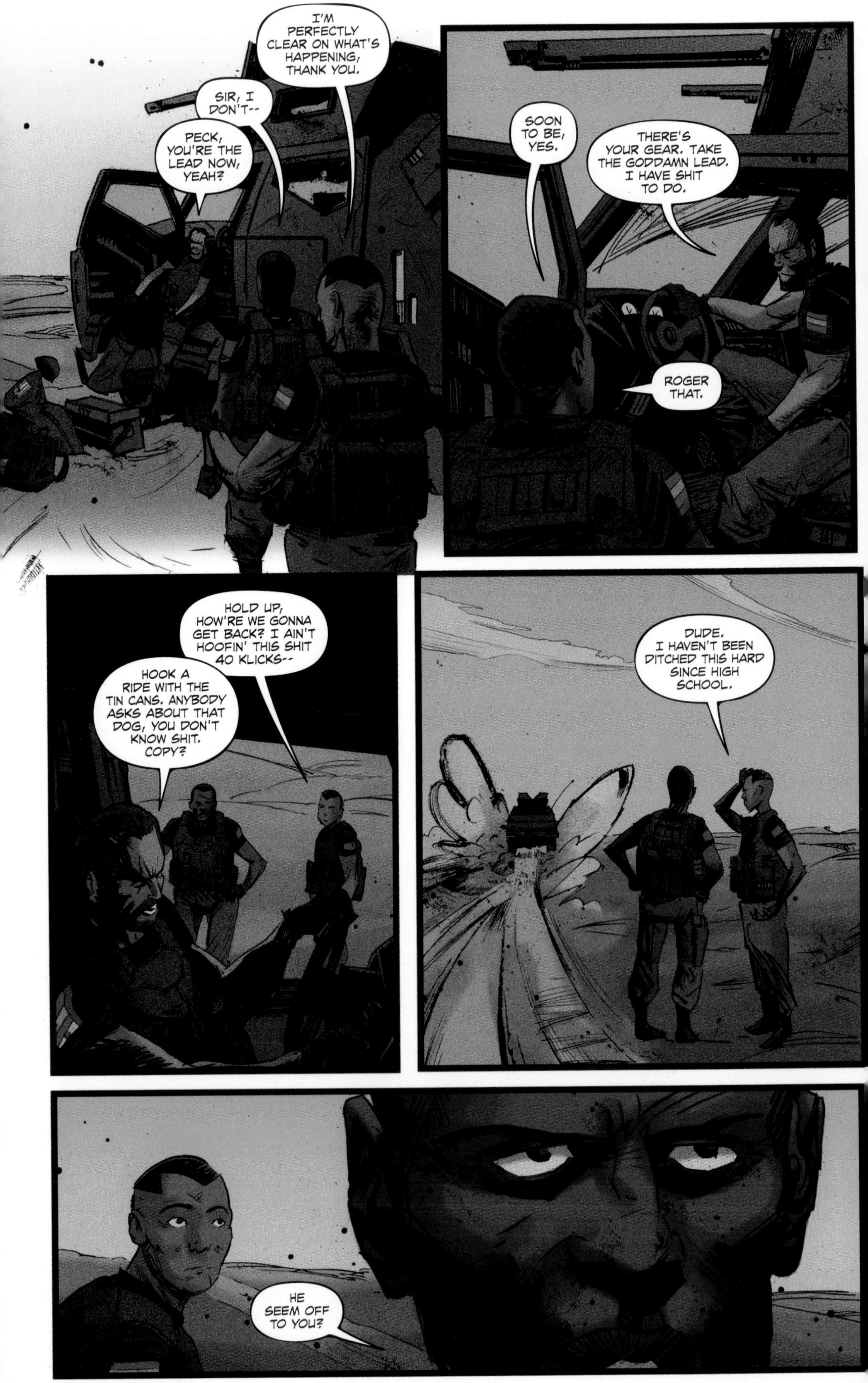

PECK, YOU'RE THE LEAD NOW, YEAH?
SIR, I DON'T--
I'M PERFECTLY CLEAR ON WHAT'S HAPPENING, THANK YOU.
SOON TO BE, YES.
THERE'S YOUR GEAR. TAKE THE GODDAMN LEAD. I HAVE SHIT TO DO.
ROGER THAT.
HOLD UP, HOW'RE WE GONNA GET BACK? I AIN'T HOOFIN' THIS SHIT 40 KLICKS--
HOOK A RIDE WITH THE TIN CANS. ANYBODY ASKS ABOUT THAT DOG, YOU DON'T KNOW SHIT. COPY?
DUDE. I HAVEN'T BEEN DITCHED THIS HARD SINCE HIGH SCHOOL.
HE SEEM OFF TO YOU?

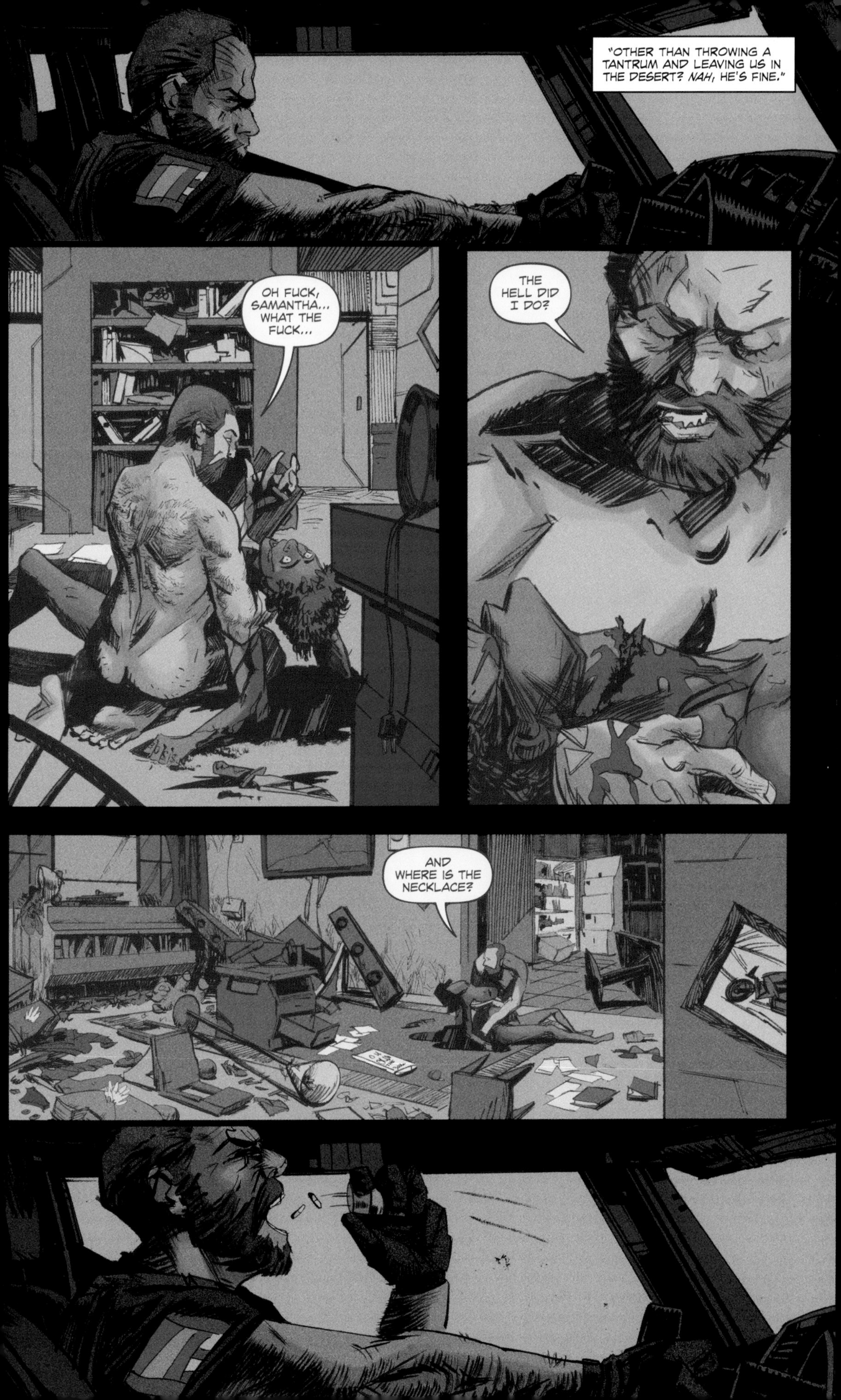
"OTHER THAN THROWING A TANTRUM AND LEAVING US IN THE DESERT? *NAH*, HE'S FINE."
OH FUCK, SAMANTHA... WHAT THE FUCK...
THE HELL DID I DO?
AND WHERE IS THE NECKLACE?

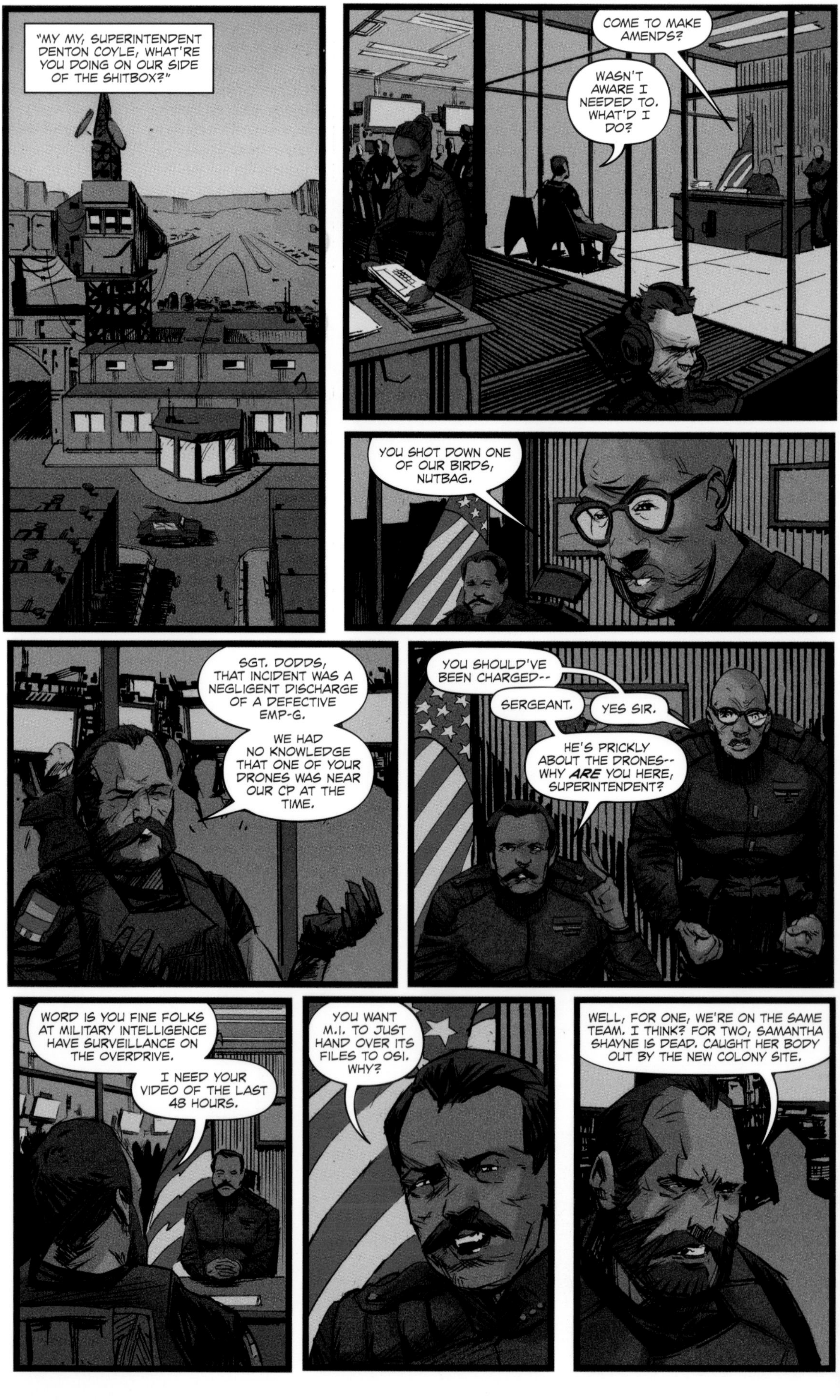
"MY MY, SUPERINTENDENT DENTON COYLE, WHAT'RE YOU DOING ON OUR SIDE OF THE SHITBOX?"
COME TO MAKE AMENDS?
WASN'T AWARE I NEEDED TO. WHAT'D I DO?
YOU SHOT DOWN ONE OF OUR BIRDS, NUTBAG.
SGT. DODDS, THAT INCIDENT WAS A NEGLIGENT DISCHARGE OF A DEFECTIVE EMP-G.
WE HAD NO KNOWLEDGE THAT ONE OF YOUR DRONES WAS NEAR OUR CP AT THE TIME.
YOU SHOULD'VE BEEN CHARGED--
SERGEANT.
YES SIR.
HE'S PRICKLY ABOUT THE DRONES-- WHY *ARE* YOU HERE, SUPERINTENDENT?
WORD IS YOU FINE FOLKS AT MILITARY INTELLIGENCE HAVE SURVEILLANCE ON THE OVERDRIVE.
I NEED YOUR VIDEO OF THE LAST 48 HOURS.
YOU WANT M.I. TO JUST HAND OVER ITS FILES TO OSI. WHY?
WELL, FOR ONE, WE'RE ON THE SAME TEAM. I THINK? FOR TWO, SAMANTHA SHAYNE IS DEAD. CAUGHT HER BODY OUT BY THE NEW COLONY SITE.

THE HELL WAS SHE DOING WAY OUT THERE?

BODY WAS DUMPED. ONE OF THE TERRA FORM® TRACTORS TURNED IT TO BURGER BEFORE WE FOUND IT.

ODD SPOT TO DROP A BODY.

SHE WAS A C.I. I WAS THE HANDLER.

THE SITE IS OSI TERRITORY, WHICH MEANS THEY AT LEAST KNOW SOMETHING OF WHO COVERS WHAT ON STATION.

IT'S A NEAT LITTLE MESSAGE FOR ME, AND I'D VERY MUCH LIKE TO FIND WHO SENT IT.

THE MOTHER OF THE OVERDRIVE, THE LORD AND MASTER OF HARRISON'S BLACK MARKET, WAS YOUR C.I.?

SMELLS LIKE SOME BULLSHIT.

LOOK UP AN OLD HOMICIDE. PENROSE DENCH. SHAYNE'S PREDECESSOR.

SHAYNE WAS MY C.I. WOULD'VE HAD DENCH CLEAN, EXCEPT SOMEONE PUT A BULLET IN HER FIRST.

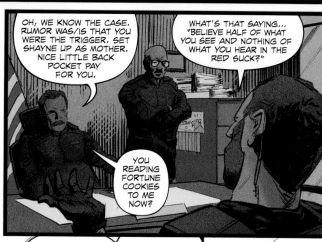

OH, WE KNOW THE CASE. RUMOR WAS/IS THAT YOU WERE THE TRIGGER. SET SHAYNE UP AS MOTHER. NICE LITTLE BACK POCKET PAY FOR YOU.

WHAT'S THAT SAYING... "BELIEVE HALF OF WHAT YOU SEE AND NOTHING OF WHAT YOU HEAR IN THE RED SUCK?"

YOU READING FORTUNE COOKIES TO ME NOW?

CAN I GET THAT FOOTAGE OR NO?

SGT. DODDS WILL BURN A COPY FOR YOU.

YOU'VE GOT TWO MONTHS LEFT, SUPERINTENDENT. TRY TO STAY OUT OF TROUBLE, YEAH?

I'D SAY I WOULD, BUT YOU'D KNOW I'M LYING.

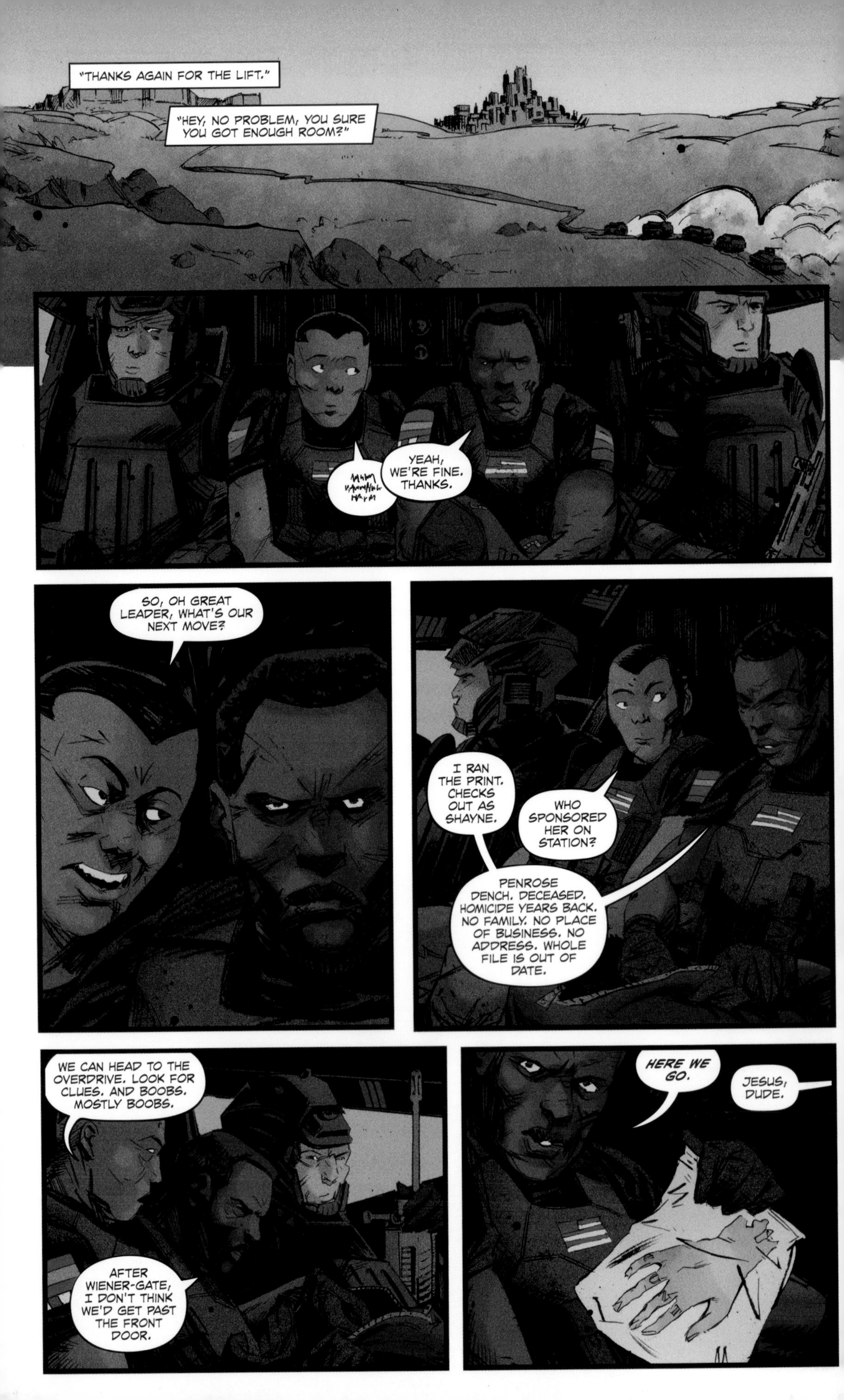
"THANKS AGAIN FOR THE LIFT."
"HEY, NO PROBLEM, YOU SURE YOU GOT ENOUGH ROOM?"
YEAH, WE'RE FINE. THANKS.
SO, OH GREAT LEADER, WHAT'S OUR NEXT MOVE?
I RAN THE PRINT. CHECKS OUT AS SHAYNE.
WHO SPONSORED HER ON STATION?
PENROSE DENCH. DECEASED. HOMICIDE YEARS BACK. NO FAMILY. NO PLACE OF BUSINESS. NO ADDRESS. WHOLE FILE IS OUT OF DATE.
WE CAN HEAD TO THE OVERDRIVE. LOOK FOR CLUES. AND BOOBS. MOSTLY BOOBS.
AFTER WIENER-GATE, I DON'T THINK WE'D GET PAST THE FRONT DOOR.
HERE WE GO.
JESUS, DUDE.

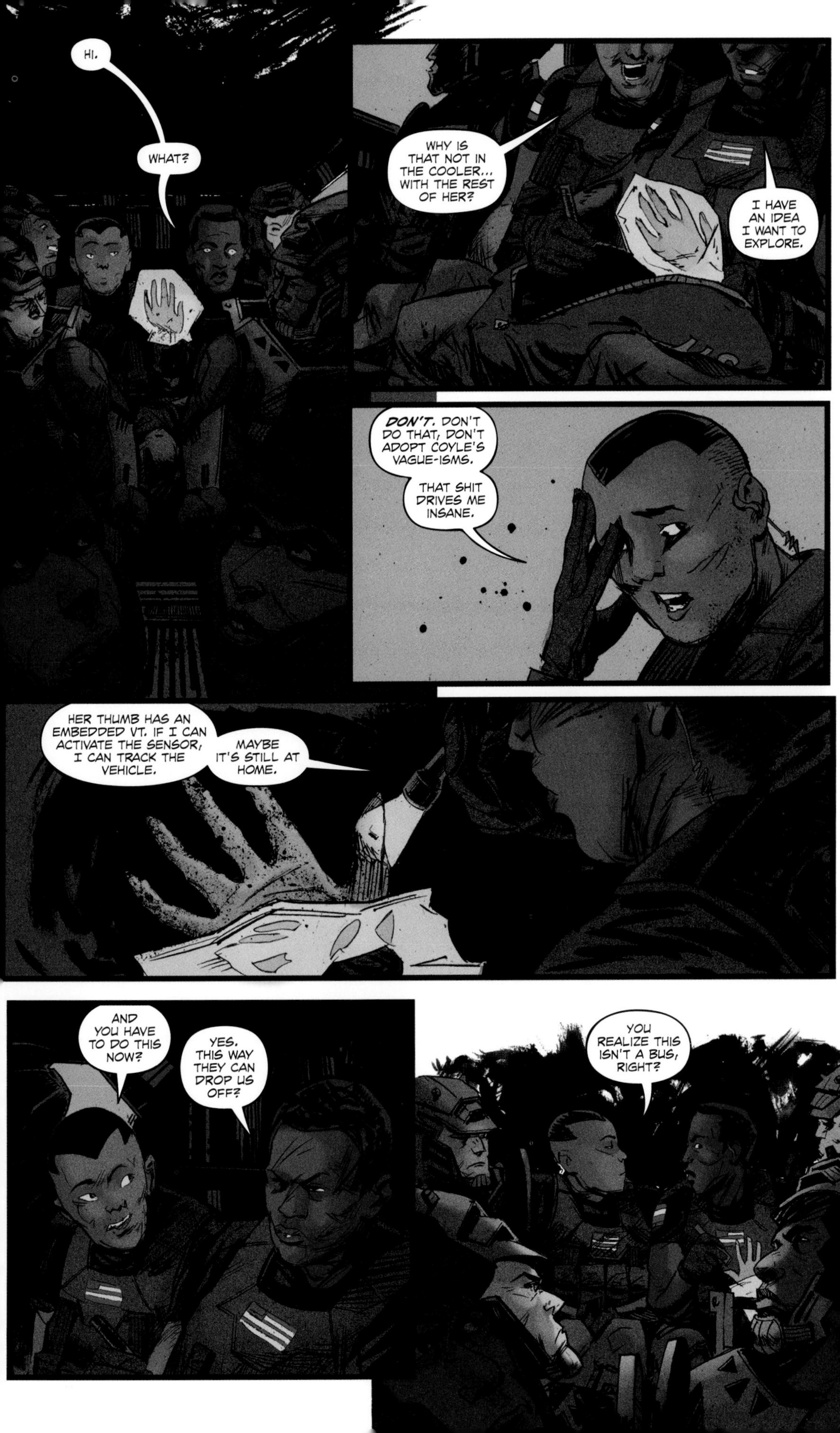
HI.
WHAT?
WHY IS THAT NOT IN THE COOLER... WITH THE REST OF HER?
I HAVE AN IDEA I WANT TO EXPLORE.
DON'T. DON'T DO THAT, DON'T ADOPT COYLE'S VAGUE-ISMS.
THAT SHIT DRIVES ME INSANE.
HER THUMB HAS AN EMBEDDED VT. IF I CAN ACTIVATE THE SENSOR, I CAN TRACK THE VEHICLE.
MAYBE IT'S STILL AT HOME.
AND YOU HAVE TO DO THIS NOW?
YES. THIS WAY THEY CAN DROP US OFF?
YOU REALIZE THIS ISN'T A BUS, RIGHT?

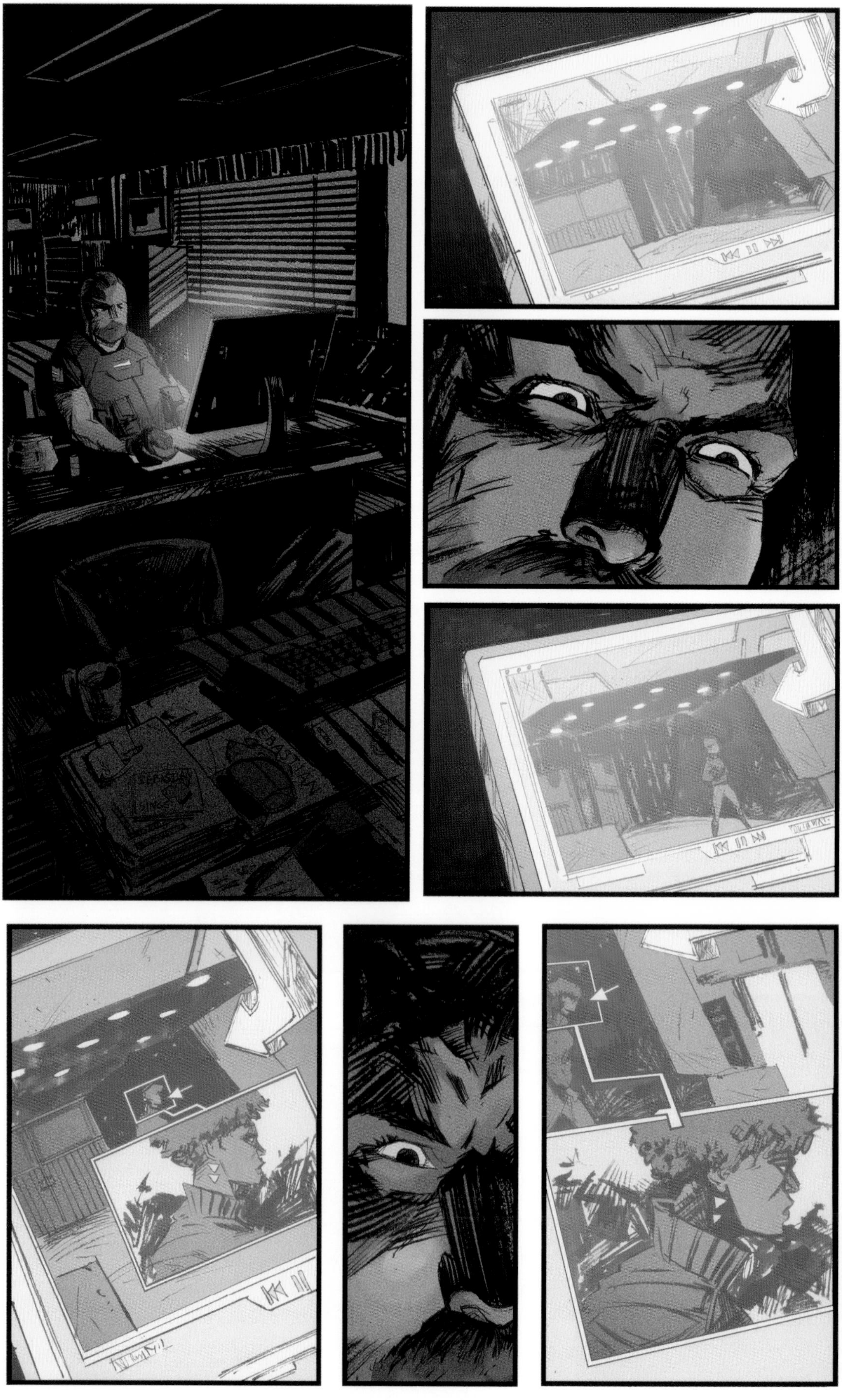

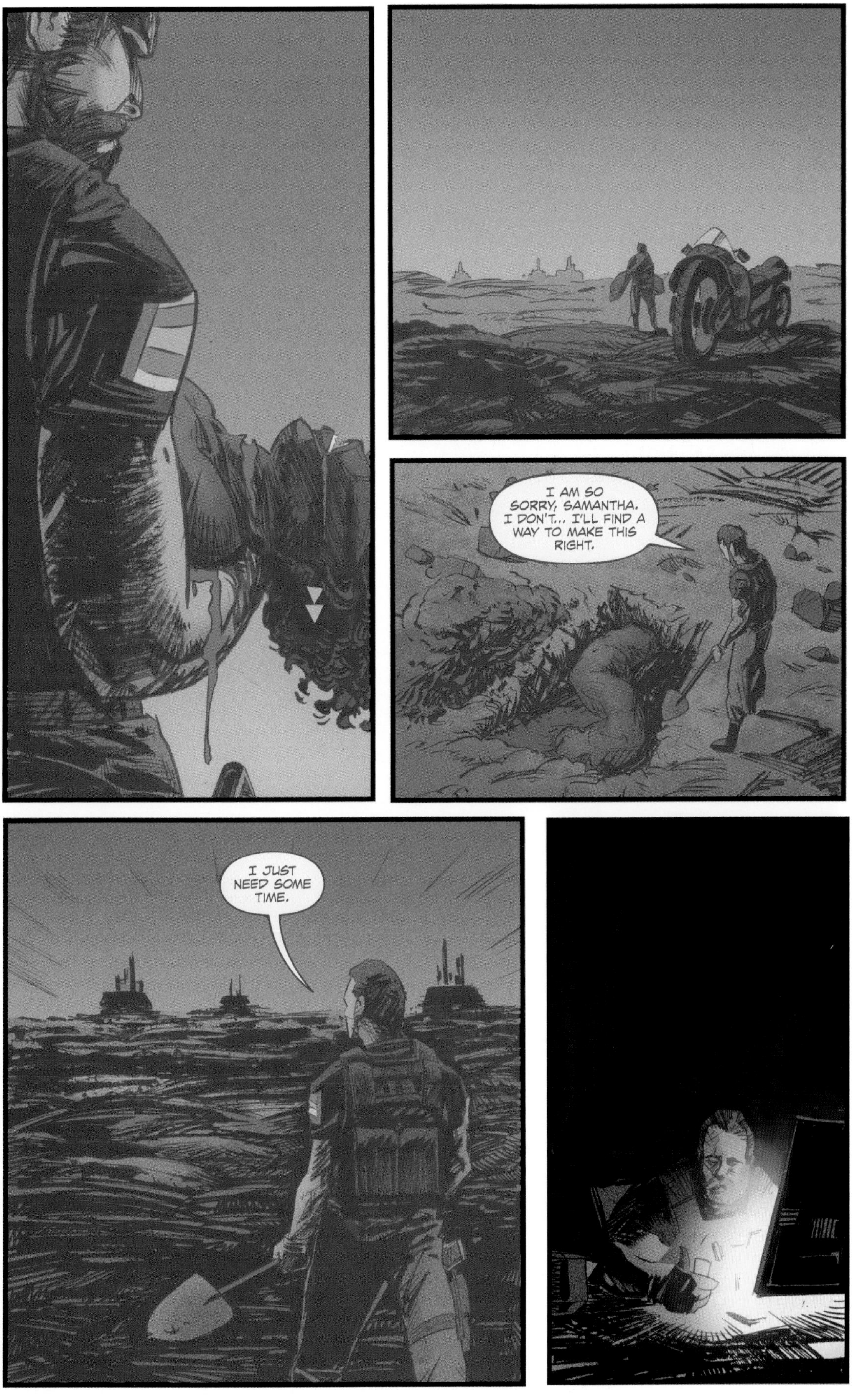
I AM SO SORRY, SAMANTHA. I DON'T... I'LL FIND A WAY TO MAKE THIS RIGHT.
I JUST NEED SOME TIME.

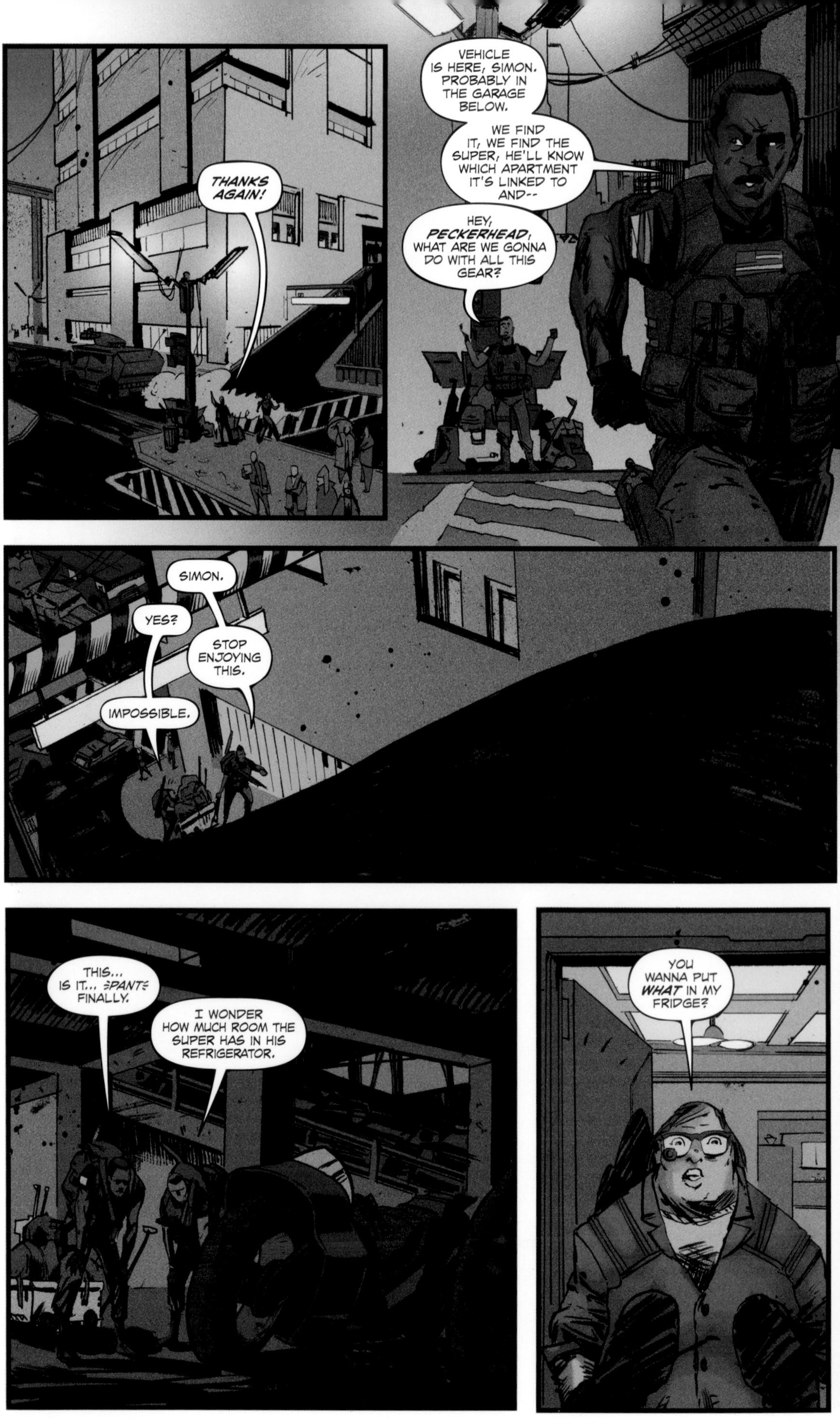
THANKS AGAIN!
VEHICLE IS HERE, SIMON. PROBABLY IN THE GARAGE BELOW.
WE FIND IT, WE FIND THE SUPER, HE'LL KNOW WHICH APARTMENT IT'S LINKED TO AND--
HEY, PECKERHEAD, WHAT ARE WE GONNA DO WITH ALL THIS GEAR?
SIMON.
YES?
STOP ENJOYING THIS.
IMPOSSIBLE.
THIS... IS IT... =PANT= FINALLY.
I WONDER HOW MUCH ROOM THE SUPER HAS IN HIS REFRIGERATOR.
YOU WANNA PUT WHAT IN MY FRIDGE?

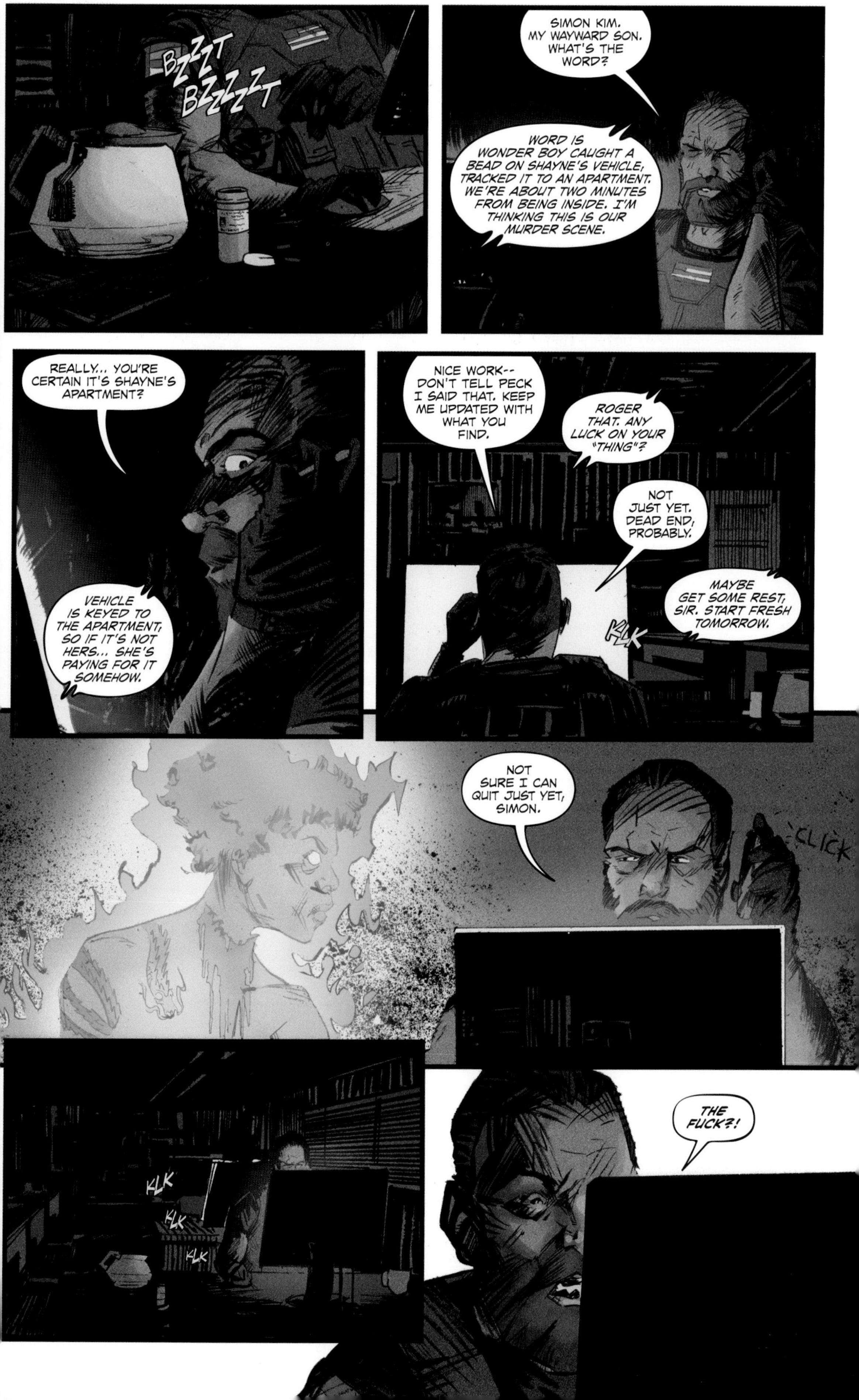
BZZZT
BZZZZZT
SIMON KIM. MY WAYWARD SON. WHAT'S THE WORD?
WORD IS WONDER BOY CAUGHT A BEAD ON SHAYNE'S VEHICLE, TRACKED IT TO AN APARTMENT. WE'RE ABOUT TWO MINUTES FROM BEING INSIDE. I'M THINKING THIS IS OUR MURDER SCENE.
REALLY... YOU'RE CERTAIN IT'S SHAYNE'S APARTMENT?
VEHICLE IS KEYED TO THE APARTMENT, SO IF IT'S NOT HERS... SHE'S PAYING FOR IT SOMEHOW.
NICE WORK-- DON'T TELL PECK I SAID THAT. KEEP ME UPDATED WITH WHAT YOU FIND.
ROGER THAT. ANY LUCK ON YOUR "THING"?
NOT JUST YET. DEAD END, PROBABLY.
MAYBE GET SOME REST, SIR. START FRESH TOMORROW.
KLK
NOT SURE I CAN QUIT JUST YET, SIMON.
CLICK
KLK
KLK
KLK
THE FUCK?!

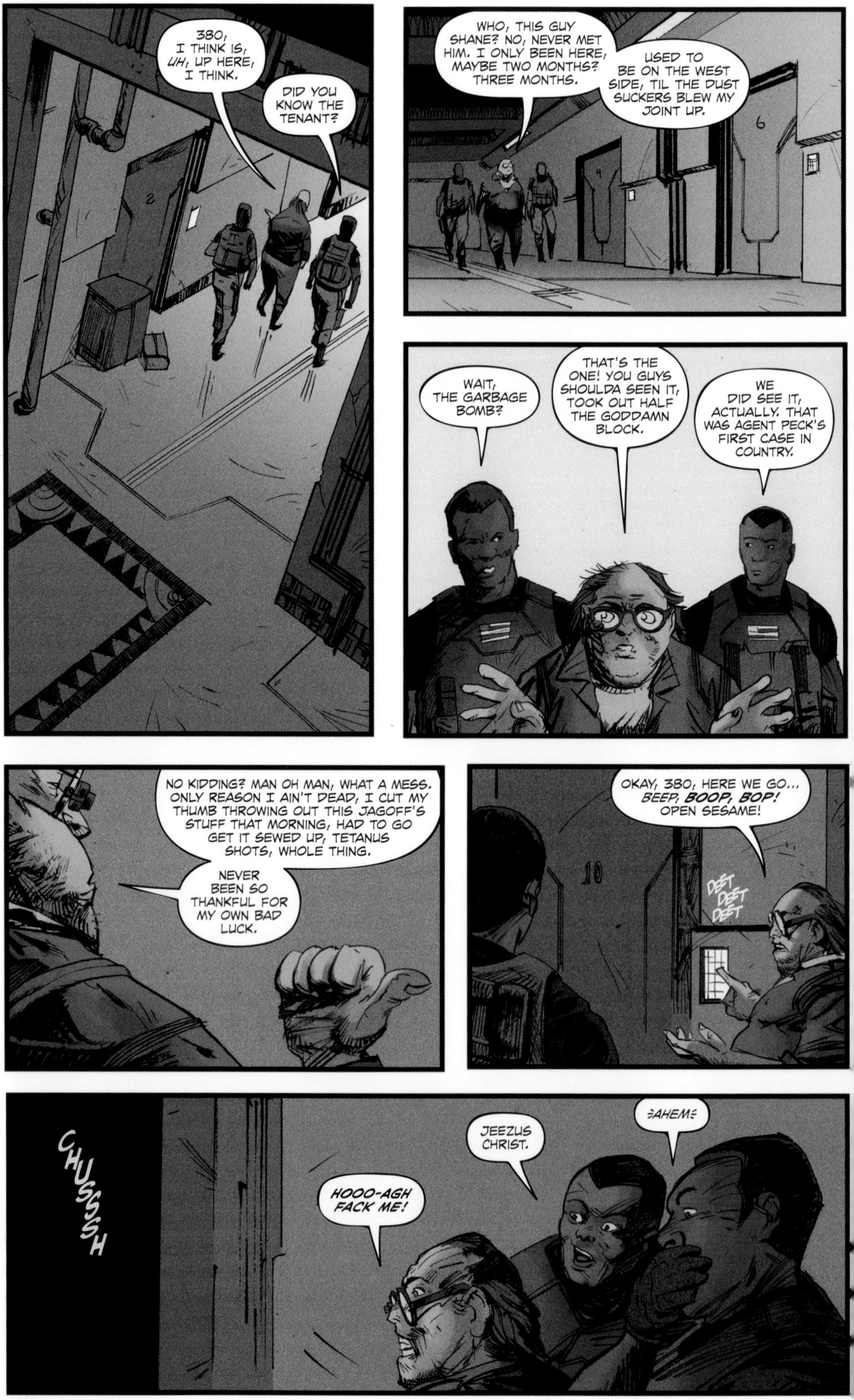
380, I THINK IS, *UH*, UP HERE, I THINK.
DID YOU KNOW THE TENANT?
WHO, THIS GUY SHANE? NO, NEVER MET HIM. I ONLY BEEN HERE, MAYBE TWO MONTHS? THREE MONTHS.
USED TO BE ON THE WEST SIDE, TIL THE DUST SUCKERS BLEW MY JOINT UP.
WAIT, THE GARBAGE BOMB?
THAT'S THE ONE! YOU GUYS SHOULDA SEEN IT, TOOK OUT HALF THE GODDAMN BLOCK.
WE DID SEE IT, ACTUALLY. THAT WAS AGENT PECK'S FIRST CASE IN COUNTRY.
NO KIDDING? MAN OH MAN, WHAT A MESS. ONLY REASON I AIN'T DEAD, I CUT MY THUMB THROWING OUT THIS JAGOFF'S STUFF THAT MORNING, HAD TO GO GET IT SEWED UP, TETANUS SHOTS, WHOLE THING.
NEVER BEEN SO THANKFUL FOR MY OWN BAD LUCK.
OKAY, 380, HERE WE GO... *BEEP, **BOOP, BOP!*** OPEN SESAME!
DEET DEET DEET
CHUSSSH
HOOO-AGH FACK ME!
JEEZUS CHRIST.
AHEM

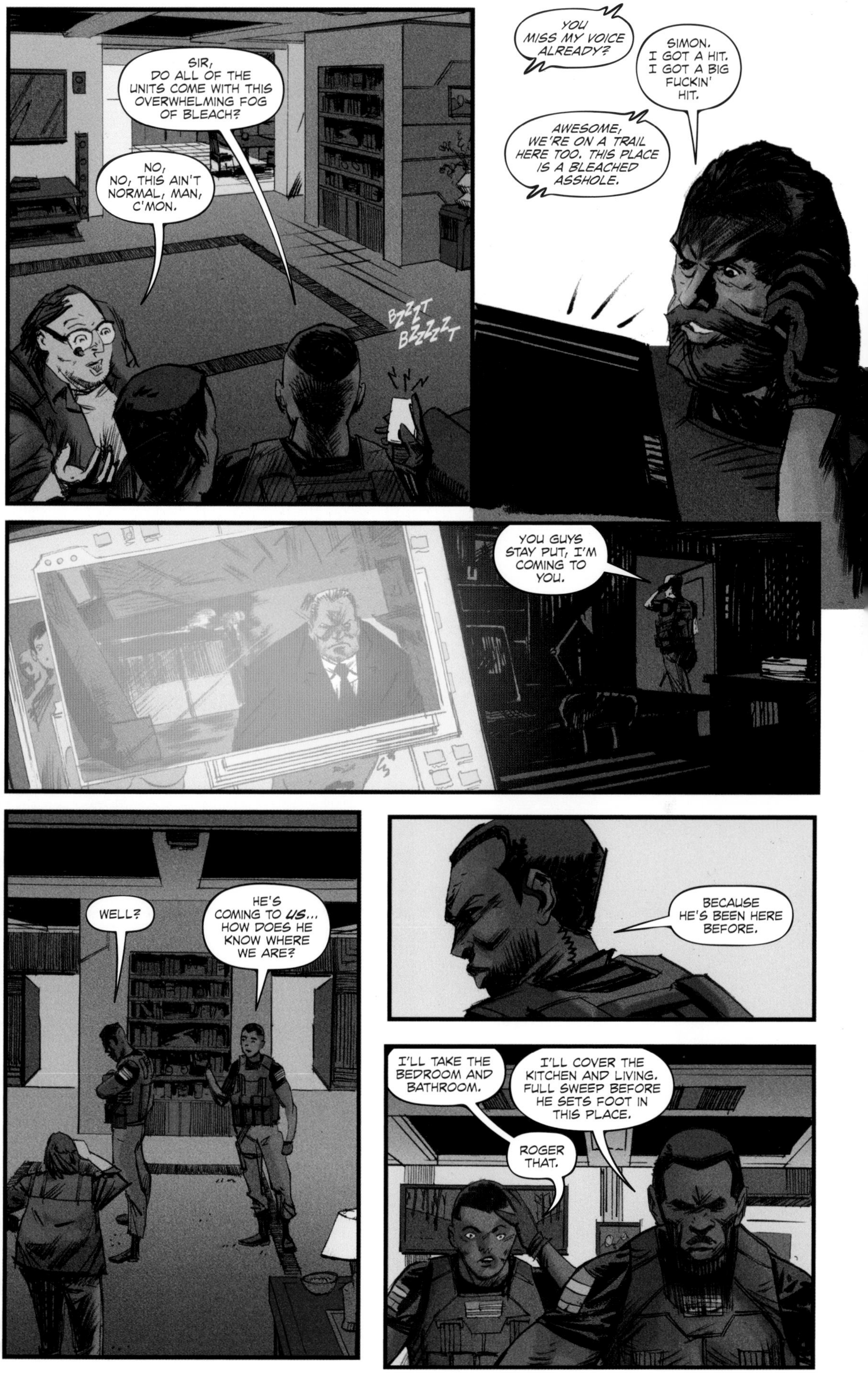
SIR, DO ALL OF THE UNITS COME WITH THIS OVERWHELMING FOG OF BLEACH?
NO, NO, THIS AIN'T NORMAL, MAN, C'MON.
BZZZT BZZZZZT
YOU MISS MY VOICE ALREADY?
SIMON. I GOT A HIT. I GOT A BIG FUCKIN' HIT.
AWESOME, WE'RE ON A TRAIL HERE TOO. THIS PLACE IS A BLEACHED ASSHOLE.
YOU GUYS STAY PUT, I'M COMING TO YOU.
WELL?
HE'S COMING TO US... HOW DOES HE KNOW WHERE WE ARE?
BECAUSE HE'S BEEN HERE BEFORE.
I'LL TAKE THE BEDROOM AND BATHROOM.
I'LL COVER THE KITCHEN AND LIVING. FULL SWEEP BEFORE HE SETS FOOT IN THIS PLACE.
ROGER THAT.

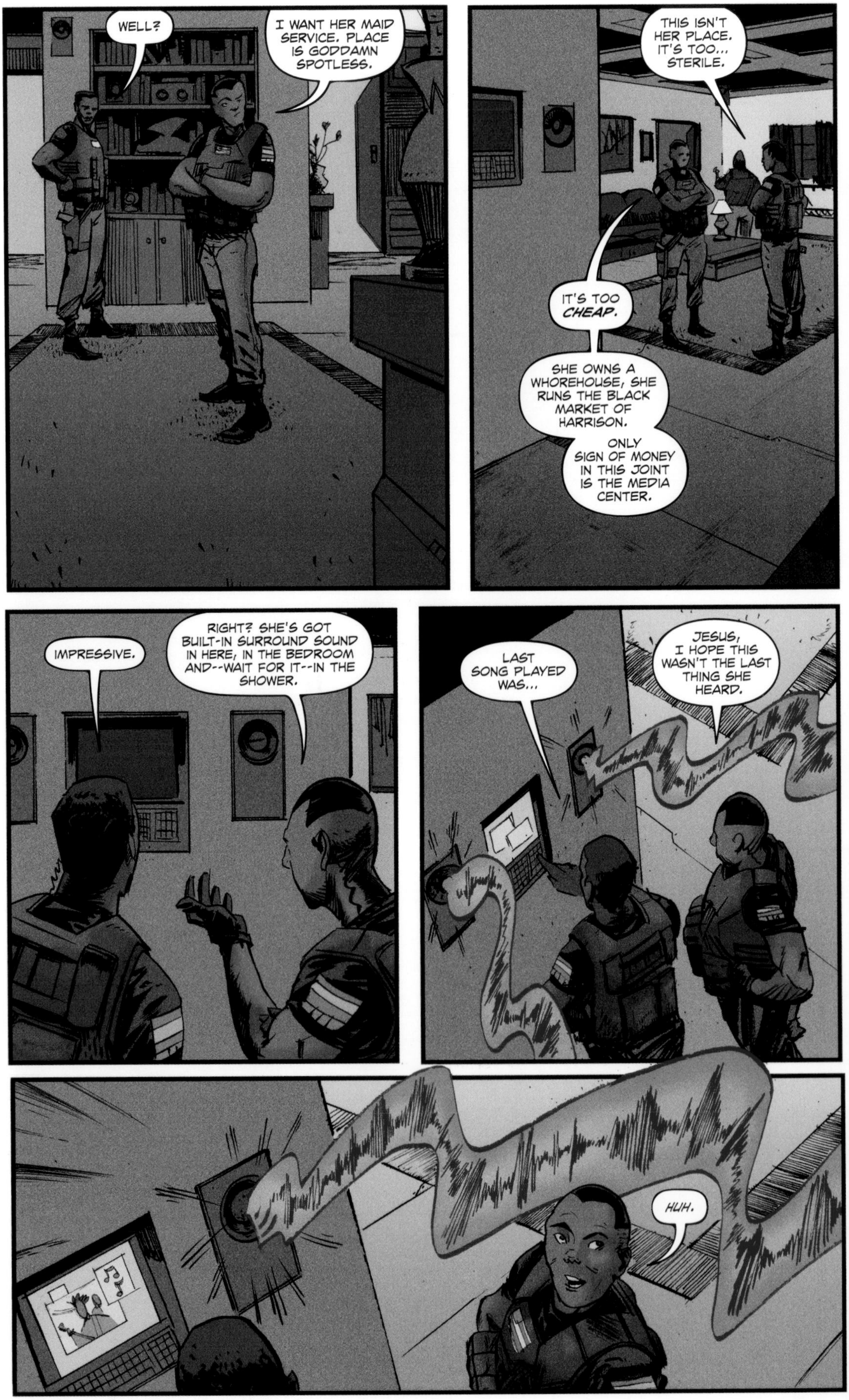
WELL?
I WANT HER MAID SERVICE. PLACE IS GODDAMN SPOTLESS.
THIS ISN'T HER PLACE. IT'S TOO... STERILE.
IT'S TOO *CHEAP*.
SHE OWNS A WHOREHOUSE, SHE RUNS THE BLACK MARKET OF HARRISON.
ONLY SIGN OF MONEY IN THIS JOINT IS THE MEDIA CENTER.
IMPRESSIVE.
RIGHT? SHE'S GOT BUILT-IN SURROUND SOUND IN HERE, IN THE BEDROOM AND--WAIT FOR IT--IN THE SHOWER.
LAST SONG PLAYED WAS...
JESUS, I HOPE THIS WASN'T THE LAST THING SHE HEARD.
HUH.

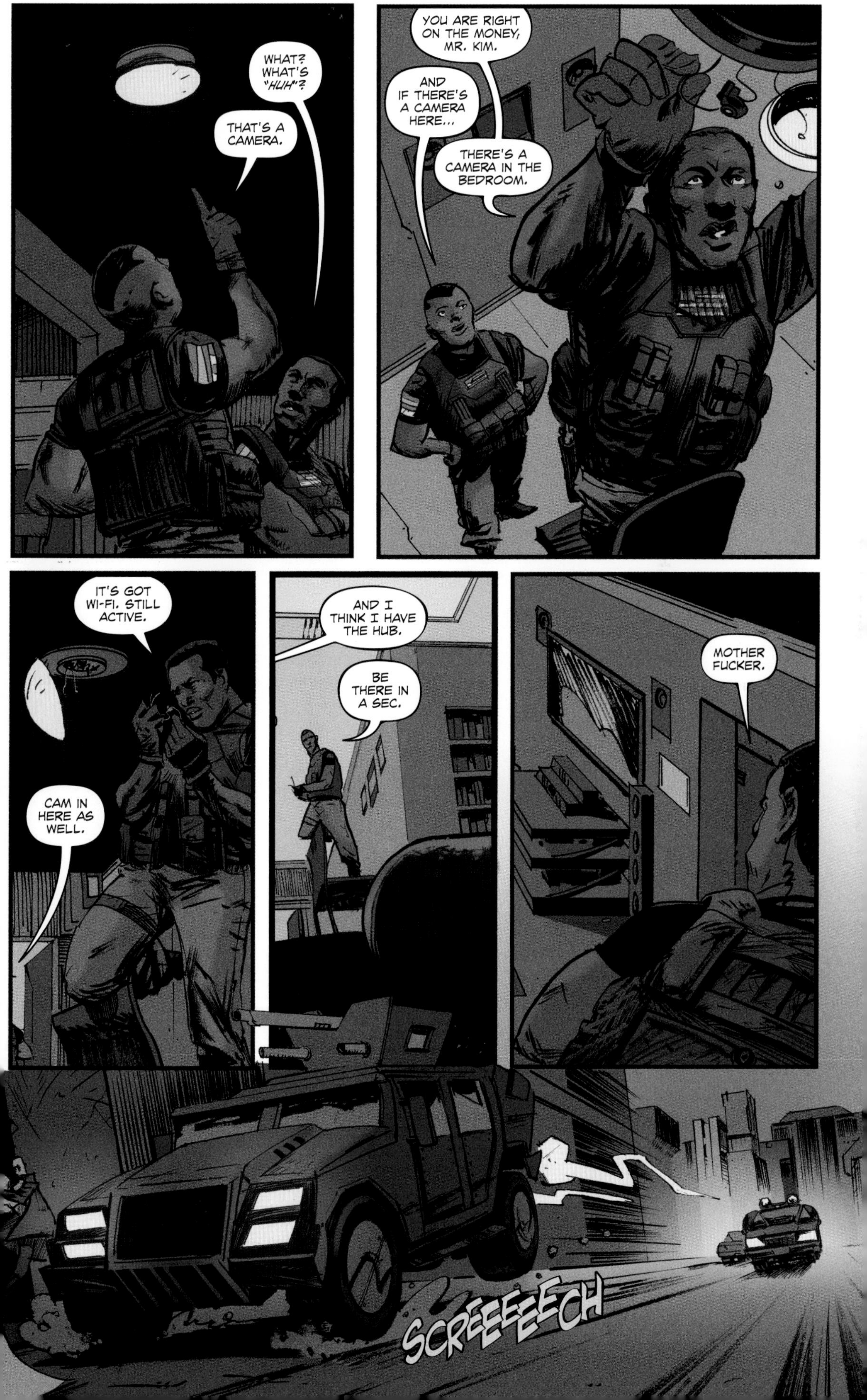
WHAT? WHAT'S "HUH"?
THAT'S A CAMERA.
YOU ARE RIGHT ON THE MONEY, MR. KIM.
AND IF THERE'S A CAMERA HERE...
THERE'S A CAMERA IN THE BEDROOM.
IT'S GOT WI-FI. STILL ACTIVE.
CAM IN HERE AS WELL.
AND I THINK I HAVE THE HUB.
BE THERE IN A SEC.
MOTHER FUCKER.
SCREEEEEECH

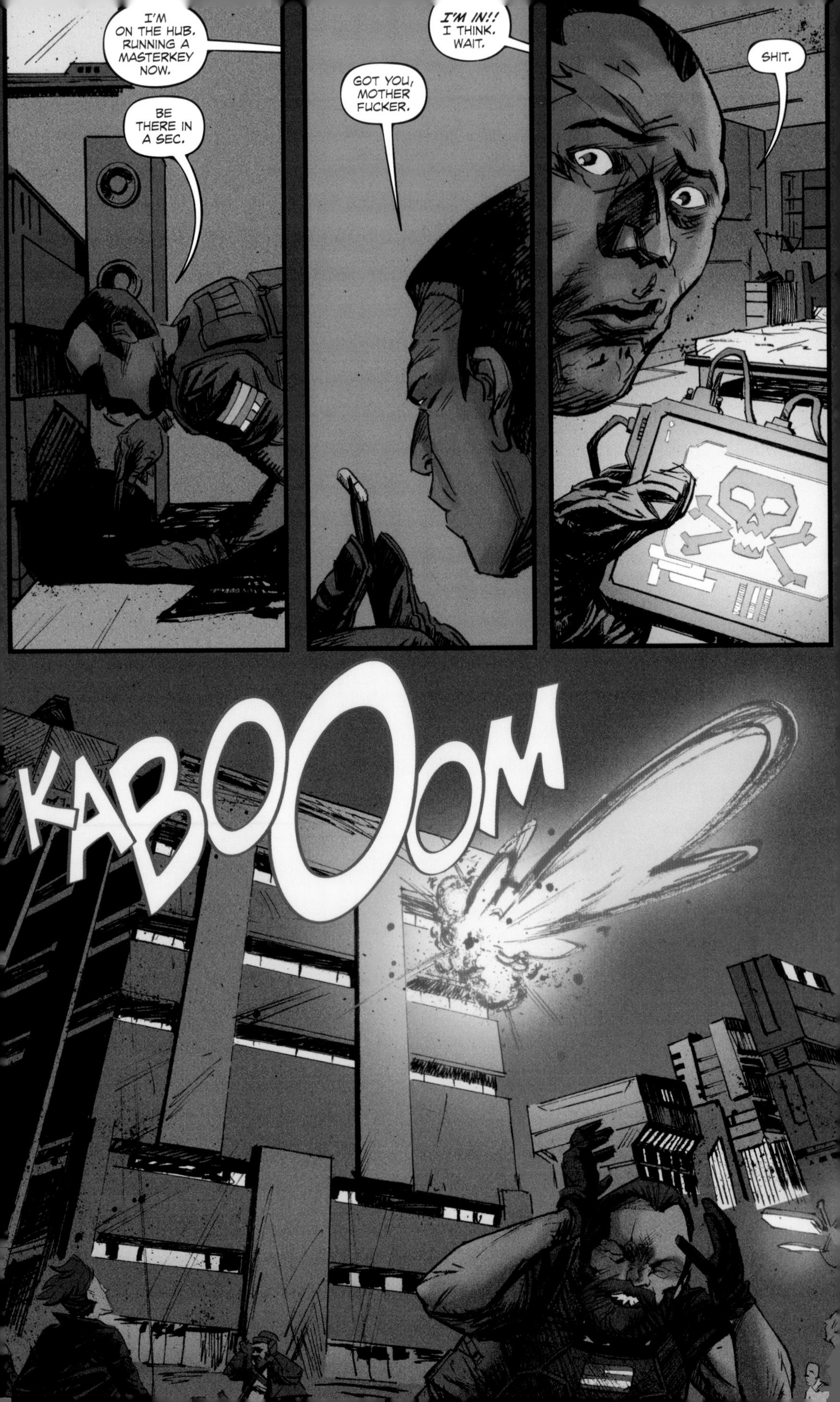
I'M ON THE HUB. RUNNING A MASTERKEY NOW.
BE THERE IN A SEC.
GOT YOU, MOTHER FUCKER.
I'M IN!! I THINK. WAIT.
SHIT.
KABOOOM

CHAPTER 05

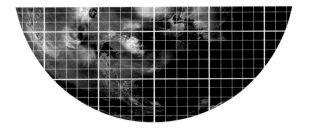

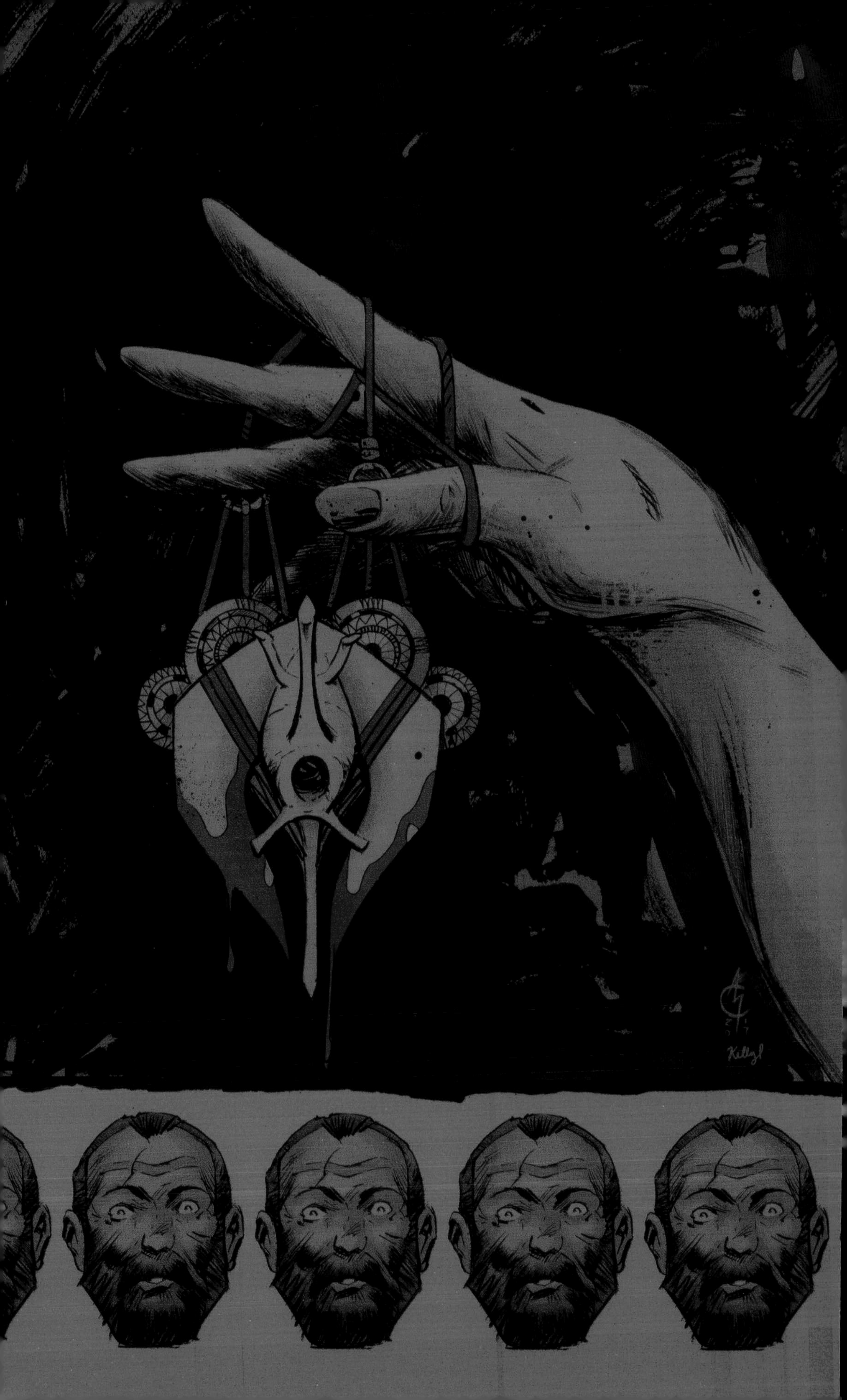

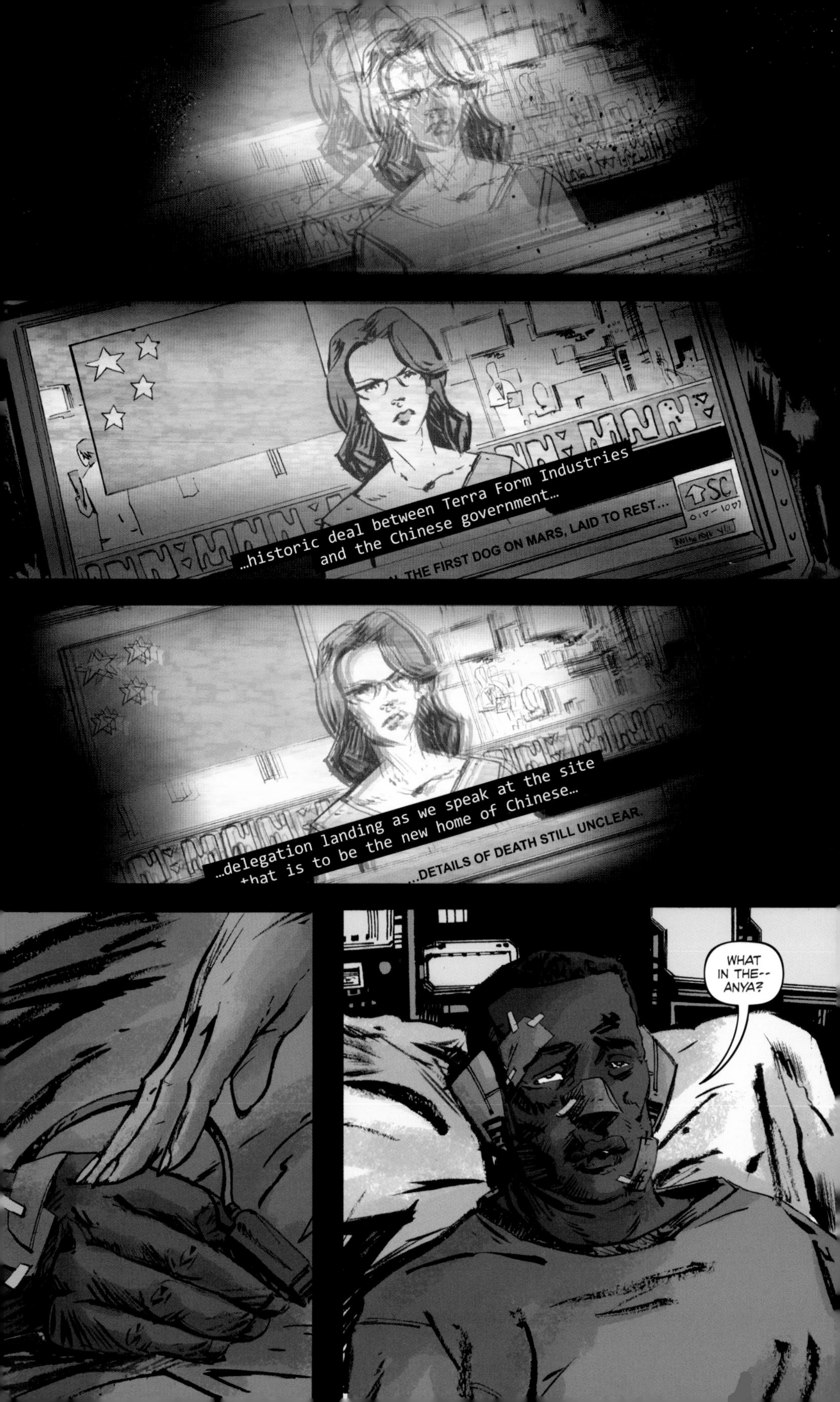
...historic deal between Terra Form Industries and the Chinese government...
...THE FIRST DOG ON MARS, LAID TO REST...
...delegation landing as we speak at the site that is to be the new home of Chinese...
...DETAILS OF DEATH STILL UNCLEAR.
WHAT IN THE-- ANYA?

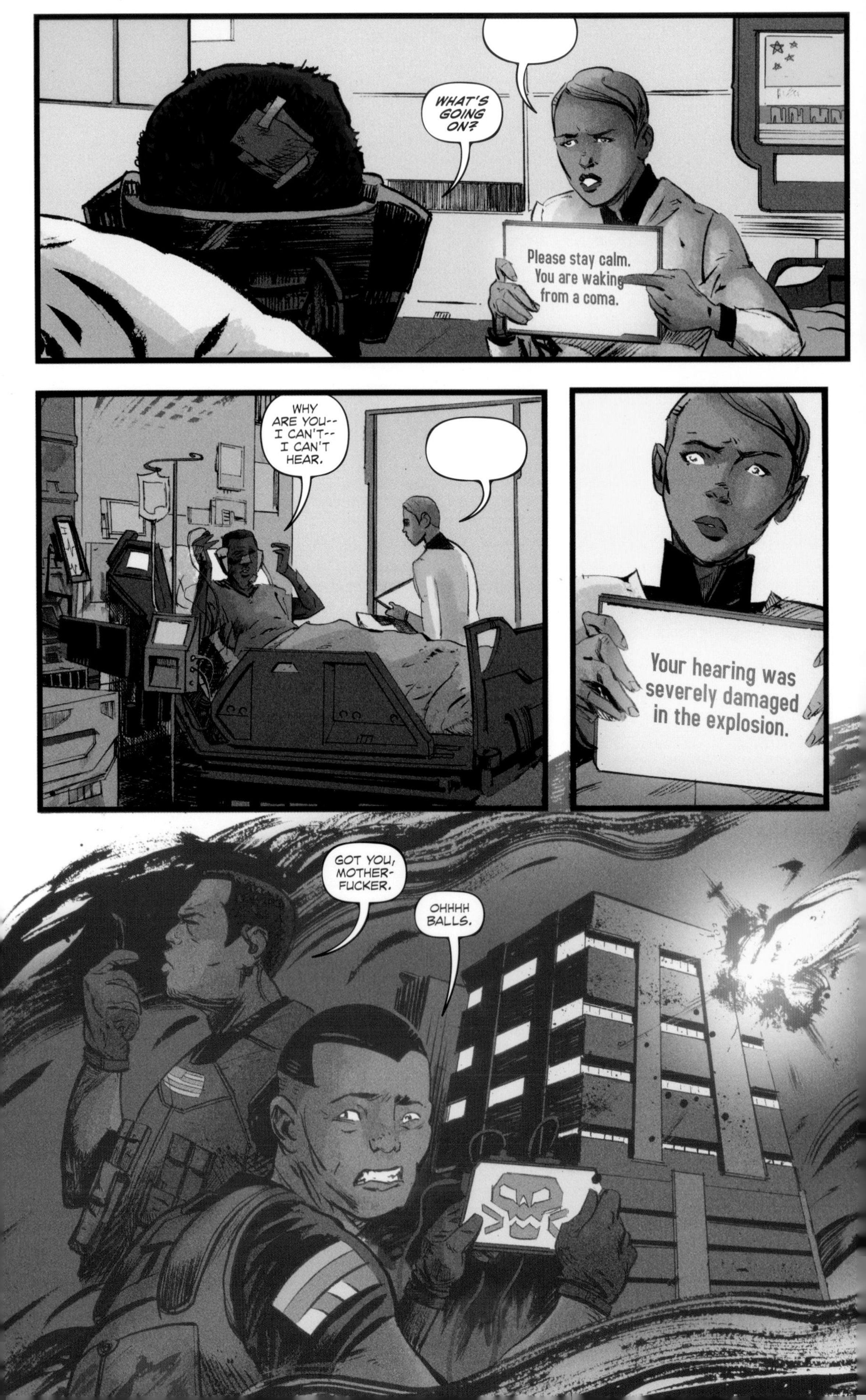
WHAT'S GOING ON?
Please stay calm. You are waking from a coma.
WHY ARE YOU-- I CAN'T-- I CAN'T HEAR.
Your hearing was severely damaged in the explosion.
GOT YOU, MOTHER-FUCKER.
OHHHH BALLS.

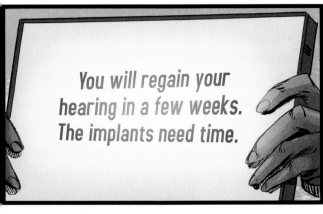
You will regain your hearing in a few weeks. The implants need time.

IS SIMON...?

I'm so sorry.

AND COYLE? HAS HE BEEN CHARGED?

??

BETTER QUESTION-- WHERE IS MY GUN?

YOU NEED to REST.

NO, I NEEEED TO F-FIND... DENNTONNNNN COYLLLLLLE--♪

CHAPTER 05

When the game stops, it will be called on account of darkness. But it is a long day.

Robert Penn Warren, *All the King's Men*

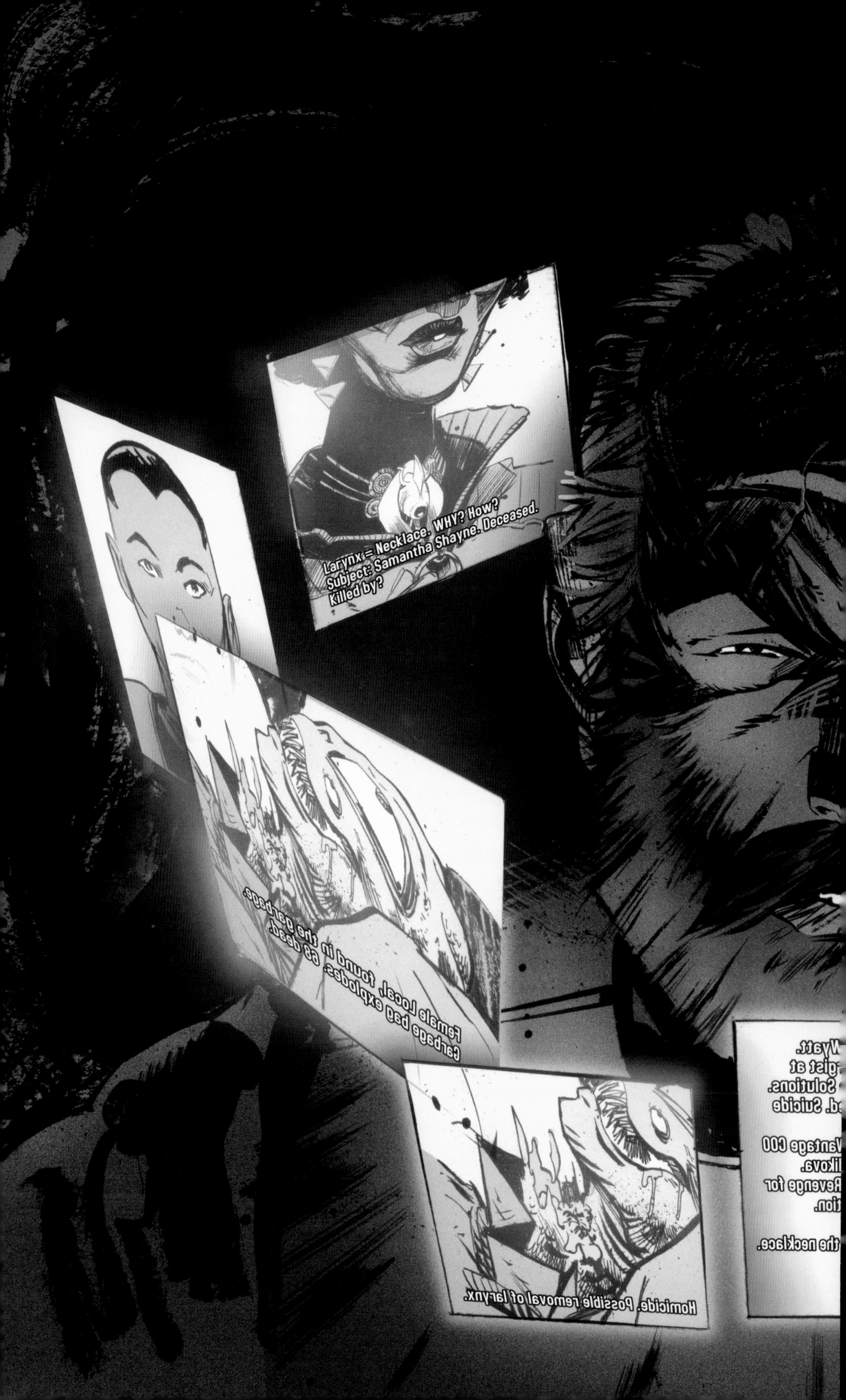
Larynx = Necklace. WHY? How?
Subject: Samantha Shayne. Deceased.
Killed by?
Female Local, found in the garbage.
Garbage bag explodes. 68 dead.
Homicide. Possible removal of larynx.
Wyatt.
gist at
Solutions.
ed. Suicide
Wantage COO
ilkova.
Revenge for
tion.
the necklace.

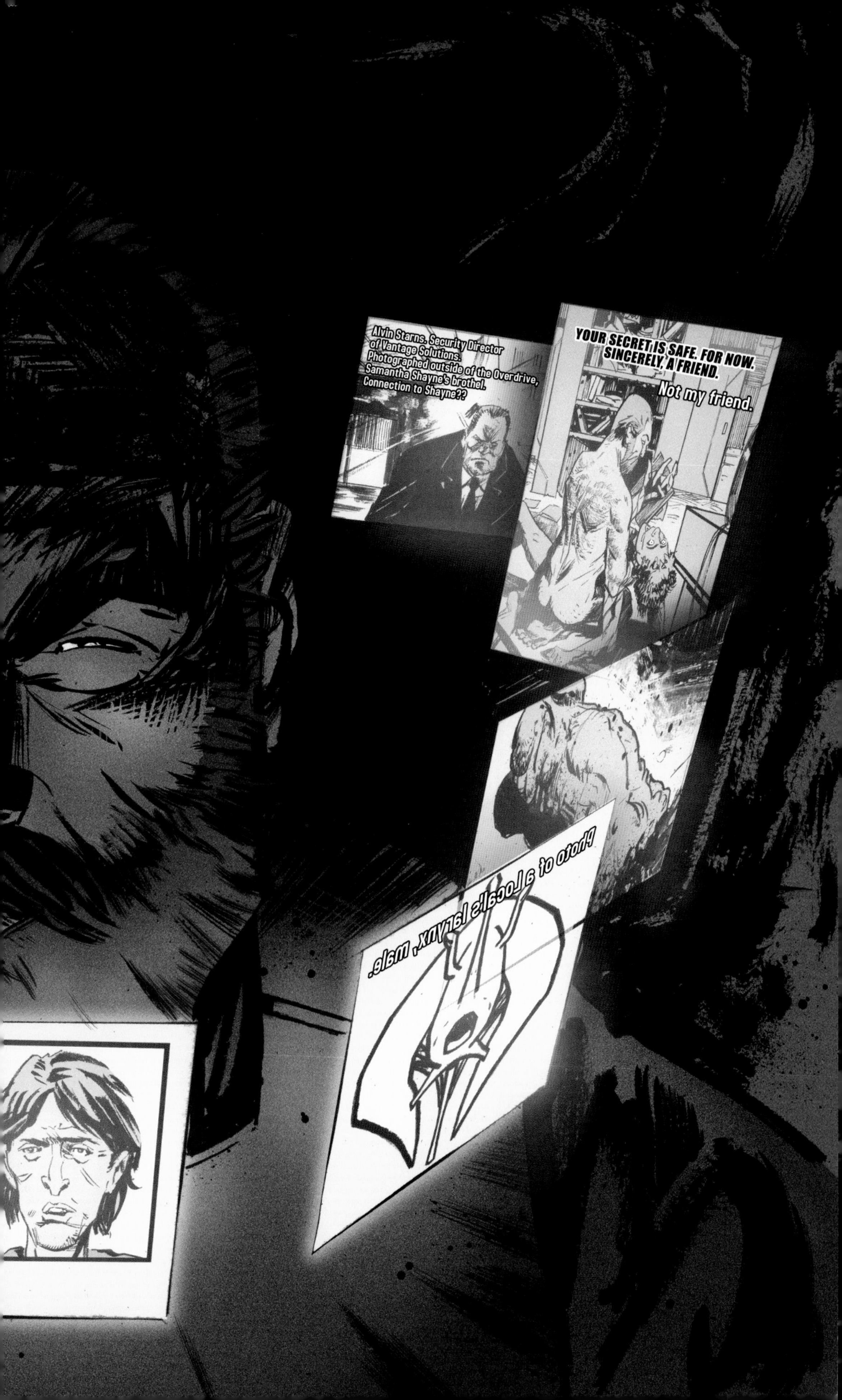

Alvin Starns. Security Director of Vantage Solutions. Photographed outside of the Overdrive, Samantha Shayne's brothel. Connection to Shayne??
YOUR SECRET IS SAFE. FOR NOW. SINCERELY, A FRIEND.
Not my friend.
Photo of a Local's larynx, male.

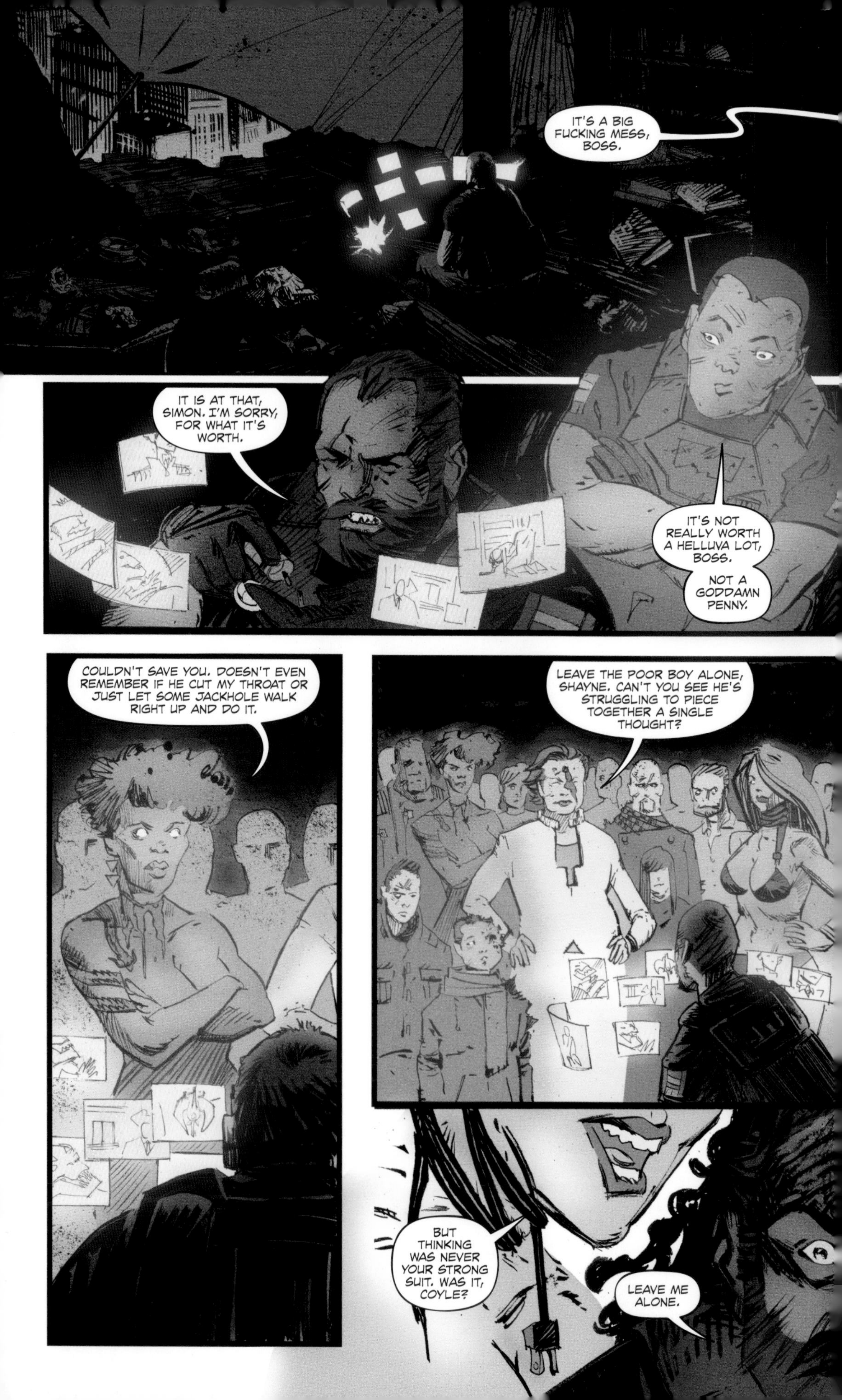
IT'S A BIG FUCKING MESS, BOSS.
IT IS AT THAT, SIMON. I'M SORRY, FOR WHAT IT'S WORTH.
IT'S NOT REALLY WORTH A HELLUVA LOT, BOSS.
NOT A GODDAMN PENNY.
COULDN'T SAVE YOU. DOESN'T EVEN REMEMBER IF HE CUT MY THROAT OR JUST LET SOME JACKHOLE WALK RIGHT UP AND DO IT.
LEAVE THE POOR BOY ALONE, SHAYNE. CAN'T YOU SEE HE'S STRUGGLING TO PIECE TOGETHER A SINGLE THOUGHT?
BUT THINKING WAS NEVER YOUR STRONG SUIT. WAS IT, COYLE?
LEAVE ME ALONE.

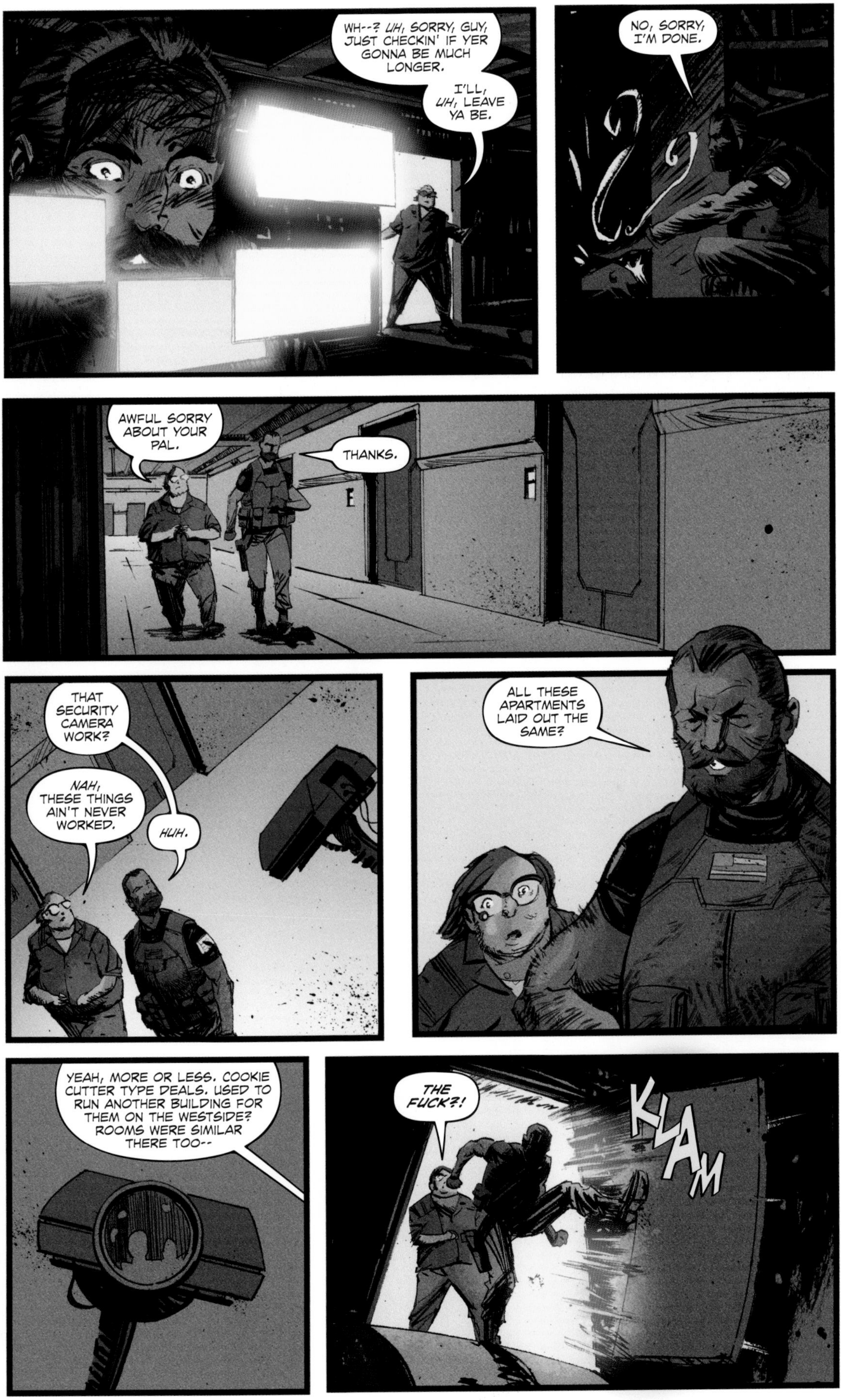
WH--? UH, SORRY, GUY, JUST CHECKIN' IF YER GONNA BE MUCH LONGER.
I'LL, UH, LEAVE YA BE.
NO, SORRY, I'M DONE.
AWFUL SORRY ABOUT YOUR PAL.
THANKS.
THAT SECURITY CAMERA WORK?
NAH, THESE THINGS AIN'T NEVER WORKED.
HUH.
ALL THESE APARTMENTS LAID OUT THE SAME?
YEAH, MORE OR LESS. COOKIE CUTTER TYPE DEALS. USED TO RUN ANOTHER BUILDING FOR THEM ON THE WESTSIDE? ROOMS WERE SIMILAR THERE TOO--
THE FUCK?!
KLAM

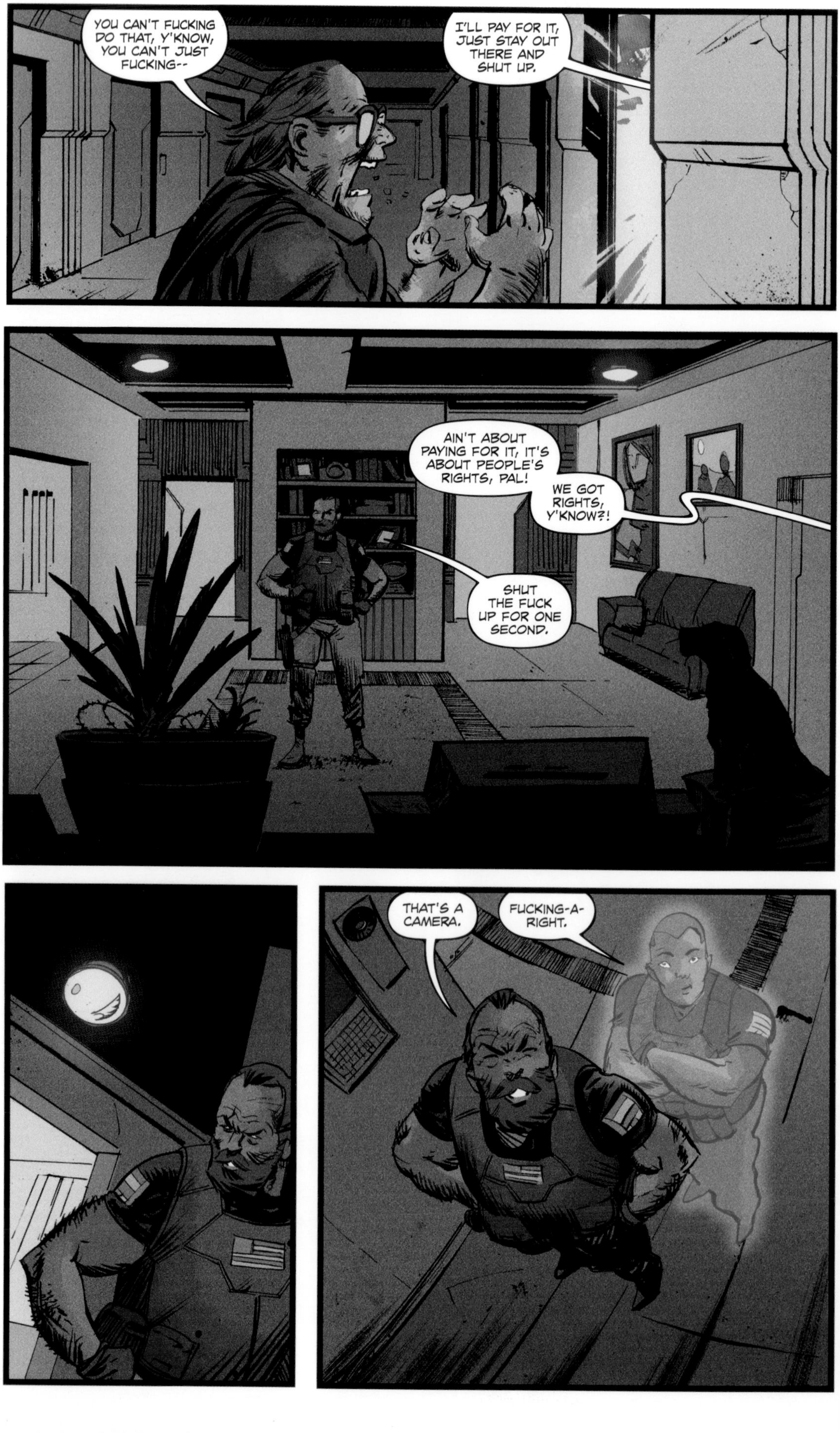

YOU CAN'T FUCKING DO THAT, Y'KNOW, YOU CAN'T JUST FUCKING--
I'LL PAY FOR IT, JUST STAY OUT THERE AND SHUT UP.
AIN'T ABOUT PAYING FOR IT, IT'S ABOUT PEOPLE'S RIGHTS, PAL!
WE GOT RIGHTS, Y'KNOW?!
SHUT THE FUCK UP FOR ONE SECOND.
THAT'S A CAMERA.
FUCKING-A-RIGHT.

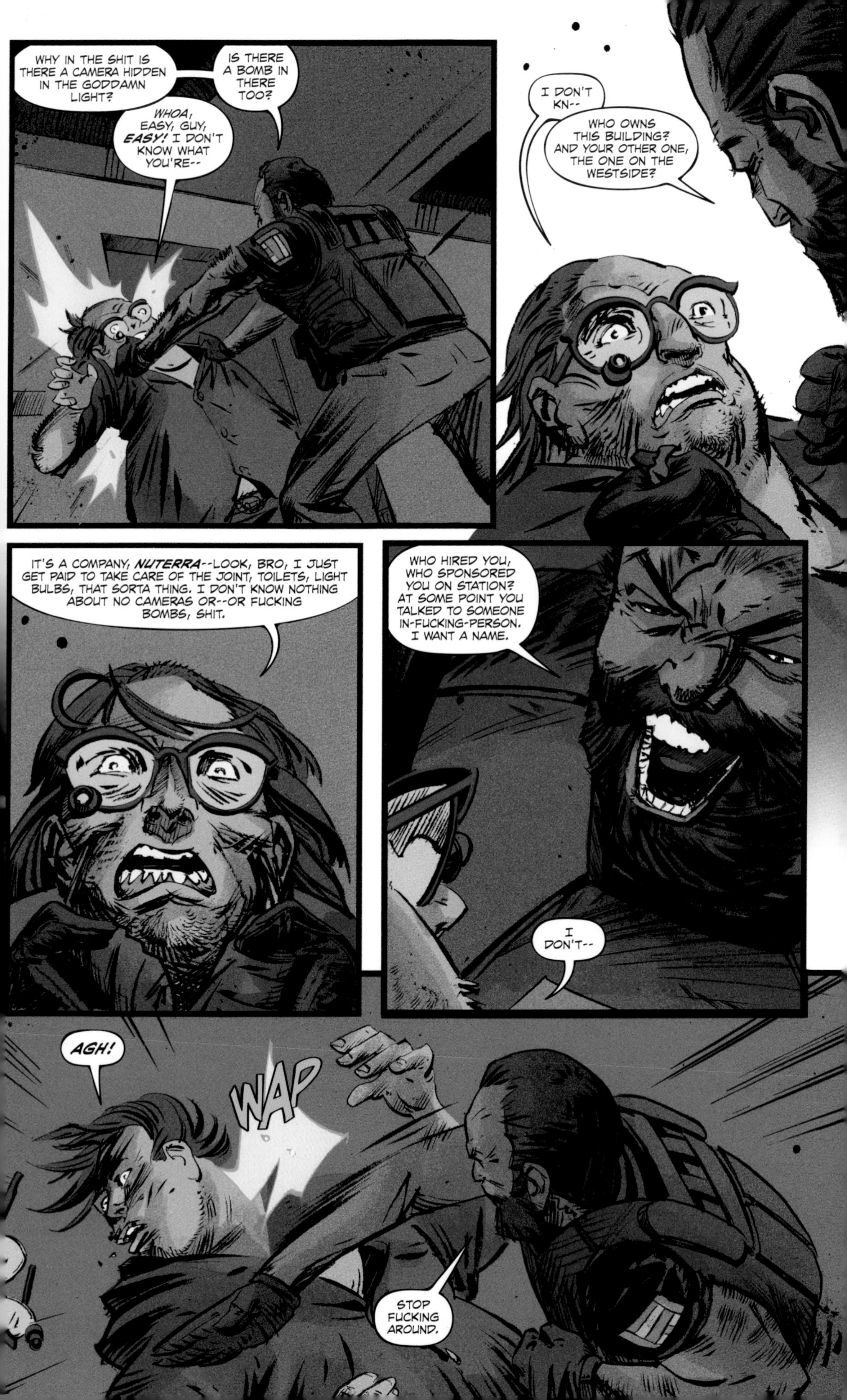
WHY IN THE SHIT IS THERE A CAMERA HIDDEN IN THE GODDAMN LIGHT?
IS THERE A BOMB IN THERE TOO?
WHOA, EASY, GUY, EASY! I DON'T KNOW WHAT YOU'RE--
I DON'T KN--
WHO OWNS THIS BUILDING? AND YOUR OTHER ONE, THE ONE ON THE WESTSIDE?
IT'S A COMPANY, NUTERRA--LOOK, BRO, I JUST GET PAID TO TAKE CARE OF THE JOINT, TOILETS, LIGHT BULBS, THAT SORTA THING. I DON'T KNOW NOTHING ABOUT NO CAMERAS OR--OR FUCKING BOMBS, SHIT.
WHO HIRED YOU, WHO SPONSORED YOU ON STATION? AT SOME POINT YOU TALKED TO SOMEONE IN-FUCKING-PERSON. I WANT A NAME.
I DON'T--
AGH!
WAP
STOP FUCKING AROUND.

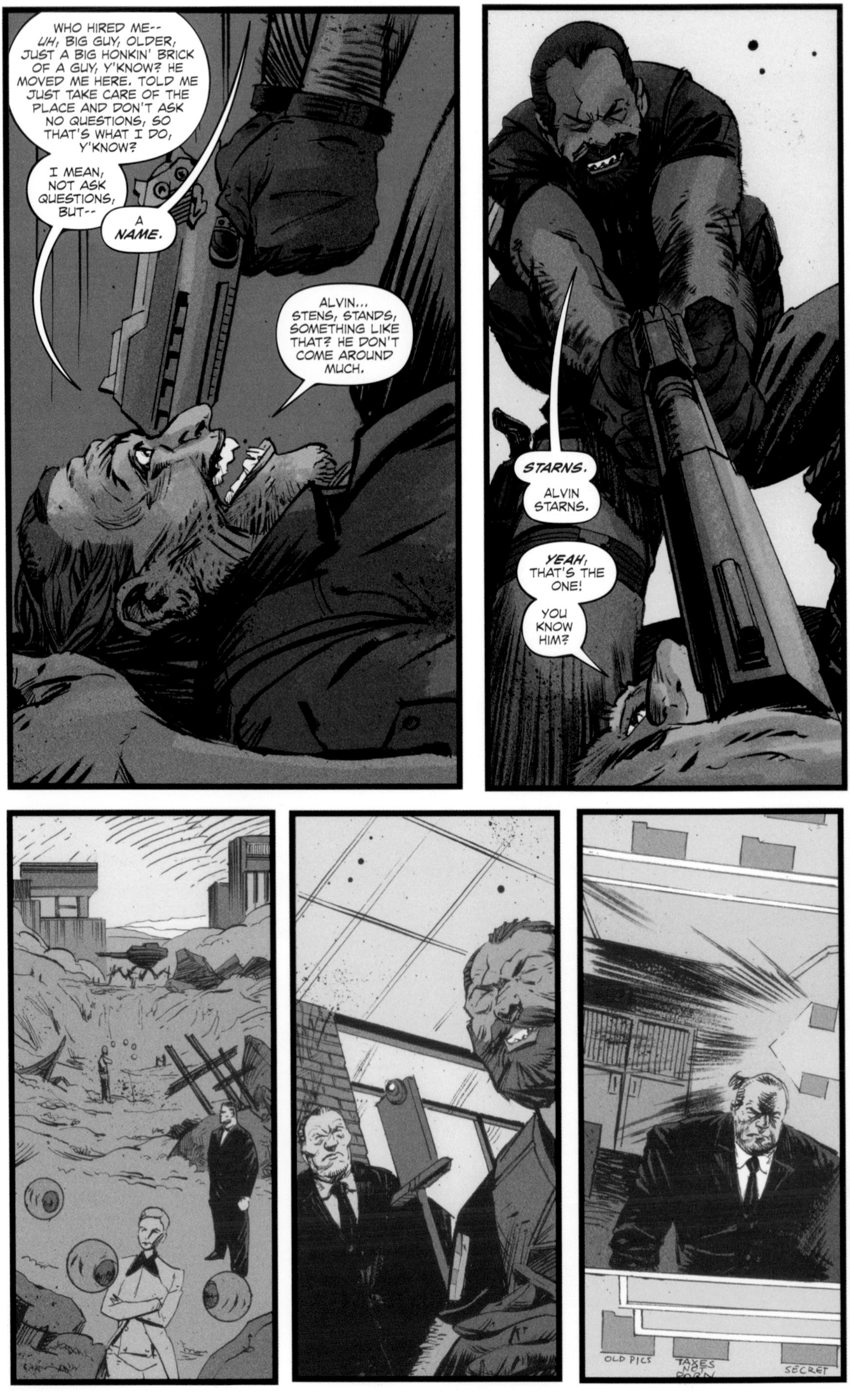
WHO HIRED ME-- UH, BIG GUY, OLDER, JUST A BIG HONKIN' BRICK OF A GUY, Y'KNOW? HE MOVED ME HERE. TOLD ME JUST TAKE CARE OF THE PLACE AND DON'T ASK NO QUESTIONS, SO THAT'S WHAT I DO, Y'KNOW?
I MEAN, NOT ASK QUESTIONS, BUT--
A *NAME.*
ALVIN... STENS, STANDS, SOMETHING LIKE THAT? HE DON'T COME AROUND MUCH.
STARNS.
ALVIN STARNS.
YEAH, THAT'S THE ONE!
YOU KNOW HIM?
OLD PICS
TAXES NOT
SECRET

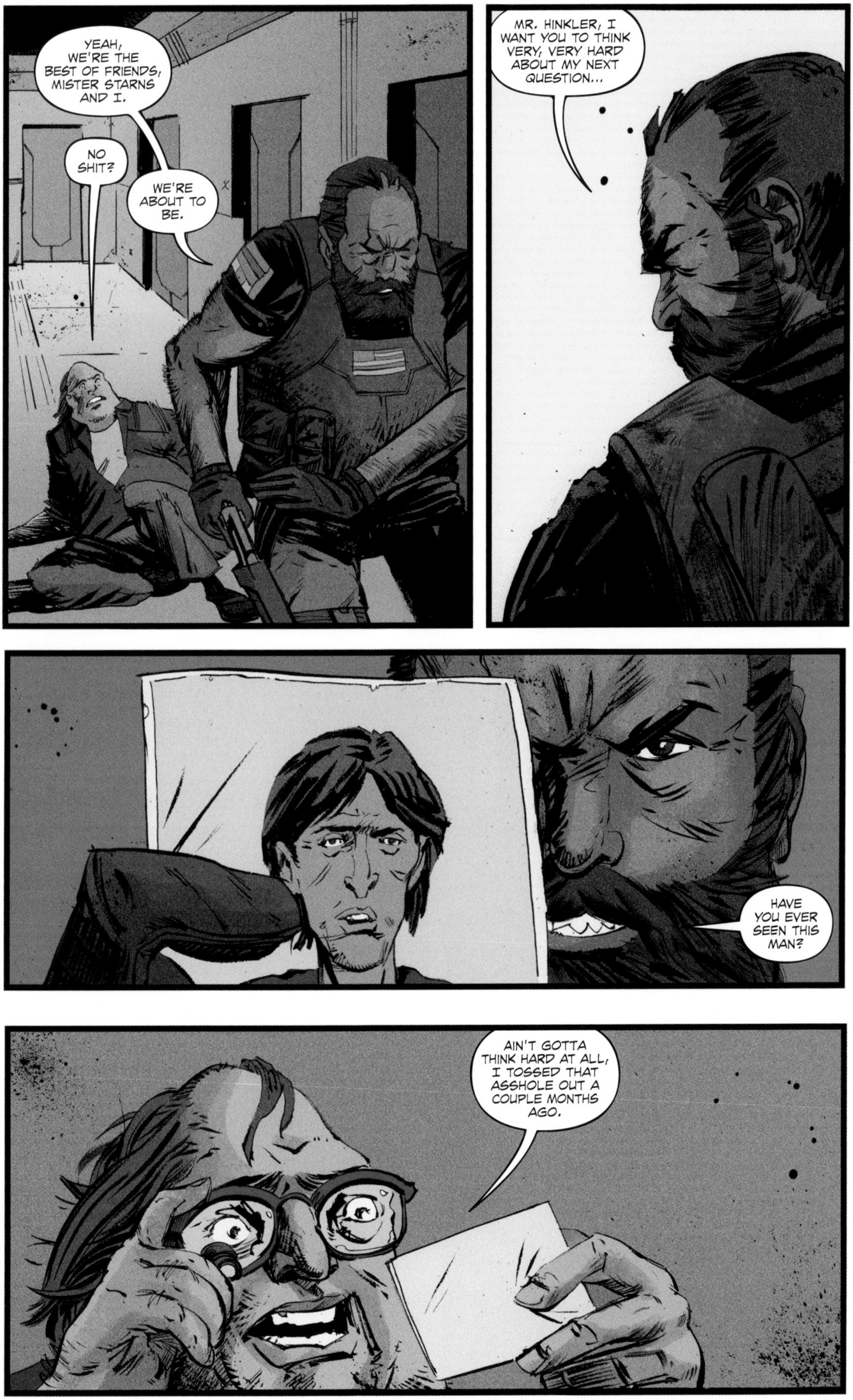
YEAH, WE'RE THE BEST OF FRIENDS, MISTER STARNS AND I.
NO SHIT?
WE'RE ABOUT TO BE.
MR. HINKLER, I WANT YOU TO THINK VERY, VERY HARD ABOUT MY NEXT QUESTION...
HAVE YOU EVER SEEN THIS MAN?
AIN'T GOTTA THINK HARD AT ALL, I TOSSED THAT ASSHOLE OUT A COUPLE MONTHS AGO.

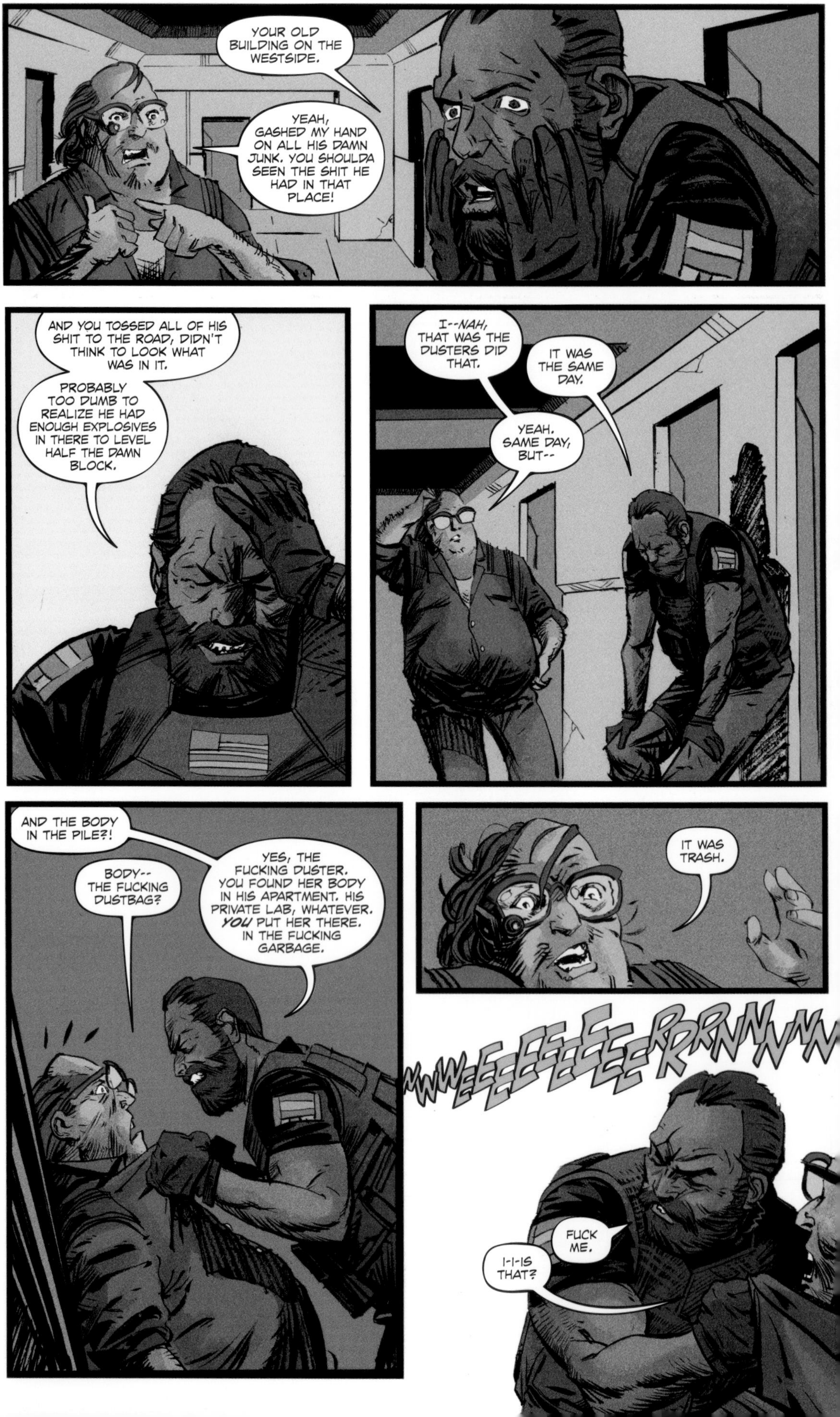
YOUR OLD BUILDING ON THE WESTSIDE.
YEAH, GASHED MY HAND ON ALL HIS DAMN JUNK. YOU SHOULDA SEEN THE SHIT HE HAD IN THAT PLACE!
AND YOU TOSSED ALL OF HIS SHIT TO THE ROAD, DIDN'T THINK TO LOOK WHAT WAS IN IT.
PROBABLY TOO DUMB TO REALIZE HE HAD ENOUGH EXPLOSIVES IN THERE TO LEVEL HALF THE DAMN BLOCK.
I--NAH, THAT WAS THE DUSTERS DID THAT.
IT WAS THE SAME DAY.
YEAH. SAME DAY, BUT--
AND THE BODY IN THE PILE?!
BODY-- THE FUCKING DUSTBAG?
YES, THE FUCKING DUSTER. YOU FOUND HER BODY IN HIS APARTMENT. HIS PRIVATE LAB, WHATEVER. YOU PUT HER THERE. IN THE FUCKING GARBAGE.
IT WAS TRASH.
NNWEEEEEEEEEEERRRNNNNN
FUCK ME.
I-I-IS THAT?

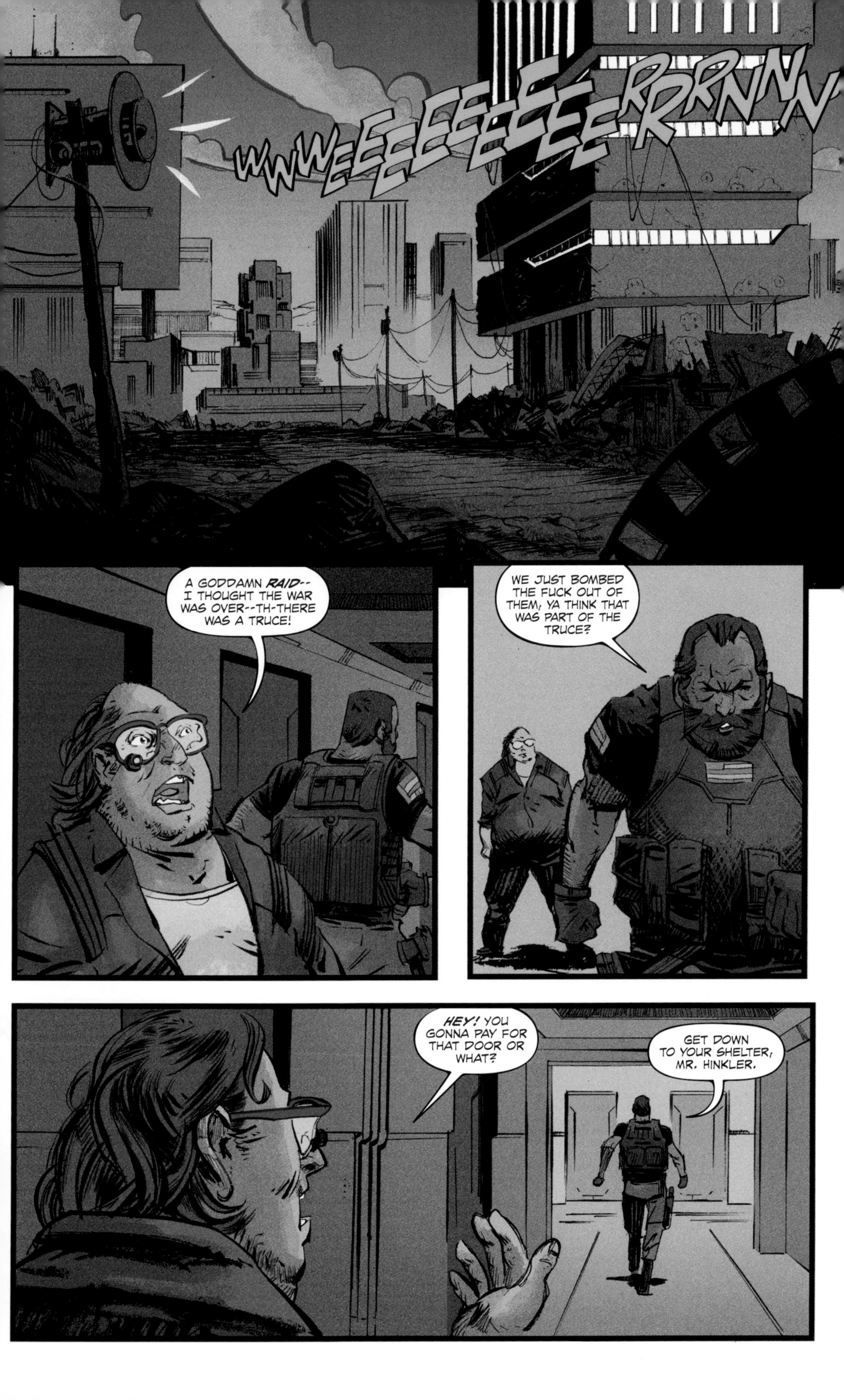
WWWEEEEEEEEEERRRNNN
A GODDAMN RAID-- I THOUGHT THE WAR WAS OVER--TH-THERE WAS A TRUCE!
WE JUST BOMBED THE FUCK OUT OF THEM, YA THINK THAT WAS PART OF THE TRUCE?
HEY! YOU GONNA PAY FOR THAT DOOR OR WHAT?
GET DOWN TO YOUR SHELTER, MR. HINKLER.

ALL HARRISON VICTORS, BE ADVISED, HOSTILES ARE INBOUND. THIS IS NOT A DRILL. REPORT TO YOUR STAGING AOR.

REPEAT, THIS IS NOT A DRILL.

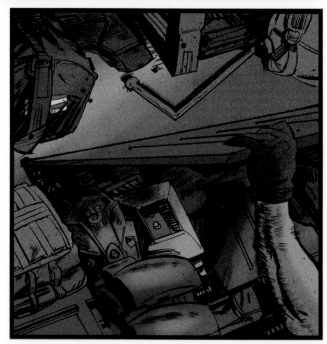

WHAT, YER GONNA GO PLAY WAR?

NOT QUITE.

SHOULD I REMIND YOU, YOU LEAVE THIS DUMB ROCK IN TWO WEEKS? YOU CAN LET IT BE...

NO.

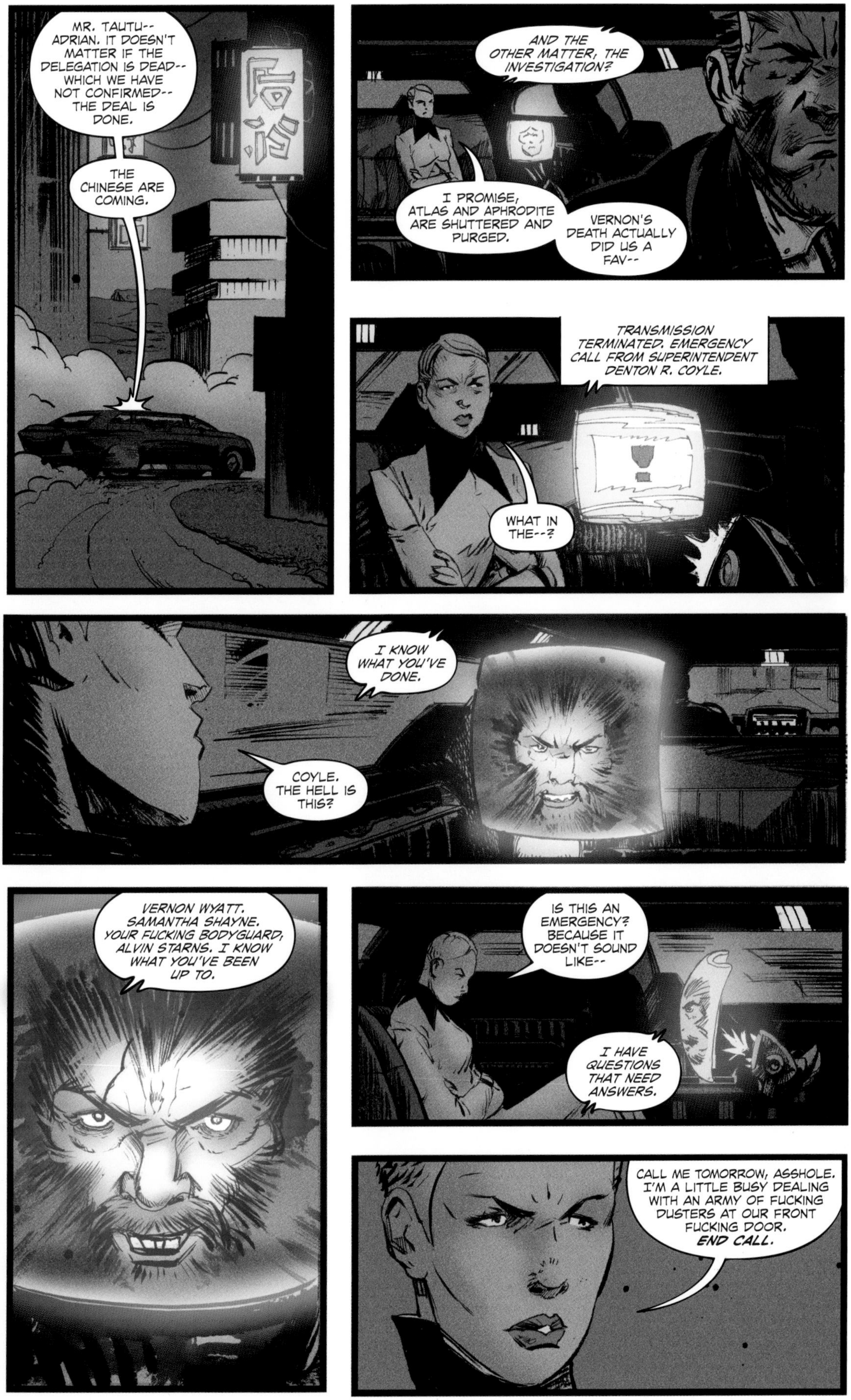
MR. TAUTU-- ADRIAN. IT DOESN'T MATTER IF THE DELEGATION IS DEAD-- WHICH WE HAVE NOT CONFIRMED-- THE DEAL IS DONE.
THE CHINESE ARE COMING.
AND THE OTHER MATTER, THE INVESTIGATION?
I PROMISE, ATLAS AND APHRODITE ARE SHUTTERED AND PURGED.
VERNON'S DEATH ACTUALLY DID US A FAV--
TRANSMISSION TERMINATED. EMERGENCY CALL FROM SUPERINTENDENT DENTON R. COYLE.
WHAT IN THE--?
I KNOW WHAT YOU'VE DONE.
COYLE. THE HELL IS THIS?
VERNON WYATT. SAMANTHA SHAYNE. YOUR FUCKING BODYGUARD, ALVIN STARNS. I KNOW WHAT YOU'VE BEEN UP TO.
IS THIS AN EMERGENCY? BECAUSE IT DOESN'T SOUND LIKE--
I HAVE QUESTIONS THAT NEED ANSWERS.
CALL ME TOMORROW, ASSHOLE. I'M A LITTLE BUSY DEALING WITH AN ARMY OF FUCKING DUSTERS AT OUR FRONT FUCKING DOOR. END CALL.

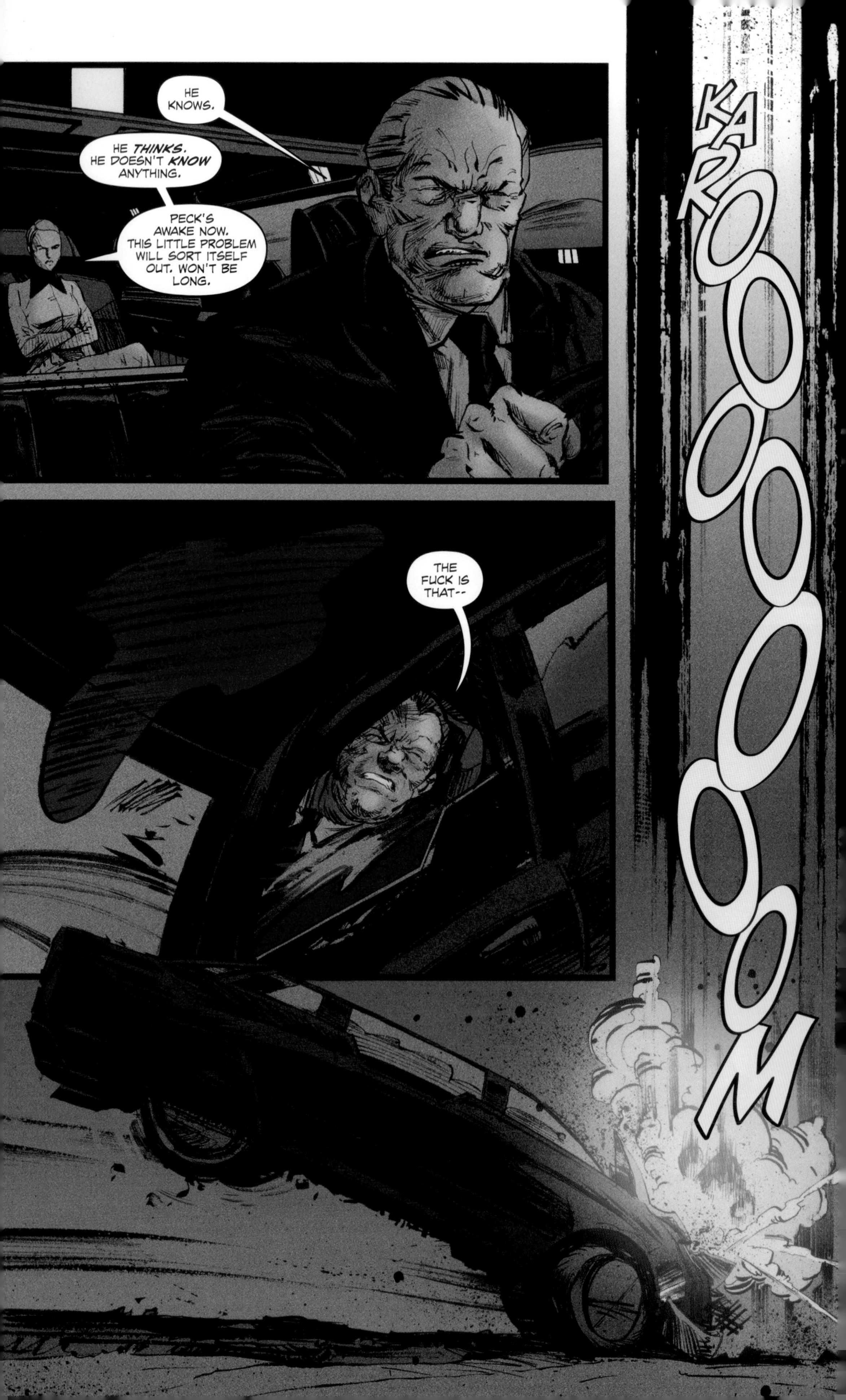

HE KNOWS.
HE *THINKS.* HE DOESN'T *KNOW* ANYTHING.
PECK'S AWAKE NOW. THIS LITTLE PROBLEM WILL SORT ITSELF OUT. WON'T BE LONG.
KAROOOOOOOOOM
THE FUCK IS THAT--

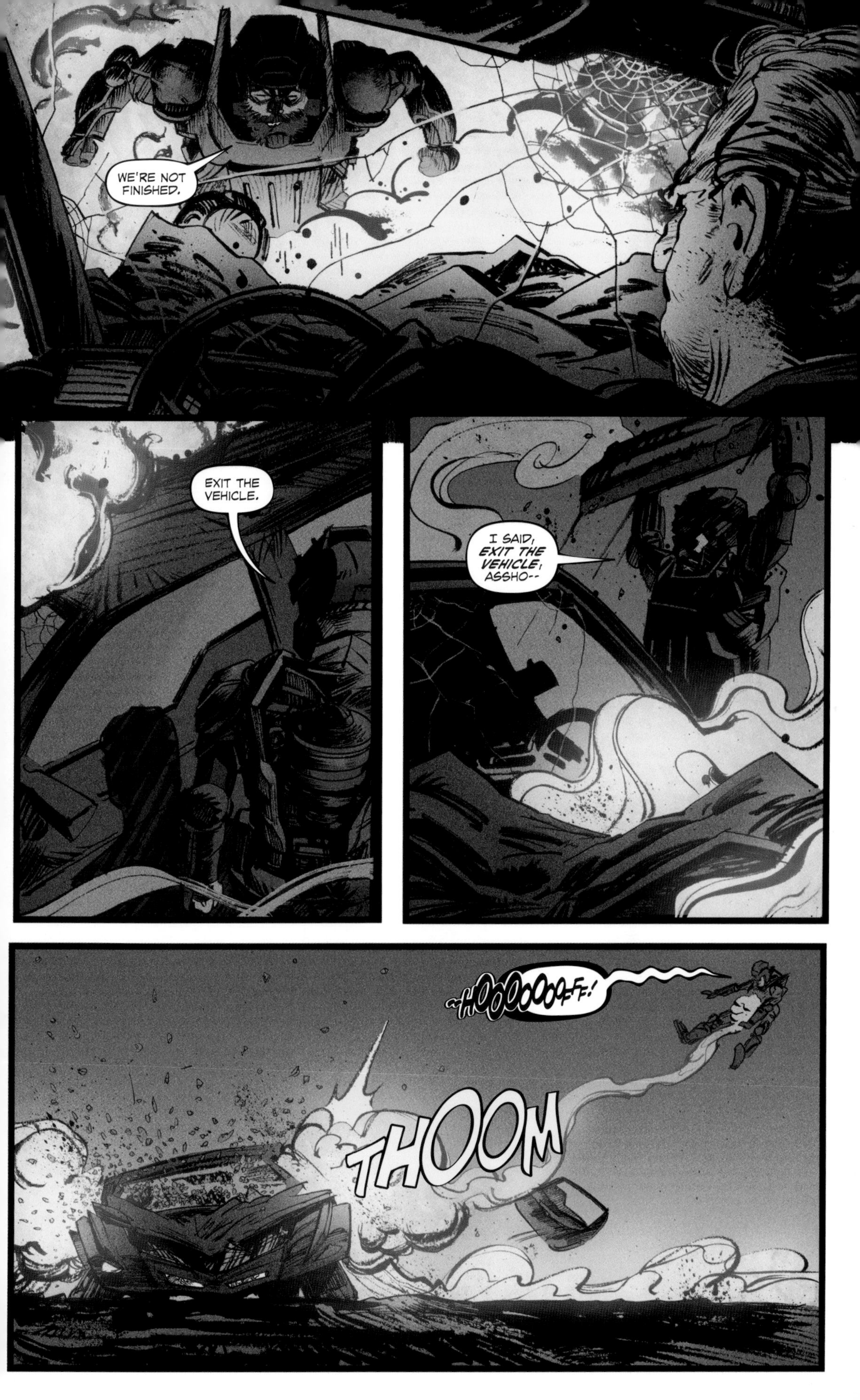
WE'RE NOT FINISHED.
EXIT THE VEHICLE.
I SAID, EXIT THE VEHICLE, ASSHO--
HOOOOOOFF!
THOOM

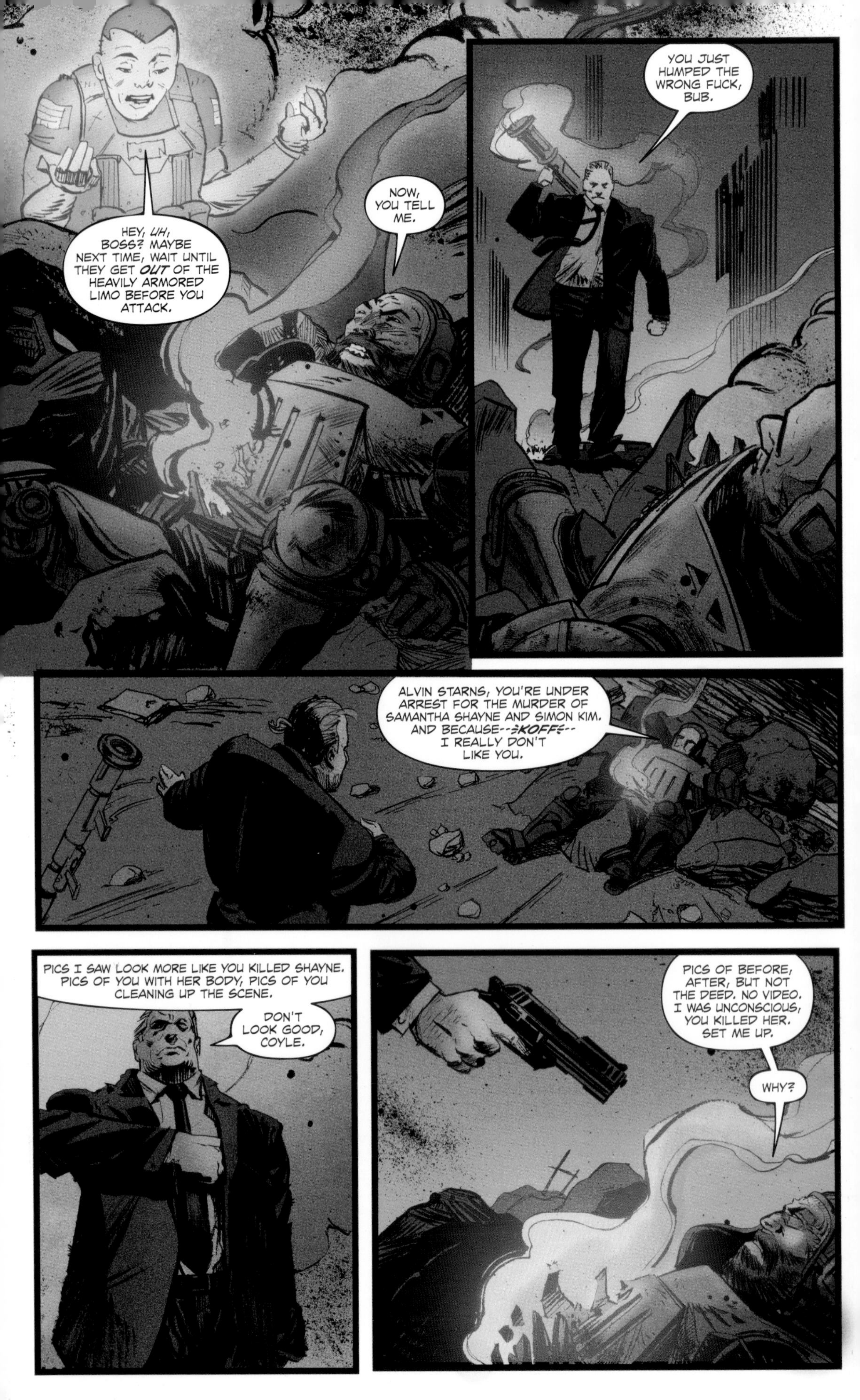
HEY, UH, BOSS? MAYBE NEXT TIME, WAIT UNTIL THEY GET OUT OF THE HEAVILY ARMORED LIMO BEFORE YOU ATTACK.
NOW, YOU TELL ME.
YOU JUST HUMPED THE WRONG FUCK, BUB.
ALVIN STARNS, YOU'RE UNDER ARREST FOR THE MURDER OF SAMANTHA SHAYNE AND SIMON KIM. AND BECAUSE--KOFF--I REALLY DON'T LIKE YOU.
PICS I SAW LOOK MORE LIKE YOU KILLED SHAYNE. PICS OF YOU WITH HER BODY, PICS OF YOU CLEANING UP THE SCENE.
DON'T LOOK GOOD, COYLE.
PICS OF BEFORE, AFTER, BUT NOT THE DEED. NO VIDEO. I WAS UNCONSCIOUS, YOU KILLED HER. SET ME UP.
WHY?

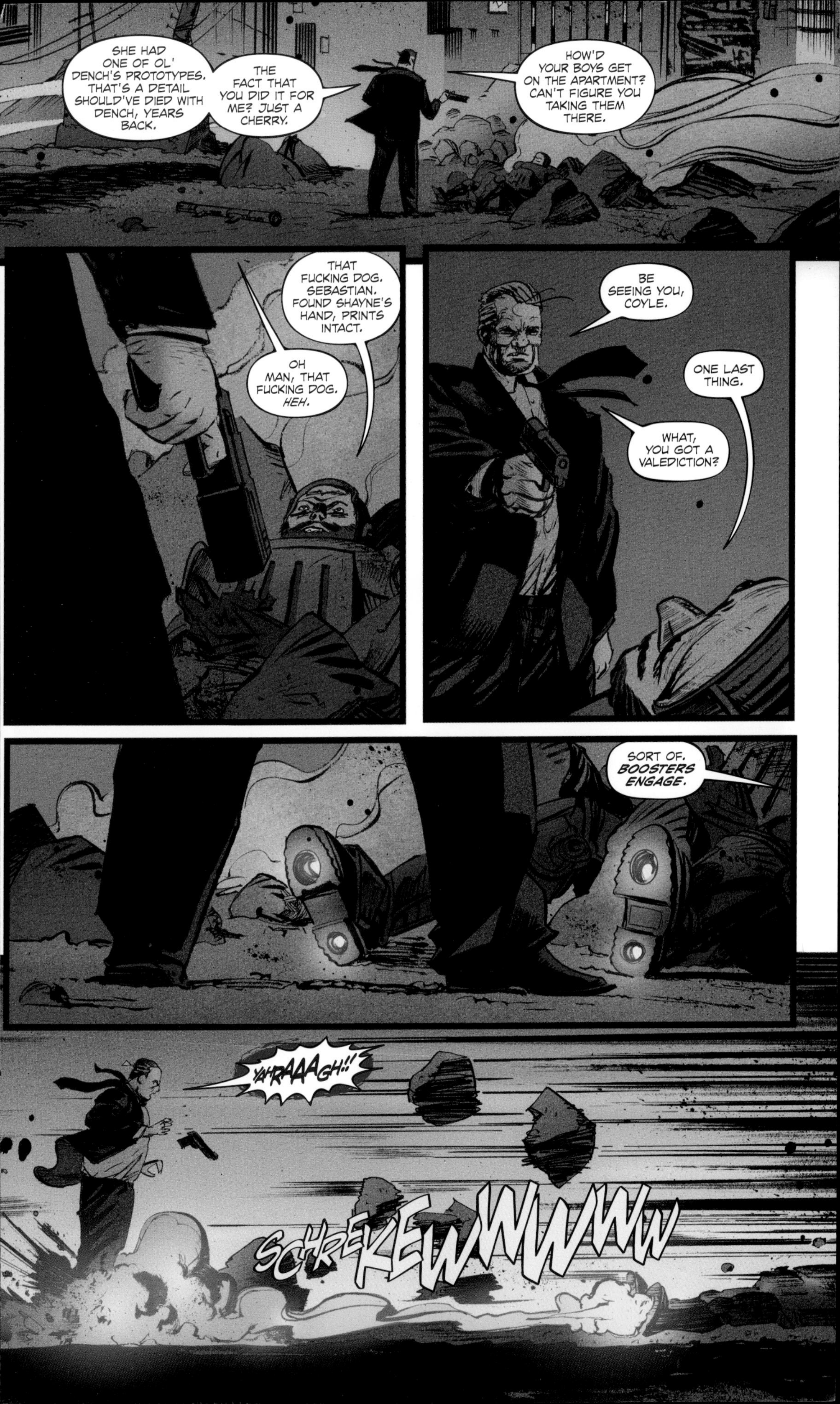
SHE HAD ONE OF OL' DENCH'S PROTOTYPES. THAT'S A DETAIL SHOULD'VE DIED WITH DENCH, YEARS BACK.
THE FACT THAT YOU DID IT FOR ME? JUST A CHERRY.
HOW'D YOUR BOYS GET ON THE APARTMENT? CAN'T FIGURE YOU TAKING THEM THERE.
THAT FUCKING DOG. SEBASTIAN. FOUND SHAYNE'S HAND, PRINTS INTACT.
OH MAN, THAT FUCKING DOG. *HEH.*
BE SEEING YOU, COYLE.
ONE LAST THING.
WHAT, YOU GOT A VALEDICTION?
SORT OF. ***BOOSTERS ENGAGE.***
YAHRAAAGH!!
SCHREKEWWWWW

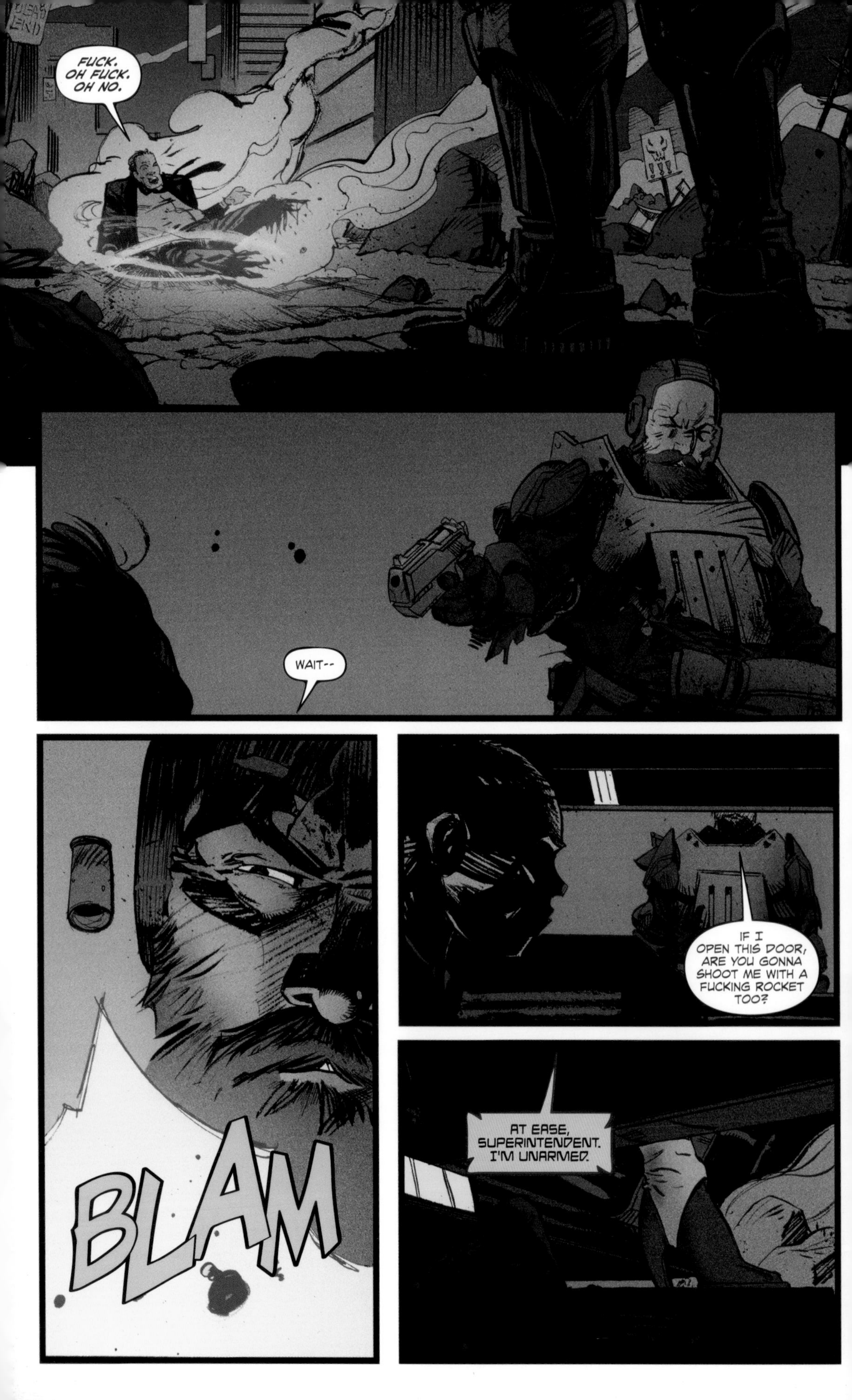
FUCK. OH FUCK. OH NO.
WAIT--
BLAM
IF I OPEN THIS DOOR, ARE YOU GONNA SHOOT ME WITH A FUCKING ROCKET TOO?
AT EASE, SUPERINTENDENT. I'M UNARMED.

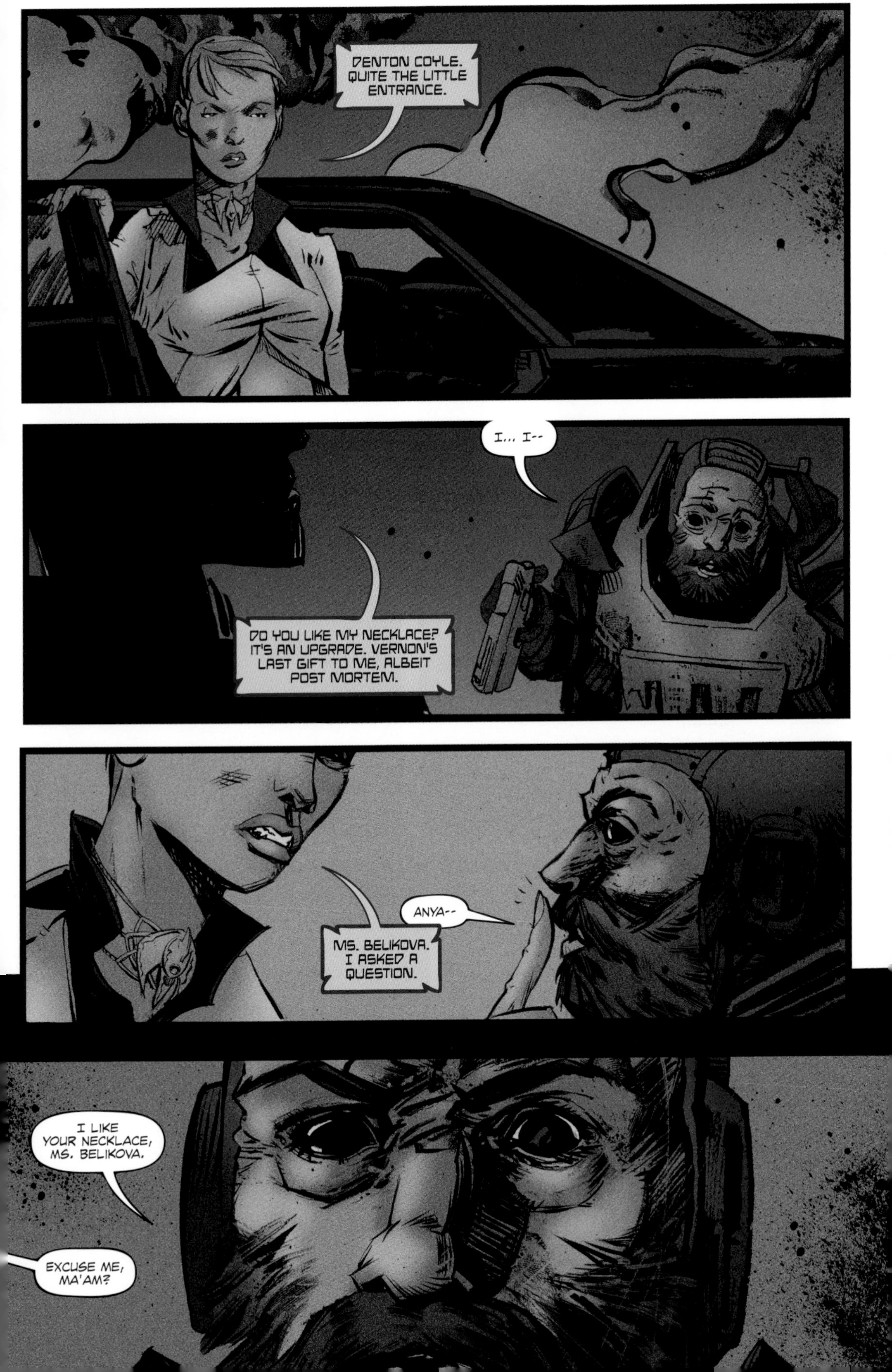
DENTON COYLE. QUITE THE LITTLE ENTRANCE.
I... I--
DO YOU LIKE MY NECKLACE? IT'S AN UPGRADE. VERNON'S LAST GIFT TO ME, ALBEIT POST MORTEM.
ANYA--
MS. BELIKOVA. I ASKED A QUESTION.
I LIKE YOUR NECKLACE, MS. BELIKOVA.
EXCUSE ME, MA'AM?

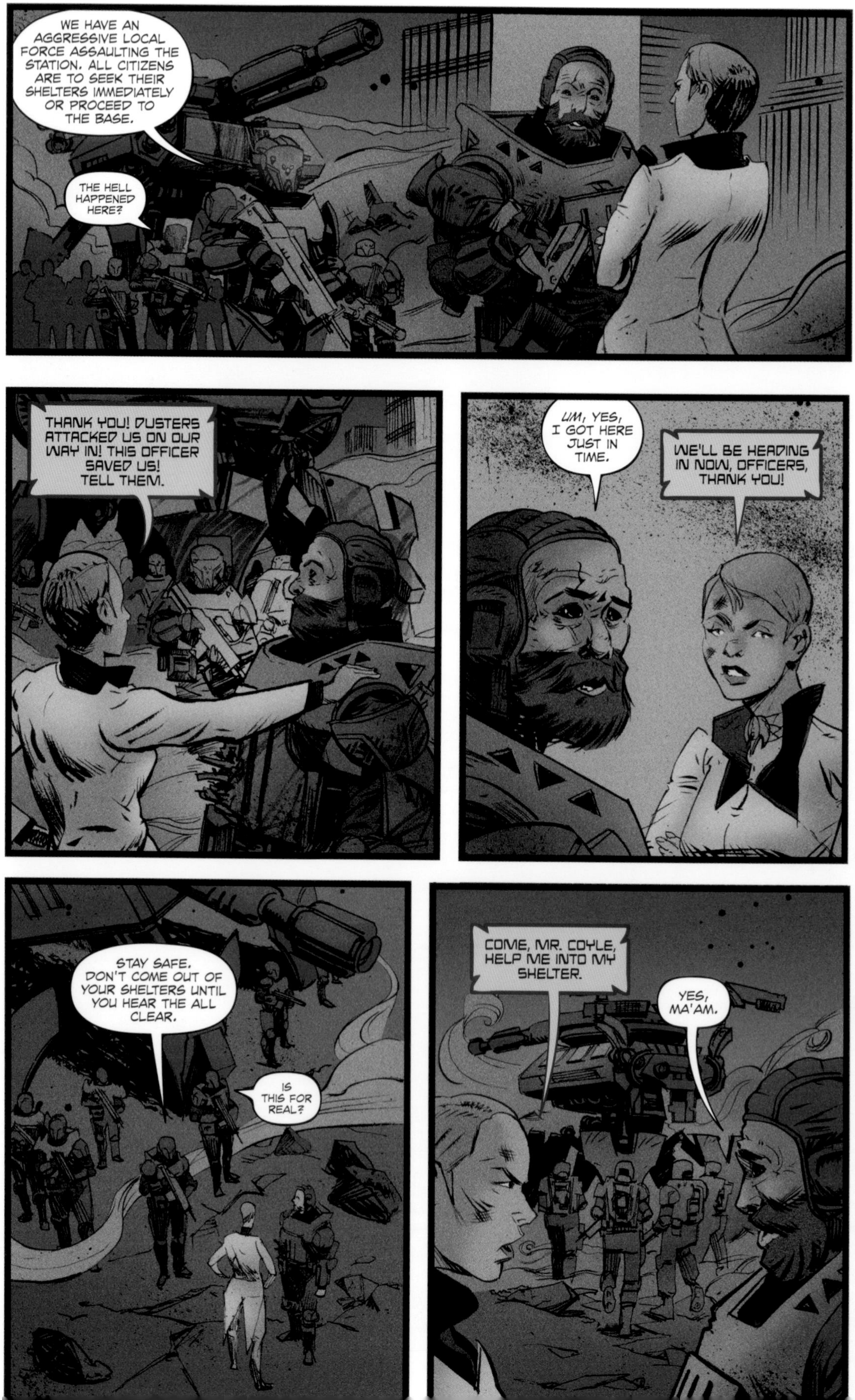
WE HAVE AN AGGRESSIVE LOCAL FORCE ASSAULTING THE STATION. ALL CITIZENS ARE TO SEEK THEIR SHELTERS IMMEDIATELY OR PROCEED TO THE BASE.
THE HELL HAPPENED HERE?
THANK YOU! DUSTERS ATTACKED US ON OUR WAY IN! THIS OFFICER SAVED US! TELL THEM.
UM, YES, I GOT HERE JUST IN TIME.
WE'LL BE HEADING IN NOW, OFFICERS, THANK YOU!
STAY SAFE. DON'T COME OUT OF YOUR SHELTERS UNTIL YOU HEAR THE ALL CLEAR.
IS THIS FOR REAL?
COME, MR. COYLE, HELP ME INTO MY SHELTER.
YES, MA'AM.

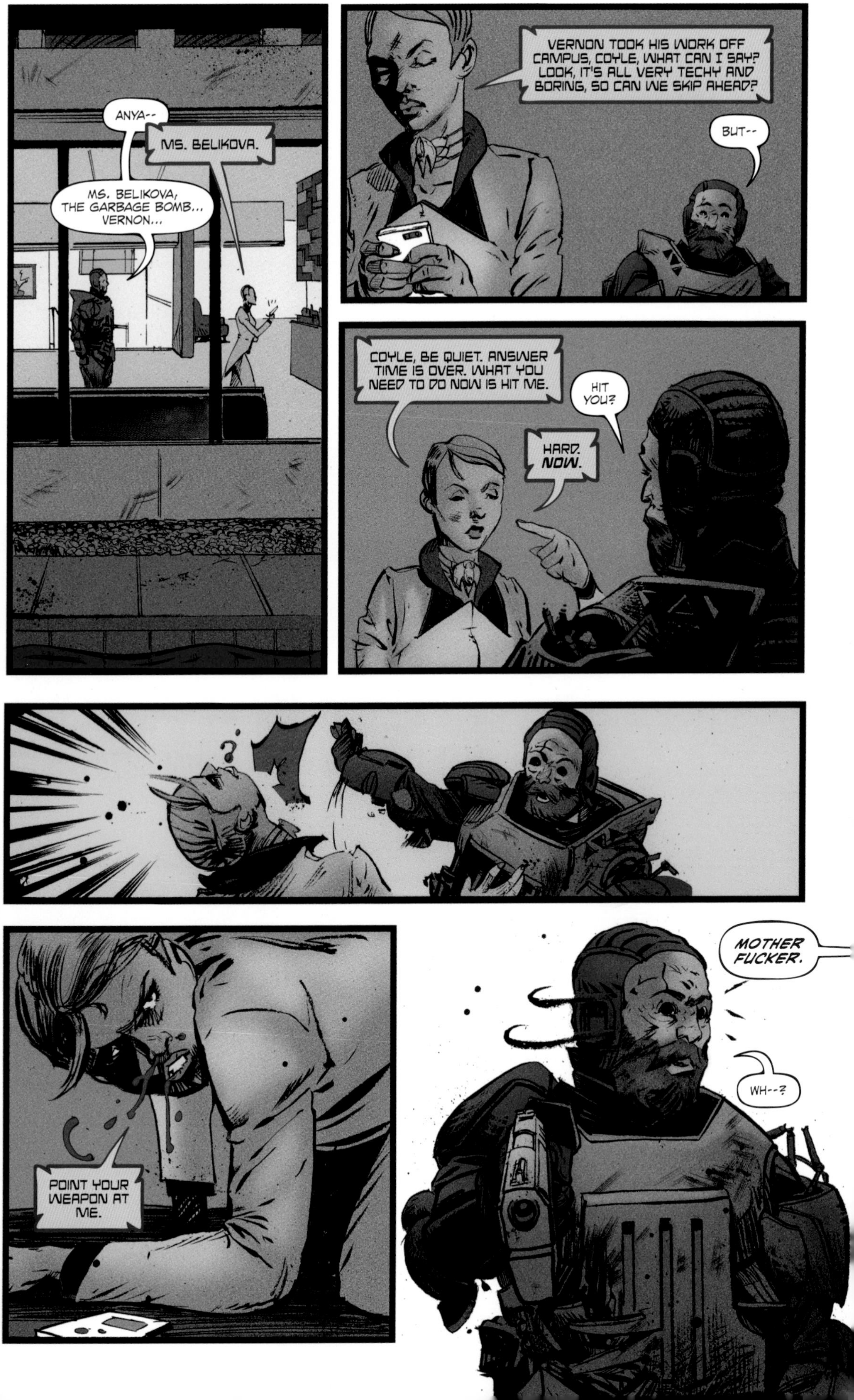

ANYA--
MS. BELIKOVA.
MS. BELIKOVA, THE GARBAGE BOMB... VERNON...
VERNON TOOK HIS WORK OFF CAMPUS, COYLE, WHAT CAN I SAY? LOOK, IT'S ALL VERY TECHY AND BORING, SO CAN WE SKIP AHEAD?
BUT--
COYLE, BE QUIET. ANSWER TIME IS OVER. WHAT YOU NEED TO DO NOW IS HIT ME.
HIT YOU?
HARD. NOW.
?
POINT YOUR WEAPON AT ME.
MOTHER FUCKER.
WH--?

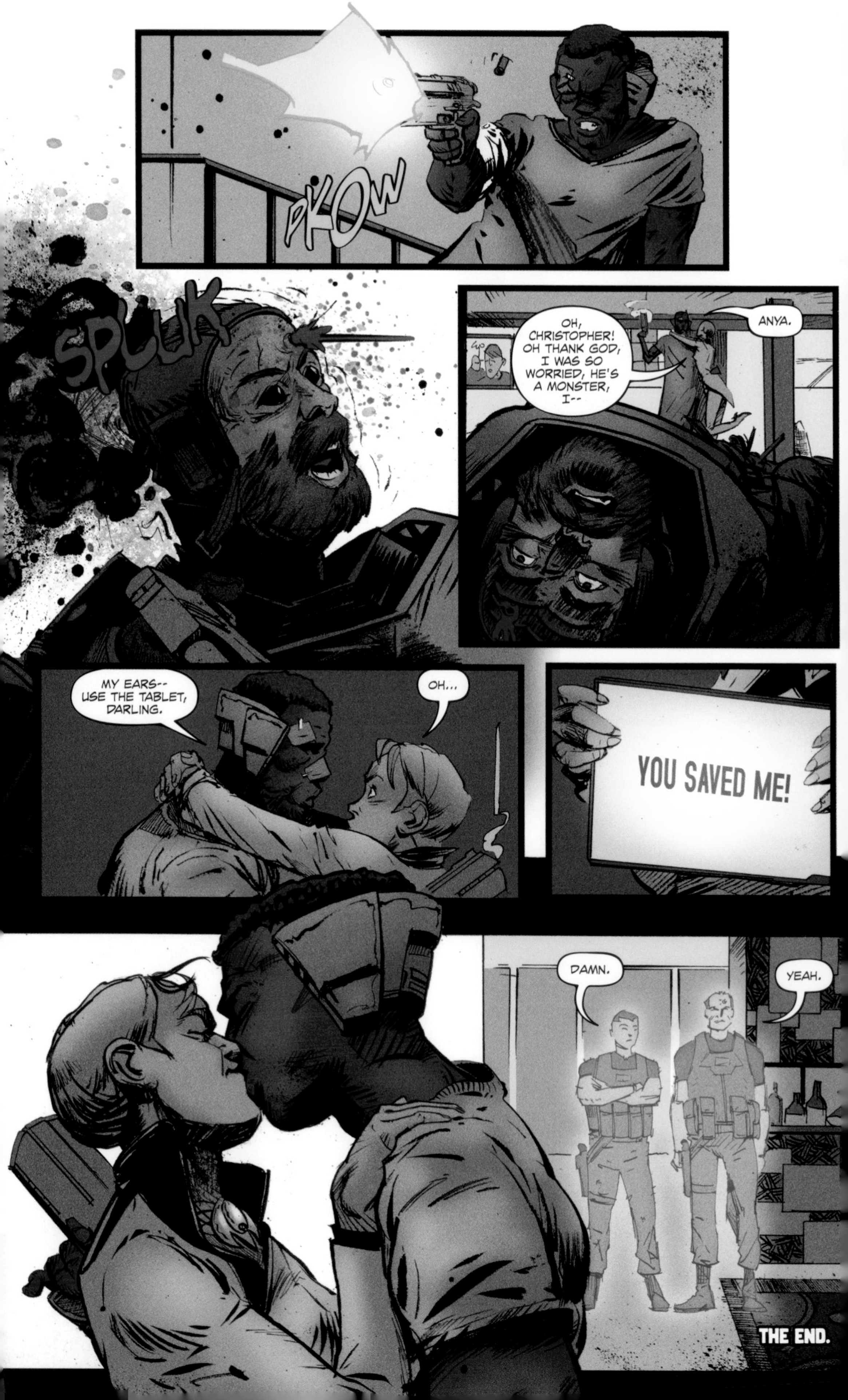
PKOW
SPLUK
OH, CHRISTOPHER! OH THANK GOD, I WAS SO WORRIED, HE'S A MONSTER, I--
ANYA.
MY EARS-- USE THE TABLET, DARLING.
OH...
YOU SAVED ME!
DAMN.
YEAH.
THE END.

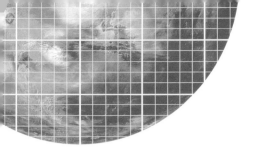

—ABOUT THE CREATORS

NEAL HOLMAN
is a writer, art director, and producer for Floyd County Productions, the Emmy Award-winning animation studio behind *ARCHER*, *UNSUPERVISED*, *CHOZEN* and other works for the FX Networks and FOX. His previous credits include *FRISKY DINGO* and *SEALAB 2021* for Cartoon Network. Holman believes he is generally regarded as nice, but realizes he has a socially unacceptable amount of chest hair that prohibits "friends." His coworkers point out that the hair is not just on his chest, but literally everywhere except his head and also "nice" might be a bit of a stretch. Holman points out that his coworkers are mean, spiteful people. His wife would like him to "stop, just stop" and "help me with this baby."

CLAYTON McCORMACK
is a veteran artist of the independent comics scene, and while *REDLINE* represents his first major series publication, he has also had work featured on the pages and covers of books by IDW, Image, Boom, Sean Murphy's *CAFE RACER*, and *HEAVY METAL* magazine. His previous work also includes being the writer, artist, and creator of the multiaward-winning online graphic novel *DEAD MEAT*, and one time he and his friends discovered a pirate ship after following a map they found in an old picture frame hidden in his attic.

KELLY FITZPATRICK
is a comic book colorist and illustrator and has worked on hundreds of comics since 2013 with publishers such as Aftershock, Archie, Boom, Dark Horse, DC, Dynamite, Image, Oni, and Young Animal. She has garnered numerous awards and recognition for her work including many Autostraddle Comic Awards (Favorite Indie Book, Favorite Single Issue, Favorite Comic, as well as being nominated for Best Colorist and Favorite Big 2 Book) and a Ghastly Award nomination, and was recognized by Comicbook.com as one of the 10 Best Colorists of 2014. She also has a problem with drinking too much coffee and petting stray cats.

CHRISTOPHER CRANK
letters a bunch of books put out by Oni Press, Image and Dark Horse. He also has a podcast with comic artist Mike Norton and members of Four Star Studios in Chicago (crankcast.net) and makes music (sonomorti.bandcamp.com). Catch him on Twitter: @ccrank.

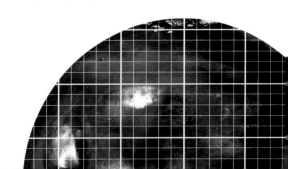

MORE GREAT SCI-FI FROM ONI PRESS

ONI PRESS
$10
THE BUNKER
JOSHUA HALE FIALKOV | JOE INFURNARI
VOLUME 1

THE BUNKER, VOLUME 1
By Joshua Hale Fialkov
& Joe Infurnari
136 pages, softcover,
color interiors
ISBN 978-1-62010-442-2

ONI PRESS
$10
THE LIFE AFTER
JOSHUA HALE FIALKOV • GABO
1
10/10

THE LIFE AFTER VOLUME 1
By Joshua Hale Fialkov
& Gabo
136 pages, softcover,
color interiors
ISBN 978-1-62010-389-0

ZANDER CANNON
KAIJUMAX
SEASON ONE

KAIJUMAX SEASON ONE: TERROR AND RESPECT
By Zander Cannon
168 pages, softcover,
color interiors
ISBN 978-1-62010-270-1

"JEFF STEINBERG IS AN AT TIMES ABSURD BUT ALWAYS HILARIOUS BREATH OF FRESH AIR." COMICBOOK.COM
JEFF STEINBERG
CHAMPION OF EARTH
FIALKOV!
FLEECS!
ANDERSON!
BOWLAND!

JEFF STEINBERG: CHAMPION OF EARTH
By Joshua Hale Fialkov,
Tony Fleecs, and Luigi Anderson
176 pages, softcover,
color interiors
ISBN 978-1-62010-431-6

ONI PRESS
$10
LETTER 44
SOULE • ALBURQUERQUE • MAJOR • JACKSON
VOLUME 1: ESCAPE VELOCITY

LETTER 44, VOL 1: ESCAPE VELOCITY
By Charles Soule,
Alberto Jiménez Alburquerque,
Guy Major, and Dan Jackson
160 pages, softcover,
color interiors
ISBN 978-1-62010-388-3

WARREN ELLIS
WASTELAND
COMPENDIUM
ANTONY JOHNSTON & CHRISTOPHER MITTEN

WASTELAND COMPENDIUM, VOLUME ONE
By Antony Johnston,
Christopher Mitten, and more
744 pages, softcover,
black and white interiors
ISBN 978-1-62010-412-5

For more information on these and other fine Oni Press comic books and graphic novels, visit **www.onipress.com**. To find a comic specialty store in your area visit **www.comicshops.us**.

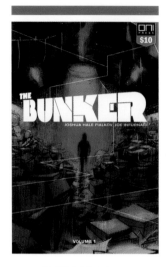

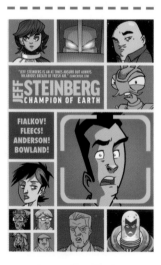